The Success of the Left in Latin America

RECENT TITLES FROM THE HELEN KELLOGG INSTITUTE
FOR INTERNATIONAL STUDIES

Scott Mainwaring, *series editor*

The University of Notre Dame Press gratefully thanks the Helen Kellogg Institute for International Studies for its support in the publication of titles in this series.

Ana María Bejarano
Precarious Democracies: Understanding Regime Stability and Change in Colombia and Venezuela (2011)

Carlos Guevara Mann
Political Careers, Corruption, and Impunity: Panama's Assembly, 1984–2009 (2011)

Gabriela Ippolito-O'Donnell
The Right to the City: Popular Contention in Contemporary Buenos Aires (2012)

Susan Fitzpatrick-Behrens
The Maryknoll Catholic Mission in Peru, 1943–1989: Transnational Faith and Transformation (2012)

Barry S. Levitt
Power in the Balance: Presidents, Parties, and Legislatures in Peru and Beyond (2012)

Sérgio Buarque de Holanda
Roots of Brazil (2012)

José Murilo de Carvalho
The Formation of Souls: Imagery of the Republic in Brazil (2012)

Douglas Chalmers and Scott Mainwaring, eds.
Problems Confronting Contemporary Democracies: Essays in Honor of Alfred Stepan (2012)

Peter K. Spink, Peter M. Ward, and Robert H. Wilson, eds.
Metropolitan Governance in the Federalist Americas: Strategies for Equitable and Integrated Development (2012)

Natasha Borges Sugiyama
Diffusion of Good Government: Social Sector Reforms in Brazil (2012)

Ignacio Walker; translated by Krystin Krause, Holly Bird, and Scott Mainwaring
Democracy in Latin America: Between Hope and Despair (2013)

Laura Gómez-Mera
Power and Regionalism in Latin America: The Politics of MERCOSUR (2013)

For a complete list of titles from the Helen Kellogg Institute for International Studies, see http://www.undpress.nd.edu

THE SUCCESS
OF THE
LEFT
IN LATIN AMERICA

Untainted Parties,
Market Reforms,
and Voting Behavior

ROSARIO QUEIROLO

University of Notre Dame Press

Notre Dame, Indiana

Library of Congress Cataloging-in-Publication Data

Queirolo, Rosario.
   The success of the left in Latin America : untainted parties,
market reforms, and voting behavior / Rosario Queirolo.
      pages   cm. — (The Helen Kellogg Institute for International Studies)
   Includes bibliographical references and index.
   ISBN 978-0-268-03979-0 (pbk.) — ISBN 0-268-03979-8 (paper)
   1. Latin America—Politics and government—21st century.
2. Right and left (Political science)—Latin America.   3. Liberalism—
Latin America.   4. Socialism—Latin America.   5. Political parties—
Latin America.   6. Political culture—Latin America.   7. Latin America—
Economic conditions—21st century.   8. Unemployment—Political
aspects—Latin America.   I. Title.
   F1414.3.Q45   2013
   320.09809'05—dc23

                                                      2013029854

To my mother and father,
and to Álvaro

CONTENTS

ABBREVIATIONS

AD   Acción Democrática

APC   Alianza Patriótica por el Cambio

APRA   Alianza Popular Revolucionaria Americana

BNES   Brazil's 2002 National Election Study

COPEI   Comité de Órganización Política Electoral Independiente

ECLAC   Economic Commission for Latin America and the
        Caribbean

EP-FA   Encuentro Progresista–Frente Amplio

FA   Frente Amplio

FDN   Frente Democrático Nacional

FMLN   Frente Farabundo Martí para la Liberación Nacional

FSLN   Frente Sandinista de Liberación Nacional

IADB   Inter-American Development Bank

ISI   Import Substitution Industrialization

MAS   Movimiento al Socialismo

MVR   Movimiento Quinta República

NE   Nuevo Espacio

PAN   Partido de Acción Nacional

PC   Partido Colorado

PFL   Partido do Frente Liberal

PGP   Partido por el Gobierno del Pueblo

PI   Partido Independiente

PLN   Partido Liberación Nacional

PMDB   Partido do Movimiento Democratico Brasileiro

PMS   Partido Mexicano Socialista

PN   Partido Nacional

PRD   Partido Revolucionario Democrático

PRI   Partido Revolucionario Institucional

PRT   Partido Revolucionario de los Trabajadores

PSDB   Partido da Social Democracia Brasileira

PT   Partido dos Trabalhadores

PUSC   Partido Unidad Social Cristiana

SRI   Structural Reform Index

UNE   Unidad Nacional de la Esperanza

VRL   Vote-Revealed Leftism

TABLES

FIGURES

PREFACE AND ACKNOWLEDGMENTS

Why, since the beginning of the twenty-first century, have so many Latin American countries elected governments that identify themselves with the ideological Left? This is a question for which journalists, political analysts, and political scientists have sought explanations. The most common ones suggest this shift is a backlash against the neoliberal economic model implemented in the 1980s and 1990s. Others have pointed out that the primary factor is a need for change. Popular discontent with traditional parties unable to solve the problems of poverty, corruption, and inequality, it is argued, has impelled Latin Americans to vote for political parties that are perceived as being more likely to deliver a better standard of living. But it may not be that simple. Alternative arguments question the very existence of a movement toward the Left. And the differences among left-wing governments may be more significant than their similarities.

The Success of the Left in Latin America is the first book that disentangles these arguments. It does so by answering three questions: (1) Is the success of leftist parties something new and general in the region? (2) What particular features of market-oriented economic reforms, and what economic and political conditions, have benefited left-leaning parties? (3) Why are Latin Americans voting for left-oriented parties? Is their vote expressing a policy mandate or an outcome mandate?

My central argument is that the recent rise of leftist parties in Latin America has come about as a result of voters punishing political parties that were unable to improve the economic well-being of their electorates. Left-of-center parties took advantage of this popular discontent and capitalized on social and economic dissatisfaction because they were untainted, that is, outside the governing coalitions and in the opposition. Moreover, the electoral possibilities of success for leftist parties depend on the number of "untainted opposition" parties available in the political system. In countries like Brazil and Uruguay, where leftist parties embody the only untainted opposition, it was easier to capitalize on popular discontent than in Mexico, where a party on the Right also represented an untainted opposition.

This book demonstrates that greater levels of market reforms did not produce more votes for political parties on the Left. Rather than neoliberal economic reforms, the key macro variable is unemployment. Left-leaning parties in Latin America increase their electoral chances when unemployment is high. In other words, Latin Americans are less policy oriented than outcome oriented, and rather than ideologically concerned about neoliberal polices, they care about economic results.

In addition to explaining the recent electoral success of leftist parties, *The Success of the Left in Latin America* questions a predominant scholarly preconception that depicts Latin Americans as random and unpredictable voters. The results of recent elections indicate that Latin American electorates are capable of holding politicians accountable by voting against those parties that did not provide what was expected and rewarding those in which they still believe.

The idea for this book began in a graduate seminar taught by Mitchell Seligson at the University of Pittsburgh in 2002. The main purpose of that course was to teach students how to think, write, and develop good research ideas. At that moment, the movement of Latin America to the Left was a new phenomenon, and my idea to study it was severely criticized. However, history and the decisions of Latin Americans transformed that small ideological movement into a very large one, and I continued to refine my arguments and hypotheses, eventually transforming them into a dissertation proposal. At that stage, I was also very fortunate to have an excellent dissertation committee that helped me through the research process. So, first of all, I want to thank the four members of the committee: Barry Ames, John Markoff, Aníbal Pérez-Liñán, and Mitchell Seligson. They have been inspiring teachers, sage advisers, and incisive and constructive critics.

Several professors, colleagues, and friends provided insightful feedback at particular stages of this project and read specific chapters. In particular, I wish to thank María José Alvarez, Juan Ariel Bogliaccini, Fernanda Boidi, Luis E. González, Mark Hallerberg, Germán Lodola, Mary Malone, Juan Carlos Rodríguez-Raga, and Margit Tavits for their suggestions, criticisms, and encouragement. James McCann took on the task of reviewing the micro-level chapter and provided insightful comments. Matthew Daniels's editorial assistance did much to make my English more readable. A large component of this book is based on public opinion data, and I owe a debt of gratitude to those who gave me access to the data and in some cases helped me to reconstruct codebooks: James McCann, Alejandro Poiré, Barry Ames, Lucio Renno, Michael Coppedge, Adriana Raga and Luis E. González of CIFRA, Agustín Canzani and Ignacio Zuasnábar of EquiposMori, and Rachel Meneguello and Simone Aranha of CESOP/Unicamp.

Part of the data analyzed in the book was collected thanks to a Graduate Student Field Research Grant provided by the Center of Latin American Studies at the University of Pittsburgh. The idea started in Pittsburgh, but the book was mainly written in Uruguay, while I was working at the Universidad de Montevideo and Eileen Hudson was chair of the department. I am deeply grateful to her for generating such an open and creative place to work in and for her inspiring friendship. Colleagues and students at the Instituto de Ciencia Política at Universidad de la República have listened to my ideas and provided me with insightful feedback.

At the University of Notre Dame Press, I thank Stephen Little and Rebecca R. DeBoer, who guided me through the publishing process; Sheila Berg, for her amazing editing of the text; and the two anonymous reviewers of the manuscript, who offered invaluable comments and helped me to "punch the main story home." All the aforementioned deserve my acknowledgment. Any remaining errors are my own.

Last, but not least, I want to thank Elsa Velasco and Luis Queirolo for trusting in me at all times and for pushing me to go further. They have been with me from the start and never tire of being loving parents. Álvaro Cristiani deserves special acknowledgment; his unconditional support and patience during the writing of this book was fundamental for me, and his generosity in taking care of our main common enterprises, Antonia, Felipe, Josefina, and Juan Pedro, during so many working weekends is something for which I will always be grateful.

Latin America is a region still searching for alternatives to improve the life of its people. The evidence presented in this book indicates that the "leftist tide" could be one strategy for doing so. Regardless of whether the Left has come to stay or whether its influence wanes, it is hoped that during its predominance in the region it will help consolidate democracy and improve living conditions for all Latin Americans.

INTRODUCTION

The Rise of Leftist Parties in Latin America

The Existence of a Leftist Trend

Since the final years of the twentieth century, many Latin American countries have elected governments that identified themselves with the ideological Left. In 1999 Hugo Chávez, a former participant in a plot to overthrow the government, was elected president of Venezuela after campaigning against market-oriented reforms and promising to upend the old social order and improve the lives of the poor. Brazil also veered toward the Left with the victory of the Partido dos Trabalhadores (PT) candidate, Luiz Inácio "Lula" da Silva, in the 2002 general elections. Lula was reelected in the second round of the 2006 election. The permanence of the PT was tested in the 2010 election: Lula was not allowed to compete for reelection again, but Brazilians voted for his political protégée, Dilma Rousseff, who became the first female president of the country. In Argentina a left-wing political faction of the Peronist Party headed by Néstor Kirchner won the 2003 election; and again in 2007 the party's candidate, this time Kirchner's wife, Cristina Fernández, won the presidency. In neighboring Uruguay, the Frente Amplio, a left-leaning coalition party that has steadily increased its electoral base since its founding in 1971, finally gained the presidency in 2004. The Frente Amplio was reelected in 2009, and José Mujica, a former member of the Tupamaros urban guerrilla group, became president. Chile was governed by Concertación, a Center-Left coalition, from its return to democracy in 1989 until 2010, when a right-of-center coalition headed by Sebastián Piñera won the election. Prior to 2010, the Chilean government alternated between social democrats and socialists. The Concertación party's candidate, Michelle Bachelet, a member of the Socialist Party who campaigned in favor of a more egalitarian income distribution, also won the 2005 presidential election. Also in 2005, Bolivians elected Evo Morales, the presidential candidate of the Movimiento al Socialismo (MAS) and an important leader of the coca producers' union, giving him the reins of one of the poorest and most unequal countries in Latin America. In Mexico, Manuel López Obrador, the presidential candidate for the Partido Revolucionario Democrático (PRD), lost the election held in July 2006 by less than 1 percent of the votes in a very controversial contest. At the end of 2006, Nicaragua and Ecuador chose leftist political parties to lead their governments. Daniel Ortega, president of Nicaragua from 1985 to 1990 and leader of the Frente Sandinista de Liberación Nacional (FSLN), was reelected in November 2006. In Ecuador, Rafael Correa won the presidency in the second round of the election with the support of leftist political parties and indigenous movements. More recently, Alvaro Colom and his Center-Left party, Unidad Nacional de la Esperanza (UNE), won the 2007 election in Guatemala; and in the 2008 presidential election in Paraguay, Fernando Lugo, candidate of Alianza Patriótica por el Cambio (APC), a coalition that includes leftist parties and social organizations, defeated the Colorado Party, which had governed for sixty-one years. The last country that elected a left-of-center government is El Salvador. After several years during which the right-wing Alianza Republicana Nacional, known as Arena, had been in charge of the government, the Frente Farabundo Martí para la Liberación Nacional (FMLN) won the 2009 election, bringing to the presidency Mauricio Funes, the first FMLN candidate who is not a former guerrilla commander.

At the beginning of the twenty-first century, it was possible to question the very existence of a movement toward the Left, as countries such as Colombia and Mexico had elected governments that positioned

Figure 0.1. Latin American Countries with Left-of-Center Governments, 2010

themselves closer to the ideological Right. After a decade, however, al-most two-thirds of the region is under the "pink tide" (fig. 0.1), a term used by *New York Times* reporter Larry Rohter in 2005 to express the idea that a diluted trend leftward is sweeping the continent. Rohter, de-scribing the success of the leftist Frente Amplio in Uruguay, refers to ideo-logical changes in the region as "not so much a red tide as a pink one" (Rohter 2005). There is no doubt that, pink or red, most of the govern-ments elected during the first ten years of the century are located on the left of the ideological spectrum.

The movement of Latin America toward the Left led journalists, political analysts, and political scientists to look for explanations. The most widespread of these explanations suggests that Latin Americans' vote for leftist political parties is a backlash against the neoliberal model implemented in the region during the 1980s and 1990s. The *Economist* stated this argument as follows: "Rightly or wrongly, voters blamed the slowdown on the free-market reforms known as the Washington Consensus. As happens in democracies, they started to vote for the opposition— which tended to be on the left" (*Economist,* May 20, 2006). BBC News explained that "another common element of the 'pink tide' is a clean break with what was known at the outset of the 1990s as the 'Washington consensus,' the mixture of open markets and privatization pushed by the United States that failed to narrow the gap between the rich and millions of poor" (BBC News, March 2, 2005). The media usually make this claim in the aftermath of an election won by a leftist candidate. After the 2009 election in El Salvador, the *New York Times* reported that "El Salvador joined a growing number of Latin American countries that have elected leftist governments. In part, the left-wing victories reflect broad disappointment with the failure of free-market policies to bring significant economic growth and reduce the region's yawning inequality" (*New York Times,* March 16, 2009). The neoliberal response argument was popular not only among journalists and political analysts but also within academia (Arnson and Perales 2007; Baker and Greene 2011; Castañeda 2006; Hershberg and Rosen 2006; Lora, Panizza, and Quispe-Agnoli 2004; Roberts 2008; Rodríguez Garavito, Barrett, and Chavez 2005).

However, this is not the only answer. Others have pointed out that the primary factor behind this shift to the Left is a need for change. Popular discontent with traditional parties unable to solve the problems of poverty, corruption, and inequality led Latin Americans to vote for political parties perceived as being more likely to deliver a better standard of living (Arnold and Samuels 2011; Bruhn 2006; Castañeda and Navia 2007; Cleary 2006; Levitsky and Roberts 2011; Murillo, Oliveros, and Vaishnav 2011). To put it simply, Latin America's shift to the Left is rooted less in ideology than in a desire to punish incumbents for poor economic performance.

This book disentangles truth from falsehood in each of the former two arguments. It examines the following questions: What is the real impact that market-oriented economic reforms have had on the vote for leftist parties in Latin America? Are Latin Americans voting against the Washington Consensus and in favor of the Left depending on their ideological stances? Or, on the contrary, is the current preference for leftist parties the result of voters' discontent with traditional parties and poor economic performance? The two arguments can be summarized as follows: Are Latin Americans policy oriented or outcome oriented? Is the so-called pink tide the result of a "policy mandate" or a "performance mandate" (Baker and Greene 2011)?

Not all countries in the region moved to the Left after the implementation of economic reforms in the 1980s and 1990s. The Dominican Republic is an example of a country that greatly liberalized its economy but does not see leftist parties in an ascending phase. In contrast, Uruguay is one of the least reformed countries in Latin America, yet the Left won the 2004 presidential election and was reelected in 2009. Taking into consideration that most Latin American countries implemented neoliberal reforms, a central question is which particular features of these reforms, and which economic and political conditions, have benefited left-leaning parties' electoral performance. Are purely economic outcomes, such as inflation or unemployment, more important than market-oriented reforms in understanding the vote for leftist parties? If so, the election of leftist governments in the region would respond to a "performance mandate," and it is interesting to explore under what political conditions economic factors are relevant in the movement of some countries to the Left.

Macro factors, however, tell only part of the story; the increase in votes for the Left may be better explained by analyzing the micro foundations of voting behavior. The perception of economic reforms, or opinions about them, may not be related to the actual level of reforms. It is possible that, contrary to conventional wisdom, in countries where fewer reforms have been implemented inhabitants are more tired of them and consequently change their voting behavior in favor of political parties that traditionally oppose efficiency-oriented policies. In the view of many scholars of voting behavior and public opinion (e.g., Yeric and Todd 1989), citizens' perceptions are what really matter. Individuals make political decisions based on the way they *perceive* reality rather than on any *objective* reality. Or to put it differently, voters usually interpret reality depending on how politicians frame it. As a consequence, economic assessments can by no means be considered objective. Citizens can judge the country's economic performance negatively even though macro indicators show that the economy is doing fine. The same may happen with Latin Americans' perceptions of neoliberal economic reforms. In order to test whether perceptions about reforms are more important for understanding the vote for the Left than the actual level of reforms, it is necessary to run an analysis at a micro rather than a macro level.

Latin Americans may vote Left because they want more state intervention in the economy, a more egalitarian economic distribution, or more investment in social policies. After a decade of neoliberal economic reforms, they may be claiming that it's time for a change and consequently may behave in a policy-oriented way. Alternatively, it is possible to argue that voters are not policy oriented but care only about outcomes and are voting Left because the neoliberal model failed to deliver sustainable economic development and overcome the endemic problems of unemployment, inequality, and poverty. These two explanations are not incompatible; both can be true. Latin Americans may be voting Left because they do not want more market-friendly economic policies and also because they are punishing incumbent parties for poor economic performance.

Granted, not all countries in the region (or all citizens in every country) are voting for parties on the Left. It is also correct to say that not all the governments usually identified as "leftist" are the same. Some are closer to the center or could be considered social democratic, while others tend to the radical Left. Some have a more populist style, while others represent an institutional Left. Taking into account the favorable evidence for the existence of the "pink tide," several scholars have focused on trying to understand if the differences between left-wing governments are more significant than the similarities. It is common to read that Brazil, Chile, and Uruguay belong to a moderate left or "right left," which is "modern, open-minded, reformist, and internationalist, . . . springs, paradoxically, from the hard-core left of the past," and is close to a social democracy; while Bolivia, Ecuador, and especially Venezuela, are regarded as a "radical," "populist," or "wrong left," born of "the great tradition of Latin American populism," and "nationalist, strident and close-minded" (Castañeda 2006: 28). Recent classifications have become more sophisticated and have sorted leftist governments into four categories: "electoral professional left," "populist machines," "populist left," and "movement left," depending on the institutionalization of political parties and how political authority is managed (Levitsky and Roberts 2011).

I argue, however, that despite their differences, the countries in the region share certain characteristics that make the analysis of all the cases as a group conceptually relevant. In particular, left-leaning parties, or "left-of-center" parties, as Panizza (2005) called them, in Latin America can be described by their emphasis on economic redistribution, poverty reduction, and social policies in general. Rather than get into a discussion that compares leftist parties in Latin America, I discuss below the current meaning of the Left-Right ideological dimension in the region and define what a left-leaning political party is for this study.

The Left-Right Ideological Dimension in Latin America

There is debate over the validity of a Left-Right ideological dimension after the fall of the Soviet bloc. Those who argue that the ideological dimension is no longer relevant point to the crisis of ideologies, the lack of a true antagonism in the way problems can be stated, the possibility of a Third Way, and the loss of descriptive value that the dimension has undergone. Because the existence of the Left depends on the existence of the Right, and vice versa, the breakup of the Soviet bloc undermined the Left and consequently endangered the whole dimension (Bobbio 1995).

If the validity of the ideological dimension has been disputed around the world, the sense of unease is even greater in Latin America where scholars have argued that voters make limited use of ideological labels (Echegaray 2005; Kitschelt and Wilkinson 2007). Since Converse's 1964 article, there has been a great deal of debate about the extent to which citizens rely on ideology when voting and organize their political opinions around the ideological dimension. The same doubts are cast regarding the importance of ideology in predicting Latin Americans' voting behavior. Echegaray (2005) considers ideological clues an irrelevant source of guidance for Latin American voters, but he does not empirically test this contention.

Contrary to Echegaray, I argue that the ideological dimension is meaningful in Latin America; it represents an important methodological and analytical tool for examining politics in the region. Around eight in ten Latin Americans were able to place themselves on the ideological spectrum in 2010 (AmericasBarometer Dataset 2010). This number varies depending on the country; the labels "Left" and "Right" mean more to Uruguayans and Venezuelans than to Argentineans. But, as a first appraisal, ideological thinking is part of Latin Americans' political behavior, and there is empirical research pointing to ideology as a relevant voting clue (Cameron 1994; Carreirão 2002b; Singer 2002; Torcal and Mainwaring 2003). Electorates use the Left-Right, or Liberal-Conservative in the United States, continuum as a shortcut to processing political information and making their electoral decisions.

Voters might be highly ideological (Colomer 2005), but this does not mean that they are refined or consistent in their understanding of ideology (Zechmeister 2006; Arnold and Samuels 2011). It is not necessary to have a high level of political sophistication to vote ideologically. On the contrary, ideology can be understood in its weak meaning as a heuristic tool used by citizens to simplify information, evaluate political alternatives, and make political decisions more efficiently and precisely (Downs 1957; Sartori 1976). In Latin America, ideology, mainly understood in its weak meaning, is a relevant determinant of voting behavior (Singer 2002; Zechmeister 2006).

Moreover, previous research has shown that elite groups and citizens are linked by ideological commitments (Luna and Zechmeister 2005b). Country differences are also relevant in this respect. Chile and Uruguay present higher levels of ideological congruency between voters and parties, while Ecuador ranks very low. Regardless of these differences, this research indicates that ideology is indeed a relevant factor for understanding political representation in Latin America.

The research on the meaning of the Left-Right ideological dimension is more extensive in Western Europe and the United States (Fuchs and Klingemann 1990; Inglehart and Klingemann 1976; Kitschelt and Hellemans 1990) than in Latin America. However, recent studies have made substantive progress in determining what Left and Right means in the region (Castañeda and Morales 2008; Luna 2004a; Luna and Zechmeister 2005a, 2005b; Zechmeister 2006; Weyland, Madrid, and Hunter 2010). For example, Luna and Zechmeister (2005a) have found that what defines the placement of parties and electorates on the Left is a strong emphasis on deepening democracy, the defense of state intervention in the economy, a secular profile on religious and moral topics, and a profound concern for social issues.

Apart from these common characteristics, there is no doubt that the meaning of being a left-leaning political party varies among countries and even within the same country. For example, Castañeda (1993) classifies the Latin American Left into four categories: the traditional communist parties, the populist left, political and militaristic organizations, and reformers. Levitsky and Roberts (2011) use a categorization similar to that already mentioned: electoral professional left, populist machines, populist left, and movement left. Each of them has a particular set of defining features.

Leftist parties also differ over time. The breakdown of the Soviet bloc had an enormous impact on the way in which leftist parties positioned themselves in the ideological dimension in Latin American and elsewhere. In Latin America, scholars have distinguished two moments of the Left. The first one covers the period from the end of World War II to 1990; it is highly influenced by the Cuban Revolution in 1959, the Allende government in Chile from 1970 to 1973, and the revolutionary victory in Nicaragua in 1979. The second moment starts with the electoral defeat of the Sandinistas in 1990 and the collapse of the communist world (Castañeda 1993; Roberts 1998; Rodríguez Garavito, Barret, and Chavez 2005). Regardless of the difficulty of finding the main characteristics of left-leaning parties in Latin America, the task is necessary for the conceptual clarity of this study.

Starting from their most general feature, leftist parties emphasize equality. Bobbio (1995) argues that equality is the only principle capable of differentiating Left from Right regardless of time. The distinction between Right and Left originated in the National Assembly of the French

Republic, where those representatives who were more egalitarian and radical placed themselves on the left and those who were more conservative, supporters of the aristocratic order, sat on the right. The defense of policies that improve equality among citizens is a trait that leftist parties share.

A second characteristic is the emphasis placed on deepening democracy. Leftist parties want to increase the accountability of elected representatives, control political corruption, strengthen popular participation, augment popular control over collective decision making, and enhance the use of direct democracy mechanisms (Castañeda 1993; Roberts 1998; Rodríguez Garavito, Barrett, and Chavez 2005). This position vis-à-vis democracy represents a change in Latin American leftist parties before and after 1990. Before 1990, most of them dismissed democracy in favor of revolution. As Roberts points out, "Two responses to formal democratic institutions predominated in the Latin American left: outright rejection because democracy was an instrument of bourgeois class domination, or rationalized participation on instrumental grounds" (1998: 18). Today leftist parties in the region have reclaimed democracy as an integral component of their project. This change came about partly because of the breakup of the Soviet bloc and the failure of revolutionary means and partly because of the traumatic experience of dictatorships (Castañeda 1993; Roberts 1998; Rodríguez Garavito, Barrett, and Chavez 2005).

The debt crisis that the region suffered in the early 1980s and the way in which the neoliberal revolution undermined state-led models of economic development (Roberts 1998; Rodríguez Garavito, Barrett, and Chavez 2005) have led Latin American leftist parties to agree that the state, by itself, cannot manage the economy and that it is also necessary to respect the rules of the market. There are no recipes indicating the proportion of state to market intervention the combination should have, but it is clear that both components, income redistribution and correct market operations, are necessary to reduce inequalities and to improve competitiveness, social spending, and the control of inflation (Castañeda 1993). Leftist parties tend to favor state intervention in order to provide public services, redistribute income, and articulate social policies for equalizing social opportunities while keeping fiscal accounts under control (Rodríguez Garavito, Barrett, and Chavez 2005; Luna and Zech-meister 2005a).

In conclusion, there are some commonalities that make leftist parties substantially different from parties on the Right, or even from centrist parties. In this study Latin American political parties are classified as Left or Right following Coppedge (1997). *Right* parties are "1) Parties that target heirs of the traditional elite of the nineteenth century without moderating their discourse to appeal to middle- or lower-class voters; 2) Parties that employ a fascist or neofascist discourse; and 3) Parties sponsored by a present or former military government, as long as they have a conservative (organicist, authoritarian, elitist, looking to the past) message and are not primarily personalist vehicles for particular authoritarian leaders" (7–8). *Center-Right* parties are "parties that target middle- or lower-class voters in addition to elite voters by stressing cooperation with the private sector, public order, clean government, morality, or the priority of growth over distribution" (8). *Center* parties are "1) Parties that stress classic political liberalism—broad political participation, civic virtue, the rule of law, human rights, or democracy—without a salient social or economic agenda; and 2) Governing parties whose policies are so divided between positions both to the left and to the right of center that no orientation that is mostly consistent between elections is discernible" (8).

Center-Left parties are "parties that stress justice, equality, social mobility, or the complementary distribution and accumulation in a way intended not to alienate middle- or upper-class voters." *Left* parties are "parties that employ Marxist ideology or rhetoric and stress the priority of distribution over accumulation and/or the exploitation of the working class by capitalists and imperialists and advocate a strong role for the state to correct social and economic injustices. They may consider violence an appropriate form of struggle but not necessarily. They do not worry about alienating middle- and upper-class voters who are not already socialist intellectuals" (8).

In addition to these categories, Coppedge classifies parties that do not fit in the Left-Right spectrum as "personalist" or "other bloc." *Other bloc* parties are "any parties that represent an identifiable ideology, program, principle, region, interest, or social group that cannot be classified in the left-right or Christian-secular terms." *Personalist* parties are those that "1) base their primary appeal on the charisma, authority, or efficacy of their leader rather than on any principles or platforms, which are too vague or inconsistent to permit a plausible classification of the party in any other way, or they are 2) Independents; or are 3) unusually heterogeneous electoral fronts formed to back a candidate" (8–9).

Two remarks should be made. First, one of Coppedge's criteria for defining a Left party is that "they do not worry about alienating middle- and upper-class voters who are not already socialist intellectuals." This criterion was relaxed during the 1990s and 2000s because the implementation of the neoliberal model had weakened the organized labor movement and other traditional social bases of leftist parties and led them to appeal to broader electorates in order to increase their chances to govern. Second, although Coppedge's classification is far from perfect and can be easily criticized, it is by far the most complete, systematic, and exhaustive ideological classification of Latin American parties available. Moreover, a classification of this type should be broad enough to encompass changes in ideologies over time but also needs enough precision to be relevant. Coppedge's classification fulfills both criteria.

As a result, in this study a leftist party is understood according to Coppedge's definition of a Left and a Center-Left party: it stresses justice, equality, social mobility or complementary distribution and accumulation in a way intended not to alienate middle- or upper-class voters; or it employs Marxist ideology or rhetoric and stresses the priority of distribution over accumulation and/or the exploitation of the working class by capitalists and imperialists and advocates a strong role for the state to correct social and economic injustices. This definition matches the characteristics stated previously as the defining features of the Left in Latin America.

Macro and Micro Explanations of Voting Left

This book combines macro and micro perspectives to explain the recent rise of leftist parties in Latin America. By looking at these two levels of analysis, it is possible to discuss the theoretical connections between them and to see if they are compatible or if they compe:e with one another. Specifically, this book seeks to answer three concrete questions: Is the success of leftist parties in Latin America something new and general in the region? Have market-oriented economic reforms benefited left-leaning parties, or is their recent electoral success the result of certain economic and political conditions? And are Latin Americans voting for left-oriented parties following a policy mandate or an outcome mandate?

The first question points to the novelty and relevance of the phenomenon, which is analyzed in chapter 1. The second question focuses on the economic and political conditions under which leftist parties have increased their electoral support. Since most Latin American countries have implemented neoliberal reforms, a central question is which particular features of these reforms, and which economic and political conditions, have benefited left-leaning parties' electoral performance. The argument tested is that economic reforms by themselves are not sufficient conditions to produce an increase in the vote share for leftist parties, or to put it differently, that "neoliberal backlash" falls short as an explanation. Only when economic reforms generate an increase in unemployment can left-of-center parties capitalize on popular discontent and enlarge their share of the vote. In other words, when economic reforms fail, this indirectly benefits leftist parties. Outcomes lead.

The macro-level perspective represents an incomplete answer to the phenomenon and must be complemented by an analysis of the micro foundations of voting behavior. Therefore, the third question asks about the determinants of Latin Americans' vote for left-wing parties. Is the vote for leftist parties another example of economic voting theory according to which voters punish the incumbent party for bad economic results? Are electorates in Latin America mainly choosing leftist parties because their candidates are more appealing? Or, alternatively, are Latin Americans becoming more ideologically and policy oriented by voting Left as a reaction to the neoliberal paradigm in economic policy? Recent studies show contradictory evidence. On one side, Baker and Greene find evidence of a "moderate policy mandate," shown in a declining enthusiasm for market reforms: "Voters have not turned to the Left simply to oust governments that presided over episodes of economic contraction and rising inflation[;] voters intentionally chose the Left for its policy proposals"

(2011: 73). However, because they are interested in the country level rather than in what factors make some individuals more likely to vote for the Left, they compare aggregate-level attitudes and election outcomes across countries and over time instead of individual-level surveys, and as a result their study does not account for the factors that explain this voting behavior from a micro-level perspective.[1] On the other side, Arnold and Samuels (2011) argue that the leftward shift is the result of retrospective evaluations rather than any changes in mass ideological beliefs or policy or ideological content. But they do not really test the policy mandate because they only include variables as support for democracy, trust in institutions, ideological identification, and attitudes toward the United States; they do not test policy positions regarding the role of the state in the economy, market liberalization, or privatization. In conclusion, the question regarding which mandate, policy or performance, is behind Latin Americans' preference for leftist parties is still waiting for an answer.

The central argument of this book is that the recent rise of leftist parties in Latin America has come about as a result of voters punishing political parties that were unable to improve the economic well-being of their electorates. Most Latin Americans have faced economic hardship during successive governments under a variety of political parties, and recent research demonstrates that voters have long-term economic memories (Benton 2005). They not only punish the incumbent party for the material suffering but also the parties that governed before the incumbent came to power. Left-of-center parties took advantage of this popular discontent and capitalized on social and economic dissatisfaction when they were outside the governing coalitions and remained in the opposition. As a result, in voting for left-oriented parties, Latin Americans seem to be looking for credible political alternatives to the status quo rather than becoming anti-market in their policy positions. If this argument is correct, macro and micro evidence should support it.

This book shows that voters behave differently depending on the role left-leaning parties perform. Where leftist parties have always been outside the government and represent a credible opposition, citizens will vote for them as a way to try something different. In other words, Latin Americans vote in favor of the Left, but they are not becoming leftist in their policy positions. They are voting Left because they are punishing traditional parties that failed to provide economic well-being. Or to put it differently, citizens in the region are more outcome oriented than policy oriented.

Organization of This Book

The rest of this book is organized in the following way. Chapter 1 examines whether the shift to the Left in Latin America that started during the last years of the twentieth century is something new or if similar ideological cycles have occurred in the region before. In order to find comparative evidence that might help us to understand the recent electoral success of the Left, the chapter examines the electoral performance of Latin American ideological blocs from the end of World War II to 2010. The analysis finds that the recent electoral increase enjoyed by the Left is not a novelty; ideological cycles have always existed in Latin America. Moreover, the ideology of the Left was prevalent in the region not so long ago. In addition, the factors that influenced a previous shift to the Left look very similar to the ones that may be influencing the present turn toward leftist parties.

Chapter 2 analyzes the impact of neoliberal reforms on the vote for leftist parties and explores whether purely economic outcomes, such as inflation or unemployment, or certain political conditions are more important than market-oriented reforms for understanding the vote for the Left. In order to answer these questions, it uses a pooled data set of Latin American presidential elections from seventeen countries. Regressions results indicate that more market reforms did not produce more votes for left-wing parties; there is no linear relationship between the so-called neoliberal model and the Left's vote share. Overall, the unemployment rate is more important than reforms for explaining the increase in the vote for the Left. The performance mandate prevails.

Leaving aside the macro level of analysis and beginning with the micro level, chapter 3 describes the main theories that explain voting behavior from the individual perspective: economic voting theory, social class cleavages, prospect theory, partisanship theory, and the cleavages created by political processes. It then explains how each of them contributes to the testing of the dilemma policy mandate versus the performance mandate.

Chapter 4 tests the hypotheses presented in the previous chapter in three country cases: Brazil, Mexico, and Uruguay. First, it describes the three country cases and why they comprise a most-different system design. Second, it shows the empirical evidence regarding the main argument in each of them, which points in the direction that Latin Americans are not voting for left-of-center parties because they are against neoliberal reforms. Electorates in the region are voting Left because they are looking for new political alternatives that might provide an improvement in people's economic well-being. Chapter 5 focuses on alternative explanations and how they interact with the main argument, presenting ample evidence that Latin Americans are not random voters as other studies have argued. Regardless of the differences in voting behavior between Brazilians, Mexicans, and Uruguayans, all of them take into account the economic performance of the incumbent, party attachments, and ideological considerations. Chapter 6 discusses the results, draws comparative conclusions from the analyses performed separately at the macro and individual levels, and explains how the evidence of the country cases can be generalized to the rest of the region.

Chapter 1

LATIN AMERICAN IDEOLOGICAL CYCLES IN THE POSTWAR ERA

Disappointment is the universal modern malady. It is also a basic spring of
political change. People can never be fulfilled for long either in the public
or in the private sphere. We try one, then the other, and frustration compels a
change in course. Moreover, however effective a particular course may be in
meeting one set of troubles, it generally falters and fails when new troubles
arise. And many troubles are inherently insoluble. As political eras, whether
dominated by public purpose or by private interest, run their course, they
infallibly generate the desire for something different. It always becomes after
a while "time for a change."

—Arthur M. Schlesinger Jr., *The Cycles of American History*

The twenty-first century started with the Left in charge of
Latin American politics. Venezuela elected Hugo Chávez
president in 1999. In Brazil, the PT came to power in 2002,
leading Luís Inácio "Lula" da Silva to the presidency. A left-wing faction
of the Peronist Party headed by Néstor Kirchner won the 2003 presidential elections in Argentina. In Uruguay, the Frente Amplio, a coalition party identified with the Left, won the 2004 presidential and congressional elections with a majority vote. Evo Morales also attained the
presidency of Bolivia with a majority of the vote in the 2005 elections.
In Chile, the Concertación won the 2006 presidential election, bringing

17

Michelle Bachelet, a member of the Socialist Party, to the presidency.[1] In Mexico, Manuel López Obrador from the Partido Revolucionario Democrático (PRD) lost the presidential election held in July 2006 by only 1 percent of the vote. At the end of 2006, Nicaragua returned Daniel Ortega to the presidency; and in Ecuador, Rafael Correa was elected in the second round of the election with the support of leftist political parties and indigenous movements. The most recent members of this team are Guatemala, Paraguay, and El Salvador; all three have governments in which the president was elected with the support of left-wing parties; in El Salvador, the party itself is classified as leftist.

This electoral trend in favor of leftist parties can also be seen in Latin Americans' ideological self-placement. The AmericasBarometer data for 2010 reveal a slight shift to the left within the populace since 2004. The regional average was 6.17 in 2004, 5.77 in 2006, and 5.68 in 2010. However, several scholars have pointed out that this movement has been magnified because, at least from voters' perspectives, the region is still slightly to the right on the ideological spectrum (Murillo, Oliveros, and Vaishnav 2011; Seligson 2007). Or as Baker and Greene define it, "Latin American voters' aggregate preferences have moved *toward* the left but not *to* the left" (2011: 50; original emphasis). Although some journalists and political analysts refer to this shift to the Left as something new, this chapter shows that the rise of the Left in Latin America is not a novel phenomenon. There have been other moments in Latin American history when the Left took the lead. Moreover, the factors that once caused the dominance of the Left in the region may be reoccurring to produce the current situation. Rather than experience a new political phenomenon, the region, in this view, is in the leftist phase of an "ideological cycle."

There is a great deal of evidence that ideological swings and ideological cycles occur in American politics (Stimson, MacKuen, and Erikson 1995; Stimson 1999; Erikson, MacKuen, and Stimson 2002). Change is a part of politics, and the alternation of political parties in the government is a desirable feature of democracies. If alternations, swings, and changes of political parties are a part of political life, it might well be the case that these movements reflect changes in the ideological leanings of the voters. Perhaps shifts in "ideology," understood as self-placement in an ideological spectrum, do not occur, but subtler changes do. For example,

Stimson (1999) does not call it "ideology" but rather refers to the "public mood," which can be briefly described as a set of preferences, and finds that it follows clearly observable cycles in American politics, and these cycles have an impact on the kind of policies that politicians enact. In other words, in the United States "dynamic representation" exists: elected organs of the government are highly responsive to changes in the public mood (Stimson, MacKuen, and Erikson 1995). The existence of cycles implies that there are political eras in which liberalism is dominant and that after a while a conservative era takes over. The logic is as follows: the longer an electorate has experienced liberal policies, the more probable it is that it will choose a conservative government. Conversely, the electorate is likely to choose a liberal government after a number of years of living under conservative policies.

Are ideological cycles also a part of Latin American politics? In a region generally defined as unstable, volatile, and prone to institutional breakdown, is it possible to identify cycles? There is no reason to suppose that the ideological cycles that scholars find in other parts of the world do not take place in Latin America. However, there is at present no scholarly work demonstrating this effect. One possible reason for the existence of this vacuum is the scarcity of public opinion data on which to build a historical series. A deeper reason is that so much of Latin America has, for so long, been dominated by imposed political regimes that voting behavior mattered little. Since the mid-1980s, however, when Latin America shifted to electoral democracy, the voting record has become more widely accessible.

If cycles are ubiquitous in politics, why should we pay attention to them? The reason to search for prior ideological cycles, from the perspective of political science, is a comparative one. In recent years, it has become very common for journalists and political analysts to report that the "neoliberal era" is over and to claim that the movement of Latin American governments to the Left is new (Arnson and Perales 2007; Baker and Greene 2011; BBC News 2005; Castañeda 2006; Hershberg and Rosen 2006; Lora, Panizza, and Quispe-Agnoli 2004; Roberts 2008; Rodríguez, Barrett, and Chavez 2005; *Economist* 2006; *New York Times* 2009). Most analysts are mainly interested in understanding the impact of market-oriented economic reforms pursued in Latin America during the 1980s and 1990s on the recent increase in the vote for leftist parties. The only way to know for certain if this is a new electoral phenomenon and to understand its causes is to examine the ideological history of the region. It is possible that leftist parties obtained an important share of the vote in previous periods of the region's history for similar, or maybe different, reasons. It would not be a surprise to find that leftist parties increased their share of the vote in a particular period of Latin American history and that later rightist parties took the lead, and vice versa.

To find comparative evidence that might help us to understand the recent electoral strength of the Left, this chapter examines the ideological evolution of Latin America since 1945 using the electoral performance of Latin American political parties. It begins with a discussion of what is meant by the term *ideological cycle*. The second section discusses Latin American ideological cycles since 1945. The final section of the chapter focuses on the past three decades, 1980–2010, exploring the different degrees to which reforms were implemented in the region, as well as the degree to which leftist parties have increased their share of the vote.

Ideological Cycles or Trends

Ideological trends, in general, can be of three types: constant, unidirectional, or cyclical (fig. 1.1).[2] A constant is the absence of movement. In the history of the ideological distribution of votes, a constant would be represented graphically as a horizontal line. In that case, we should expect no differences in the share of the ideological blocs from 1945 to 2010. In a unidirectional trend the ideological Left might, for example, experience a steady increase in the share of the vote while the Center and the Right monotonically lose votes. Stimson (1999) understands a cycle as a public opinion trend that is eventually followed by a reversal of the same. One caveat: a cyclical ideological trend does not imply a regular trend of any kind. Cycles can be asymmetrical; they can behave in different ways, have various shapes, and do not start or finish in the same place. Common sense and primary historical knowledge would lead us to expect more ideological cycles than any of the other types of historical trends in Latin America. But this is an assumption that needs to be tested.

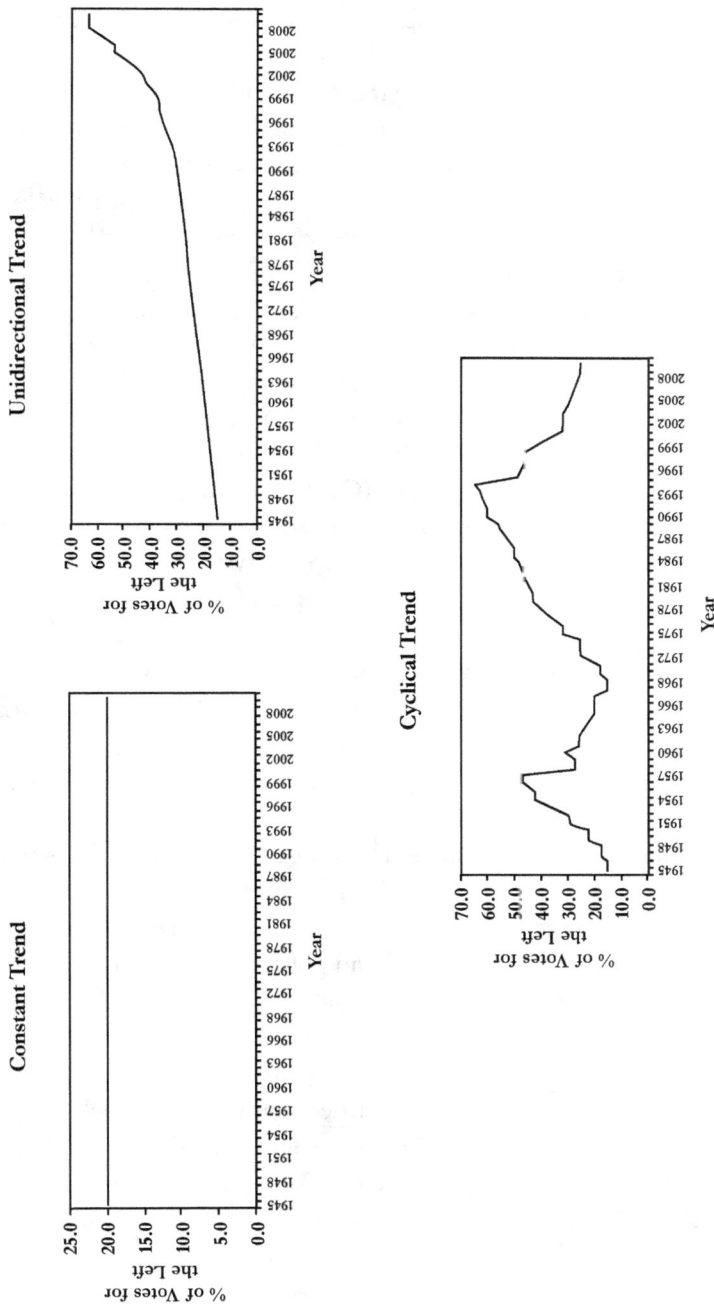

Figure 1.1. Examples of Ideological Trends

Having established the meaning of a cycle, I need now to define what I mean by an *ideological* cycle. First, an ideological cycle as used here is an electoral cycle, because it is defined by the percentage of votes that leftist parties, center parties, and rightist parties obtain in each congressional election.[3] The electoral ideological cycle may represent a public opinion cycle too. In other words, voters may alter their ideological preferences, and these changes are reflected in their vote.

The first step in analyzing the existence of ideological cycles in Latin America is to place all Latin American political parties that received votes in congressional elections during the period 1945–2010 into three categories: Left, Center, and Right. Coppedge (1997) was the first scholar to classify Latin American political parties in a systematic way using the ideological dimension. Before him, scholars studied specific types of political parties, such as communist (Caballero 1986), populist (Conniff 1982), or Christian democratic (Mainwaring and Scully 2003). Others classified countries according to their party systems (Mainwaring and Scully 1995) or compiled impressive amounts of information about Latin American political parties (Alexander 1988; Ameringer 1992; Coggins and Lewis 1992; Alcántara and Freidenberg 2001). Coppedge's classification represents an improvement over these studies in that each Latin American political party, including minor ones, is sorted into an ideological bloc in a comprehensive and exhaustive way that makes rigorous comparative analysis possible.

In the past few years, some scholars have classified Latin American political parties using expert surveys. Altman and colleagues (2009) asked 256 country experts, national and international, to classify political parties according to their ideological and policy positions. Using the same methodology, Wiesehomeier and Benoit (2009) collected information on 146 political parties in eighteen Latin American countries. These datasets are extremely useful for scholars working on parties and party systems in the region, but they both classify parties around 2009, which is a problem for examining ideological cycles. It would be an empirical mistake to categorize political parties during the 1970s, 1980s, or even before using a 2009 classification; and it would also be a theoretical error since almost every scholar working in the region knows that political parties usually switch their ideological positions. Coppedge's classification has the advantage of including a temporal dimension; it covers Latin American political parties since 1945.

Several observations regarding Coppedge's classifications are necessary. First, it should be noted that for the purpose of this chapter and the next, the analysis is performed using three ideological categories: Left, Center, and Right. The Left is composed of Left and Center-Left political parties, while the Right is made up of Right and Center-Right parties. The main reason to reduce the five categories defined by Coppedge to three is my interest in tackling the main ideological trends and cycles in the Left and the Right in Latin America, not the subtler movements between Center-Right and Right, or between Left and Center-Left, which are usually pretty fragile.

Second, Coppedge (1997) classifies political parties only up to 1995. Using his criteria, I have extended the classification to political parties that participated in parliamentary and presidential elections until 2010.[4] This expansion takes into consideration movements in the ideological dimension that some parties made because they were in power, because they were in the opposition, or simply because they redefined their ideology. For example, the Partido da Social Democracia Brasileira (PSDB) was classified by Coppedge as a Center-Left party until 1994. But in 1994, the PSDB won the presidential election under the candidacy of Fernando H. Cardoso with the support of the Partido do Frente Liberal (PFL), indicating that the party had already moved to the center. As president, Cardoso implemented policies more in line with a party with a Center-Right ideology. Since then, PSDB has been classified as Center-Right. Another case is Partido Liberación Nacional (PLN) in Costa Rica. Beginning in the early 1950s, Costa Rica had a two-party system, with the PLN on the Left and the Partido Unidad Social Cristiana (PUSC) on the Right. But at about the time of the 2006 election, the PLN split and pushed the party to the Right. The PLN was also the major supporter of the Free Trade Agreement with the United States, which was opposed by many in labor and on the Left. Neither Oscar Arias nor Laura Chinchilla, both elected from the PLN, can be considered left-wing presidents. For these reasons, the PLN has been classified as a Center-Right party since 2006. The same transformation happened in the PRD in 2000. My expanded classification uses information extracted from handbooks,[5] political party Websites, and consultations with experts from several countries.[6]

It can be argued that some of the ideological movements over time could be produced by having a different team recoding political parties before and after 1995. In order to maximize coding reliability and reduce the possible differences introduced when updating the dataset, whenever possible two country experts were consulted for each country. It is important to mention that we adhered to Coppedge's classification as much as possible. Only when both coders agreed that a party moved away from Coppedge's original classification was its ideological placement changed, but not before 1994. For example, in the cases of Peru and Paraguay, Coppedge's classification remained almost unchanged.[7]

In this chapter, two different samples of countries are used. In the first section below, the sample is composed of countries for which there is reliable data for the whole period of study (1945–2010): Argentina, Bolivia, Brazil, Chile, Colombia, Costa Rica, Ecuador, Mexico, Peru, Uruguay, and Venezuela. This section analyzes the results of *congressional* elections. In the next section, dealing with *presidential* elections in a more recent period (1980–2010), for which it is easier to gain access to reliable data for the whole region, the sample is wider and includes seventeen countries: Argentina, Bolivia, Brazil, Chile, Colombia, Costa Rica, Dominican Republic, Ecuador, El Salvador, Guatemala, Honduras, Mexico, Nicaragua, Paraguay, Peru, Uruguay, and Venezuela. Given that all of them have a presidential regime, it makes sense to examine the results obtained in the election of the main figure of the executive branch.

Finally, some political parties are impossible to sort as leftist, centrist, or rightist. In those cases, the party, and its share of the vote, is excluded from the analysis but remains in the denominator so as not alter the real share of the vote that each ideological bloc has. Examples of those political parties are personalist parties, where the charisma of the leader is more important than any ideology (e.g., Cambio 90 in Peru), or parties with an identifiable ideology or program that cannot be interpreted usingh the Left-Right dimension (e.g., the Argentine Partido Justicialista during most of the period under study), or parties for which there is not enough information available to determine their orientation.

Coppedge was able to classify into the Left-Right spectrum "97 percent of the vote cast in all but 5 elections (all in Argentina and Ecuador). Less than 10 percent of the vote is unclassified in all but 14 elections, and less than 1 percent is unclassified in 58 percent of the elections" (Coppedge 1997: 13). These percentages are high given that Latin American party systems are usually described as being highly volatile and weakly institutionalized. Scholars commonly define political parties in the region as highly personalistic and clientelistic (e.g., Ames 2001). For the period under study, the results of the classification are similar to those mentioned by Coppedge. Argentina and Ecuador are the two countries in the region with the highest percentage of the vote unclassified. This means that in those countries political parties that were not possible to classify in the Left-Right ideological spectrum, such as the Partido Justicialista or the Partido Roldosista Ecuatoriano, obtained a significant percentage of the vote. During Fujimori's government, Peru was another case in which a high percentage of the vote was impossible to categorize (59 percent) due to the presence of Cambio 90, among others. With these exceptions, the classification of Latin American political parties into ideological blocs is quite comprehensive.[8]

After classifying each party into an ideological bloc, the percentage of vote obtained by each bloc in all the legislative elections held from 1945 to 2010 was tallied. In order to build a series, it is assumed that the ideological distribution obtained in a legislative election remains unchanged until the next election. For example, in the Bolivian election of 1960, the Left obtained 77 percent of the vote, the Center 0, and the Right 23 percent. Therefore, the result for 1961 is also 77 percent, 0 percent, and 23 percent, respectively. In 1962, Bolivians held another election, and the share of the vote of each ideological bloc changed. This methodological rule was followed for every country, with two exceptions: when the country was under authoritarian rule and when the election was considered fraudulent by the country experts consulted.[9] In both cases, the solution was to substitute the result with dots in the dataset and exclude the country from the Latin American average of that year.[10] The final step was to build an average that represents the electoral weight that each ideological bloc held in every year from 1945 to 2010. The average includes only those countries for which there is reliable data: Argentina, Bolivia, Brazil, Chile, Colombia, Costa Rica, Ecuador, Mexico, Peru, Uruguay, and Venezuela. In addition, when those countries were under dictatorships or elections were suspected of being fraudulent, the country was excluded from the average. Following these criteria, the dataset excludes Brazilian congressional elections from 1965 to 1985 because they were carried out under an authoritarian regime. On the other hand, the data set includes Mexican elections since 1961. Although most scholars agree that Mexican elections during those years had a certain level of fraud, they were included because scholars also agree that the country underwent a process of democratization and political liberalization, and the regime allowed some ideological competition.[11] However, in order to avoid any possible bias, the analysis was also run excluding Mexican elections that occurred from 1961 to 1990; the results do not change significantly.[12] The 1970s are the years in which the greatest number of countries were under authoritarian regimes, and for that reason the averages for that period have been built with fewer countries. In 1977, the average is comprised by only four countries.

Cycles in Decades

For most of the twentieth century, Latin America alternated between liberal democracy and authoritarian regimes. By 1945, the region was undergoing a period of democratization and social and political participation had increased almost everywhere, and in most countries, the incorporation of the labor movement into the political arena was already complete (Collier and Collier 2002). However, the trend toward democratization was far from stable. Populist regimes hostile to political competition in Argentina and Brazil and a new wave of authoritarian regimes in the 1960s interrupted the optimistic postwar period. Despite the fragility of the period, the end of World War II was chosen as the starting point for the analysis of Latin American political cycles. The reason is that the beginning of the Cold War brought with it the appeal of alternatives to liberal democracy such as communism, socialism, and later the Cuban Revolution, which had a huge impact on the ideological alignment of Latin American political parties.

Figure 1.2 shows the trends, swings, and cycles of the ideological blocs in Latin America since 1945. The first unexpected finding is the general ideological distribution: while Left and Right always obtain between 20 and 50 percent of the votes, the Center fluctuates, most of the time around 10 to 20 percent. Latin America's ideological distribution looks more bimodal than normal. The highest point reached by the Right was in 1949. Conversely, the lowest point of the Left was in 1949, the highest in 1970. The Center hit its peak in 1976 and 1977. During those years, most of the countries were under dictatorships. Therefore, the average only takes into account the results of Colombia, Costa Rica, Mexico, and Venezuela. However, this might indicate two different ways in which the region dealt with the "socialist threat," political polarization, and radicalization during the 1960s. One was the breakdown of democratic institutions and subsequent authoritarian regimes. The other was the institutional ability of centrist parties to channel demands and manage popular discontent.

The ideological cycles in Latin America were mainly between the Right and the Left. In figure 1.2, the dotted line (representing the Right) and the thick unbroken line (representing the Left) cross each other several times. They appear to be highly and negatively correlated: when one goes up, the other goes down. In other words, the most important ideological movements in Latin America have more to do with the Left and the Right than with changes in the vote share obtained by the ideological Center.

Using an average for the whole region brings with it the risk of obscuring the differences between countries. Latin American ideological distribution can be bimodal because every country, or most of the countries in the region, has a bimodal distribution too, or can hide different types of distributions. In this case, the average fits into the first alternative. Generally speaking, most of the countries included in the average—Bolivia, Brazil, Chile, Costa Rica, Ecuador, Peru, Uruguay, and Venezuela—have a bimodal ideological distribution. The exceptions are Argentina, Colombia, and Mexico.[13]

Figure 1.2. Ideological Cycles in Latin America, 1945–2010

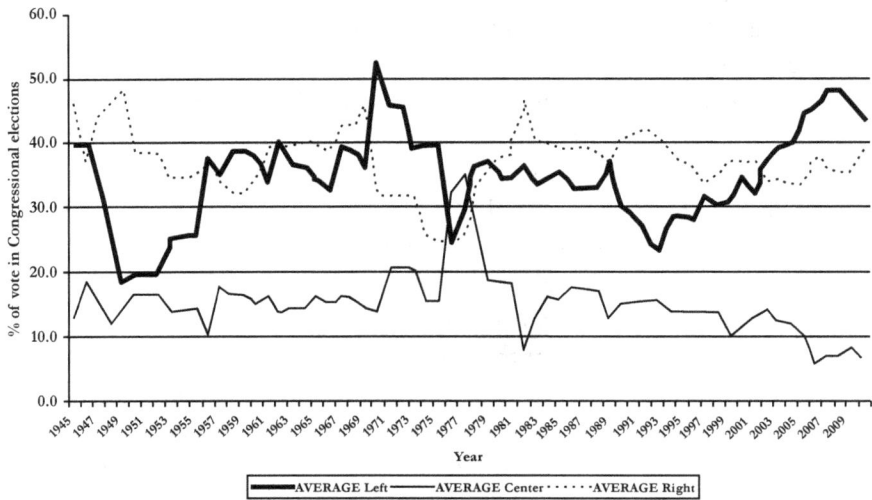

A bimodal distribution indicates that Latin American political history has not been dominated by one ideology. Only the Left obtained over 50 percent of the vote, and it did so in a single year: 1970. The region has not been predominantly leftist or rightist at any moment since the end of World War II. Neither has the Center prevailed. Politics in the region have alternated between Right and Left, with neither gaining the upper hand. This bimodal ideological distribution does not yet enable us to say that the region had a strong ideological polarization during most of the postwar period, which is one of the hazards for the stability and consolidation of democracy (Mainwaring and Scully 1995; Sani and Sartori 1983). The dearth of public opinion and elite data to measure ideological polarization in a systematic way through the whole period of study prevents us from making that argument.[14] Although the polarized image can be overstated, the vacuum of the Center is real.

There are four main ideological cycles during the period of study: 1946–1956, 1969–1976, 1979–2000, and an ongoing one since 2001.[15] In the first and third cycles the Right is the leading ideology, while in the second and fourth, the Left is predominant. The first cycle, dominated by the Right, starts at the end of World War II and lasts until 1956 and is a response to the unstable economic conditions of wartime. During the war years, the state took on more responsibilities and intervened more in the regulation of the economy in diverse ways, providing services like electricity and handling problems such as import shortages and dollar inflation. Social expenditure grew during wartime, as did inflation. For important sectors of the population, salaries and wages were undermined by the rise in the cost of living, thus generating popular discontent that was expressed in social upheavals. Income inequality also increased during those years (Bulmer-Thomas 2003). This was the economic situation in the region when World War II ended. The war had a strong and negative economic impact in Latin America because it disrupted the region's traditional markets. This trade disruption was joined by a pessimistic mood regarding the export-led model, and the two factors together encouraged a greater commitment to an alternative development model: import substitution industrialization (ISI).

The postwar years were an optimistic time in Latin America. In economic terms, this period was marked by a general confidence produced by the inward direction the regional economies had undertaken during the war, plus the expectation of the reopening of European trade (Halperín Donghi 1993). But this enthusiasm for the economic future brought conflicts regarding the best way to distribute wealth and power in the society, bringing the defenders of industrialization up against those who supported the export-oriented model. The conflict between export-led growth and the inward-looking model was resolved mostly in favor of ISI.[16] But by the middle of 1950, when almost all the countries in the region had undertaken the first stage of industrialization, the hopeful mood of 1945 was over (Halperín Donghi 1993). The main reason for this change was the end of beneficial conditions for international commerce.

The ideological cycle that began immediately after the war shows the Right increasing its share of the vote until 1949, while the Left loses votes until that year. After 1949, those trends were reversed: the Left started to win votes, while the Right lost them. This trend continued until 1956. Despite those swings, the Right was predominant during the whole cycle. The prevalent development model was the ISI. Was there something different in economic terms before and after 1949 that might have caused the swing of ideological trends in Latin America? Among the many factors that might have affected the cycle, the frame of mind produced by the deterioration in international trade conditions could be relevant. The new international economic order primarily benefited the developed countries. Latin American countries did not take advantage of this new order due to their inward-looking policies, their concentrated commodity lottery based on primary products, and the protection that developed countries established on agriculture (Bulmer-Thomas 2003).

In terms of politics, the background of the first cycle is the Cold War. The power of the Soviet Union in Latin America was not strong, and the predominance of the United States was beyond question. But the Cold War implied more than a confrontation of real power; it was also an ideological conflict, and in that respect "the forces of communism appeared more robust" in the region (Halperín Donghi 1993). The United States took several measures to maintain its supremacy in Latin America: first, through control of the Organization of American States (OAS); second, through its determination to repel any internal threat of foreign inspiration in the Americas and later the classification of communist activities as "internal threats"; and third, through the 1954 intervention in Guatemala to oust President Jacobo Arbenz. In a way, those efforts were exaggerated because the region was supportive of liberal democracy. Socialism, at least before the Cuban Revolution in 1959, was mainly seen as a device to incorporate social reform into the political agenda.

The second cycle also came about in the context of the Cold War; it started in 1969 and had ended by 1976, but the political and economic circumstances of the 1970s were very different from those of the first cycle. This second cycle coincided with disenchantment with the ISI model and was accompanied by the "socialist threat." In addition, the shape of this cycle differs from the previous one. At the beginning of the cycle, in 1969, the Right obtained 46 percent of the vote and the Left 36 percent. The following year, in 1970, the Left surpassed the Right (52 and 32 percent, respectively) and continued to outdo the Right throughout the whole cycle. But what made this cycle different was the progress of the Center. Beginning in 1970, the Center started to gain votes while the Left and Right lost them, and in 1976, it became the prevailing ideology in the region.

Dissatisfaction with the economy became widespread in the 1960s. Countries that had adopted the inward-looking model suffered from balance of payments crises, inflationary pressures, and labor strife; those that had chosen the outward model also experienced balance of payments crises plus extreme vulnerability to international economic instability. A general sense of failure existed despite the positive growth rates during the 1950s and 1960s, an improvement in several social indicators such as life expectancy, and the classification of most Latin American countries as "middle income" or "upper middle income" by the World Bank. A possible explanation for the sense of failure and the increasing popular discontent can be found in the rising inequality in income distribution, the high levels of unemployment, and an increasing informal sector in urban areas (Bulmer-Thomas 2003).

The above economic scenario was an opportunity for governments and politicians to gain votes by capitalizing on social discontent. Voters clamored for social reforms, and political and social tension grew in the first half of the 1970s. In general, between 1969 and 1976, politics in the region were under a strain. After the Cuban Revolution, which redefined Latin American–U. S. relations, socialism was seen as a possibility for some countries in the region, or at least, for some social and political groups within it. As a result, U. S. intervention in the region increased, even by supporting military regimes. In summary, the high levels of social and political turmoil, in combination with increasing inflation and the threat of socialism, contributed to the collapse of civilian governments in Latin America (Bulmer-Thomas 2003). As Halperín Donghi points out, the "more institutionalized form of armed intervention in political life responded to the increasing fear of socialist revolution" (1993: 298).

The singular shape of this cycle might be explained by looking at the history of those years. Many countries in which the Left had an important share of the vote during the first years of the 1970s, like Chile, became authoritarian regimes. This is no coincidence: one of the goals of military regimes was to stop communism or the threat embodied by leftist parties. As a result, there might be a selection bias in the ideology of countries that remained democratic during the 1970s. Those Latin American countries where the Left did not represent a challenge were not subject to the breakdown of their democratic regimes. But this argument is not true for all countries: in Costa Rica and Venezuela, the Left had a significant share of the vote, but there was no democratic breakdown. Therefore, this argument only explains part of the phenomenon.

Another explanation for the increase of the Center is methodological. During the first years of the 1970s, many Latin American governments changed from being democratic to authoritarian, and countries under dictatorships do not count in the ideological averages of the region. Despite the fact that most of the authoritarian regimes of that time were close to the Right, we excluded them from the average because it is impossible to know the popular support that those regimes received. The average for 1976 and 1977, the years in which the Center became the majority bloc, is made up of only four countries: Colombia, Costa Rica, Mexico, and Venezuela. The Center became prevalent because Colombia and Mexico have a centrist government with a majority share of the vote. It is difficult to imagine how the Left and the Right would have behaved without the breakdown of democracy in so many Latin American countries, but one possibility is that the Left would have had the same fate even without the authoritarian regimes.

The third cycle is the longest of the four; it started in 1979 and ended in 2000. It is the result of several years under dictatorships. During those twenty years, the Right always had a larger share of the vote than the Left, but the cycle had ups and downs. For example, in 1989, Latin America was equally divided between the Left and the Right; neither of the blocs was dominant. The prevalence of the Right during that period witnessed the wellspring of neoliberal economic reforms and the return to democracy in the region.

The prevailing economic model in the region changed after the debt crisis of 1982 that was produced by Mexico's threat to default. During the second half of the twentieth century, Latin American countries had become increasingly dependent on foreign borrowing to afford state spending. At the beginning of the 1980s, the debt-led growth model was no longer sustainable due to the decline in bank lending to state-owned enterprises and the opposition generated by an emerging consensus in favor of an undersized state and liberal economics (Bulmer-Thomas 2003). This new consensus was named the Washington Consensus by the economist John Williamson. Williamson (1990) described it as a set of ten policies: fiscal discipline, reordering public expenditure priorities, tax reform, liberalizing interest rates, a competitive exchange rate, trade liberalization, liberalization of inward foreign direct investment, privatization, deregulation, and property rights. Those policies were implemented in various degrees and times in Latin America, but every country in the region put into practice some of these reforms during the 1980s and 1990s.

The neoliberal reforms were implemented by authoritarian regimes (Chile) as well as by democracies (Bolivia, Dominican Republic). In terms of politics, redemocratization was the distinctive feature of the 1980s. By the mid-1980s, almost every country was moving from an authoritarian regime to a democratic one. Democracy brought a surge of political and social mobilization. Political parties in general, and leftist parties in particular, recovered their right to compete freely in elections. The transitions to democracy took the whole decade, and in some cases, like Chile and Paraguay, the process lasted into the 1990s. After the process was complete and democracy was established in the region, other issues emerged on the political agenda. While some of those topics were new, such as how to consolidate democracy, others were old and recurrent: how to make the economies grow, how to reduce the increasing levels of poverty, how to transform Latin American countries into developed ones.

The implementation of the neoliberal model was painful. Results started to appear during the 1990s: some improvement in living standards, increasing growth rates, and, most important, lower inflation. In contrast to that progress, income inequality remained, and the informal sector increased (Bulmer-Thomas 2003; Portes and Hoffman 2003; Huber and Solt 2004). By the end of the cycle, a series of financial crises (Mexico in 1994, Asia in 1997, and the Russian default in 1998) shook the model's foundations and brought into doubt its advantages.

The fourth, and last cycle, commences at the beginning of the twenty-first century and shows the predominance of the Left (see fig. 1.2). So far, it has only been possible to identify the turning point of the cycle and an incipient reversal around 2008, but the future path that it might take, and its potential end, remains unknown. This latest cycle is accompanied by a negative feeling toward the neoliberal model. Latin America seems disillusioned with the model that has prevailed during the past two decades. Concurrently, the Left has started to increase its share of the vote in several countries in the region. The convergence of these two events raises the question of a possible causal relation between them: Is the increase in the vote for the Left caused by the failure of neoliberal reforms?

The second cycle (1969–1976) also has the Left as the prevailing ideology, and it has as a background an immense wave of popular discontent with the economic situation, the failure of the previous economic model (ISI), rising inequality in income distribution, high levels of unemployment, and a growing informal sector (Bulmer-Thomas 2003). These factors are similar to the ones that are currently being blamed for "reform fatigue."[17] Taking into account these similarities, it is possible to hypothesize that the economic and social consequences of neoliberal reforms, rather than the reform policies by themselves, are influencing the electoral fortune of political parties and benefiting the Left.

Neoliberalism and Leftist Parties, 1980s to 2000s

In order to determine whether Latin American leftist parties have benefited from a failure in market-oriented economic reforms, it is necessary to examine two conditions that lie behind this assertion. The first is that the economic reforms implemented during the 1990s in all Latin American countries have failed. It is important to clarify that the argument deals with the depth of liberalization, rather than its existence, because all countries undertook some degree of market-oriented restructuring. As a result, the Washington Consensus implementation per se could not have provoked a backlash against the Right because it is a constant that cannot explain the variation in leftist parties' electoral fortunes.

The second condition is that leftist parties are increasing their share of the vote in the region. Only if these two conditions are proved true is it worth proceeding by testing the causal relationship between neoliberal economic reforms and leftist votes. The impact of market-oriented economic reforms on the vote for the Left in Latin America is the subject of the next chapter.

Condition 1: Failure of the Washington Consensus

During the 1980s and 1990s, the neoliberal model based on the so-called Washington Consensus was implemented to various degrees in Latin America. More specifically, market-oriented economic reforms started to be implemented in the 1980s or even earlier in Chile, Uruguay, Argentina, and Colombia (Morley, Machado, and Pettinato 1999).[18] In the course of the book, "Washington Consensus," "market-oriented economic reforms," "structural reforms," "neoliberal model," or "orthodox policies" are used indistinctly, and it is assumed that all these terms refer to the same set of policies described by Williamson as the Washington Consensus. The latter set of policy reforms can be summarized as fiscal discipline, public expenditure restrictions, tax reform, interest rate liberalization, a competitive exchange rate, trade liberalization, liberalization of inward foreign direct investment, privatization, deregulation, and property rights.

As shown in figure 1.3, the implementation of these reforms in Latin America has varied in terms of pace and timing. Argentina, Chile, Colombia, and Uruguay started this process early, in some cases even before the debt crisis of the 1980s (Edwards 1995; Morley, Machado, and Pettinato 1999; Lora 1997, 2001), but they did it at different speeds: in Uruguay and Colombia reforms were milder and carried out more gradually than in Chile and Argentina. In contrast, Bolivia, the Dominican Republic, El Salvador, Paraguay, and Peru started the process later (in the mid-1990s) and rapidly became deep reformers. Finally, Brazil, Costa Rica, Ecuador, Mexico, and Venezuela not only started the reforms later but also adopted fewer structural reforms. Lora (1997) distinguishes between early reformers (Argentina, Chile, Jamaica), gradual reformers (Colombia, Uruguay), recent reformers (Bolivia, El Salvador, Nicaragua, Paraguay, Peru, the Dominican Republic), and slow reformers (Brazil, Costa Rica, Ecuador, Guatemala, Honduras, Mexico, Venezuela).

The implementation of the Washington Consensus in Latin America also varied depending on the area of reform. Two leading researchers

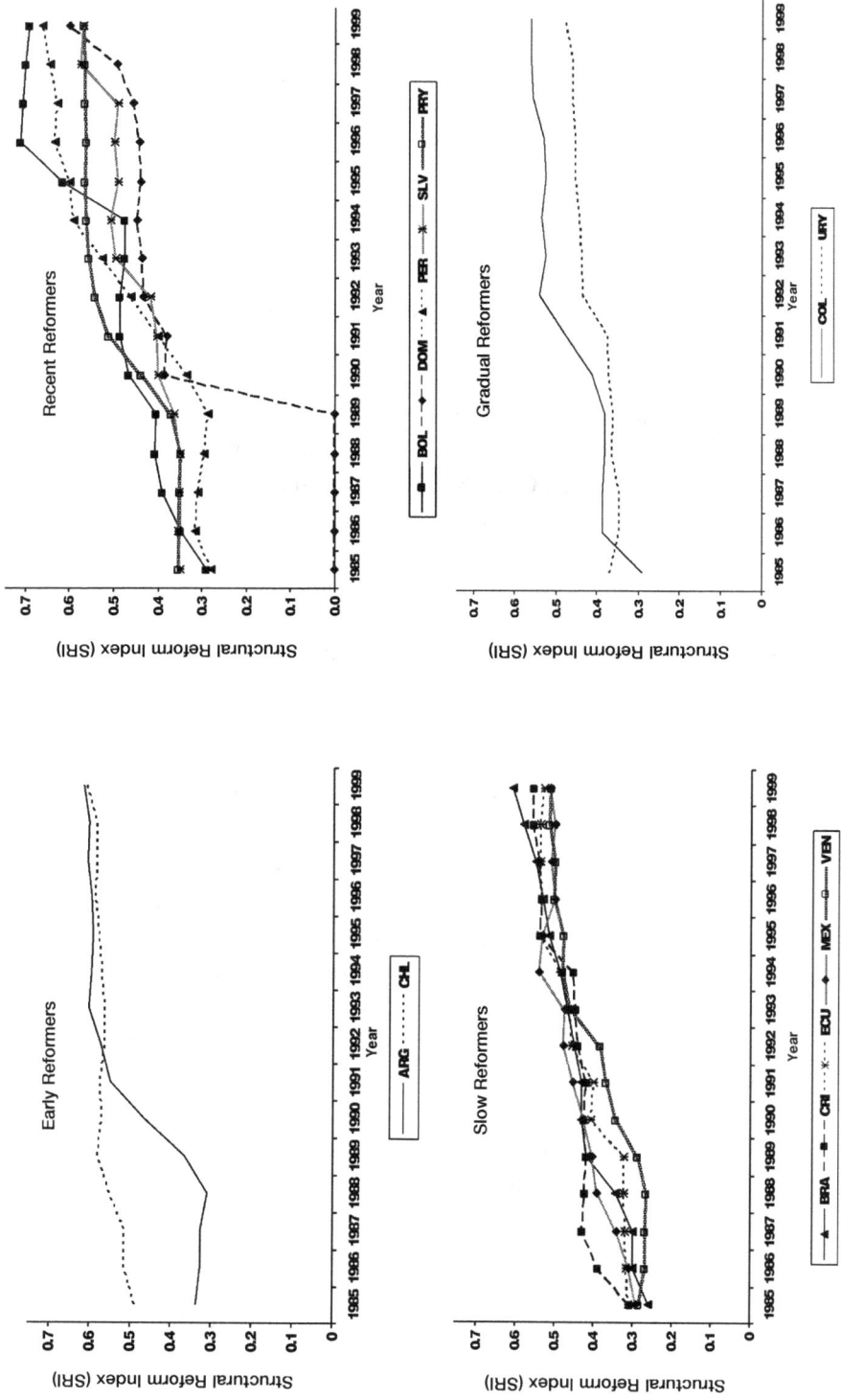

Figure 1.3. Timing and Speed of Market-Oriented Economic Reforms in Latin America

Source: Based on Lora 1997.

in the field, Eduardo Lora of the Inter-American Development Bank (IADB) and Samuel Morley of the Economic Commission for Latin America and the Caribbean (ECLAC), have developed indexes to measure the degree to which different reforms were implemented in the region. Lora (1997, 2001) measures the advance of market-oriented economic reforms from 1985 to 1999 using a *structural reform index* that encompasses the progress of neoliberal policies in five areas: trade liberalization and exchange rate unification, privatization of state companies, financial liberalization, tax reform, and deregulation of the labor market. Morley and colleagues (1999) go further by beginning their study in 1970, including an index of control of foreign capital transactions, and changing other reform indicators.[19] Despite these differences, Lora and Morley et al. arrived at very similar results: the major reformers are Chile and Uruguay from 1970 to 1982; Bolivia, Costa Rica, and Paraguay from 1985 to 1990; and Brazil, Peru, the Dominican Republic, and El Salvador after 1990.

Morley et al. (1999) distinguish between *structural reforms* and *macroeconomic reforms*. The former are defined as "the changes in regulations, tariffs, tax rates or the control of capital transactions that affect decisions at the micro level"; the latter "involve fiscal deficit control, changes in monetary policy, and exchange rate management" (Morley, Machado, and Pettinato 1999: 6). The authors argue that the success of macroeconomic policies in lowering the inflation of Latin American countries is clear, but not enough evidence exists to attribute the same achievement to structural reforms.

Since then many scholars have undertaken the task of measuring the success or failure of the Washington Consensus (Duch 2003; Escaith and Morley 2001; Huber and Solt 2004; Kuczynski and Williamson 2003; Lora and Panizza 2002; Lora, Panizza, and Quispe-Agnoli 2004; Stallings and Peres 2000), and many others have analyzed the impact of a particular policy reform (e.g., Lora 1997). Regardless of their differences, all these studies agree that after two decades of reform implementation the expected result of economic development was not achieved either in terms of sustainable economic growth or in social indicators improvement.

Table 1.1. Economic Indicators in Latin America, 1980–2004

	1980–1984	1985–1989	1990–1994	1995–1999	2000–2004
Inflation	66%	496%	367%	16%	8%
Growth*	0.81%	2.65%	4.86%	2.54%	1.93%
Unemployment	7.78%	7.41%	7.66%	9.12%	9.82%

Source: International Monetary Fund and World Development Bank.
*Annual percent change in gross domestic product, constant prices in U. S. dollars.
Results are presented in averages.

However, in order to evaluate fairly the success or failure of economic reforms, it is necessary to sort out their different goals and dimensions. The neoliberal model was implemented to introduce fiscal discipline and stabilize monetary policy, and through these mechanisms it
was expected that orthodox policies would generate economic growth.
The reforms were successful in introducing fiscal discipline and monetary stability in most Latin American countries but failed to generate the
ultimate goal: sustainable economic growth.

Curbing inflation was one of the achievements of market-oriented
economic reforms. There is no disagreement on this point. As shown in
table 1.1, inflation has been going down since the mid-1990s, and the regional average for the years 2000–2004 was only 8 percent.[20] But some
argue that the decrease in the rate of inflation should be credited to macroeconomic policy rather than to structural reforms (Morley, Machado, and
Pettinato 1999).

Economic growth did not have the same fortune. Between 1990 and
1999 the region's growth was higher than during the 1980s, showing the
immediate positive impact of structural reforms, but diminished to 1.93
percent in the 2000–2004 period. Even scholars who claimed that neoliberal reforms had produced economic growth (Lora 1997, 2001) later acknowledged that the positive and immediate impact was not sustainable:
"The reforms had only a temporary effect on growth. Our estimates suggest that in the period of most rapid reform, 1991–1993, reforms acceler-
ated annual growth by 1.3 percentage points. However, when the reform

process started decelerating, the growth effect dropped substantially, and in the period from 1997 to 1999 it accounted for only a 0.6 percentage point of additional growth" (Lora and Panizza 2002: 17). However, independently of the reforms, growth rates in the region increased substantially from 2005 to 2009 (with the exception of 2008), with an average of 4.65 for the five-year period, though other reasons, such as the commodity boom, can be pointed to as explanations for the economic success.

Opponents of neoliberal reforms usually claim that the main problem with the reforms is not the insignificant economic improvement but the social consequences that the model produced in the region: the increase in poverty, income inequality, unemployment, and the percentage of Latin Americans working in the informal sector. Several scholars have tested these claims. Huber and Solt (2004) found an improvement in poverty reduction during the 1990s, although poverty in the region remained above the 1980s level. One of their main conclusions is that countries with higher levels of neoliberalism and more aggressive liberalization strategies are associated with rising inequality and poverty. In other words, radical and rapid reformers hurt the poorest segments of society. They also noted an increase in the informalization of Latin America's economies. In most Latin American countries, unemployment rates increased because of market liberalization, public sector cutbacks, and privatization. Most formal workers who lost their jobs moved to informal sectors of the economy, and as a result informal workers became the largest class in every Latin American country (Portes and Hoffman 2003; Sabatini and Farnsworth 2006). Governments had no money to compensate the losers of economic adjustment because they had to adopt frugal fiscal policies, producing high levels of popular discontent.

Some scholars argue that targeted compensation programs presented relief for certain social groups (Weyland 2002), and they certainly did so in Argentina, Peru, and Venezuela. But those policies were not universal and were not implemented in all countries.[21] Even in countries like Venezuela where they were implemented, they did not overcome the low levels of support for neoliberal restructuring.

Although this evidence seems conclusive, an alternative view alleges that the negative social impact of the Washington Consensus was minor. Lora, Panizza, and Quispe-Agnoli state that "in spite of all the fuss about the employment implications of trade liberalization and privatization, there is very scant evidence to support it" (2004: 15). However, by examining the same studies that they reviewed, it is possible to conclude that the majority found that the neoliberal model had at least some detrimental effect on the social conditions of Latin Americans. Narayan and Petesch (2002) and the work by SAPRIN (2002) present qualitative evidence for the negative impact of reforms on the poor. From a quantitative perspective, Behrman, Birdsall, and Székely (2000) show that some reforms had the effect of increasing inequality and worsening income distribution among lower-income sectors. MacKenzie and Mookherjee (2003), in contrast, argue that privatization did not have a negative impact on employment. In conclusion, the impact of market-oriented economic reforms on the social welfare of Latin Americans remains open to question.

Scholars agree that inflation and unemployment are among the economic conditions with the greatest impact on voters' decisions (Hibbs 1979; Powell and Whitten 1993). Inflation, as Okun states, undermines "the foundations of habit and custom" (1975: 383), generates uncertainty about the future, and decreases voters' purchasing power by increasing the cost of products and services. A vast body of evidence shows that Latin Americans care about inflation and reward governments that control it (Lora and Olivera 2005; Remmer 2003). Unemployment not only has an impact on those voters who are unemployed or underemployed; it also affects a larger number of voters who become afraid of losing their jobs. Since inflation was brought under control in most of the region after the mid-1990s, it is highly probable that Latin Americans judged unemployment more serious than inflation and voted against the political parties that implemented the reforms that produced it. There is some evidence, then, to support the first statement that the neoliberal economic reforms implemented in Latin America after the debt crisis of the 1980s have failed to produce sustainable growth and unemployment.

Regardless of the objective outcomes of the neoliberal model, Latin Americans' disenchantment with it can be seen everywhere. Even the strongest supporters of the model have recognized that the outcome was not the one they were hoping for. International organizations that strongly supported the neoliberal model, such as the International Monetary Fund, the World Bank, and the Inter-American Development Bank, have acknowledged that the reforms did not produce the expected results, and they now suggest four different types of reforms to overcome this failure: "crisis proofing, completing first-generation reforms, advancing second-generation reforms, and improving equality" (IDEA 2004). Furthermore, many scholars who supported the Washington Consensus as the way to achieve development later moved away from this idea and became its critics: Sachs (2005), Stiglitz (2002), and Rodrik (2001) are examples. The international community has not been alone in showing signs of "reform fatigue." The lack of public support for the Washington Consensus can also be seen among the general public. There is a widespread loss of confidence in the benefits of pro-market reforms among opinion leaders. A less proactive stance toward reforms is the current mainstream tendency among Latin America's policy makers (Lora 2004; Panizza and Yáñez 2005).

Condition 2: Increase in the Left's Share of the Vote throughout Latin America

The evidence is conclusive to support the second statement, that Latin American leftist parties are getting more votes in the last wave of elections than they did in the 1980s or 1990s. Or, to be more precise, the statement is true by looking at the *average* share of votes for leftist parties in Latin America, but it is not the pattern followed *by every country* in the region. On average, the Left increased its share of the vote from 1980 to 2010: the mean of their vote during the 1980s was 29.5 percent; during the 1990s, 29.3 percent; and during the first presidential elections of the twenty-first century, 33.9 percent. This trend is also shown in figure 1.2, above. During the last part of the third ideological cycle, the 1990s, the Left started to increase its share of the vote. But it is at the beginning of the 2000s when it gained more votes than the Right. One could take as a pattern the recent victories of leftist parties in Brazil (2002, 2006, 2010), Bolivia (2005, 2009), Uruguay (2004, 2009), El Salvador (2009), Ecuador (2006, 2009), Paraguay (2008), Guatemala (2007), Argentina (2003, 2007), Nicaragua (2006), Venezuela (1999, 2006), and Chile (2005), but not all Latin American countries have recently elected candidates from the Left or have leftist parties that increased their share of the vote (e.g., Colombia in 2002, 2006, and 2010). In part because of the electoral rules, it is possible to have countries in which left-oriented parties augment their electoral support without winning the election (Uruguay in 1999, Chile in 2010), or the opposite, countries where a leftist candidate becomes president while right-wing parties are the majority. Figure 1.4 shows there is not a unique recognizable trend in the vote for the Left in Latin America from the 1980s to the most recent election. In terms of their tendency to vote for leftist parties, Latin American countries can be classified into four categories:[22] continuous increase, U trend, no change, and continuous decrease. These categories simplify the analysis of the evolution of leftist parties in the region by grouping countries with similar progressions. Consequently, the classification might vary depending on the results of new elections.[23]

Argentina, Brazil, Chile,[24] Guatemala, Mexico, Paraguay, El Salvador, and Uruguay are categorized as countries with continuous increase in the vote for leftist parties in presidential elections. This increase in the share of the vote was not linear for all countries; in particular, Brazil's time series has ups and downs that are an effect of the way in which the PSDB under the Cardoso government was classified. PSDB started to move from Left to Right before the 1994 election. As a result, the leftist ideological bloc lost one of their components. However, the PT compensated for this effect by increasing its electoral share of vote since the 1989 election. In Paraguay, the boost is very recent. After the return to democracy, leftist parties were almost nonexistent, and they never gained more than 0.5 percent of the vote in presidential elections until 2008, when their political support was crucial to the election of Lugo. Despite this variation, the share of the vote for leftist parties in the Southern Cone of Latin America has increased since the return of these countries to democracy in the early 1980s. In Mexico, Guatemala, and El Salvador, the increase is less pronounced but still relevant.

Bolivia, Ecuador, and Venezuela represent the U trend. In these three countries leftist parties had an important share of the vote during the 1980s but lost ground during the 1990s (similar to the continuous

Figure 1.4. Evolution of the Vote for Left and Center-Left Parties in Latin America since the 1980s

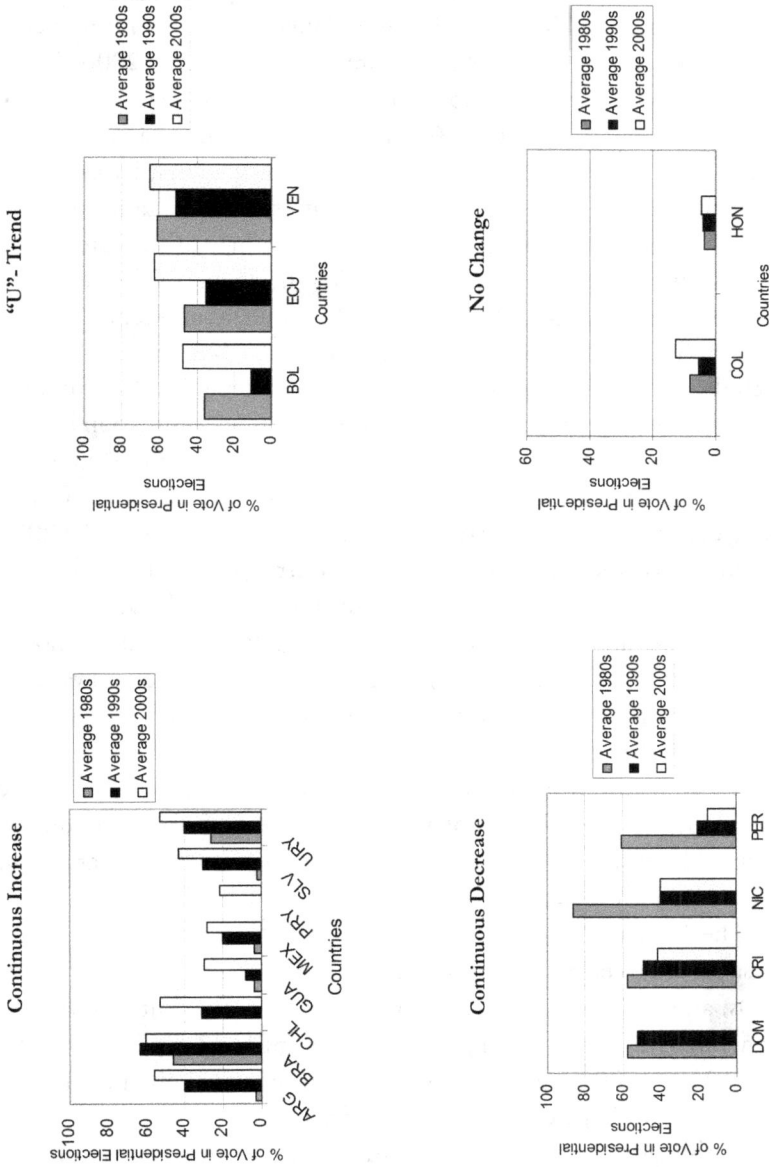

"U"- Trend

Continuous Increase

No Change

Continuous Decrease

Source: Based on Coppedge 1997 and Political Database of the Americas (Georgetown University)

decrease countries). Leftists regained their electoral appeal in the first presidential elections of the 2000s, bringing Hugo Chávez in 1999 (Venezuela), Lucio Gutiérrez in 2002 and later Rafael Correa in 2006 (Ecuador), and Evo Morales in 2005 (Bolivia) to the presidency.

The Dominican Republic, Costa Rica, Nicaragua, and Peru show a trend of continuous decrease in the share of the vote that leftist parties have had since the 1980s. In comparison with the rest of Latin America, the Left in these four countries had a significant share of the vote during the "lost decade," which later shrank during the decade of the neoliberal model implementation. During the 2000 presidential elections, leftist parties in this group experienced various fortunes, but none was able to reach the 1980s voting levels. In the Dominican Republic, they continue to obtain a minimal percentage of the vote. Nicaragua's situation is quite different; despite the fact that left-wing parties do not get the same support they did two decades earlier, the current government under Daniel Ortega is leftist, and his party, the FSLN, won a plurality in the 2006 election. Peru and Costa Rica are two countries where the traditional party systems changed dramatically during the past two decades, and traditional left-wing parties almost disappeared (APRA in Peru) or moved to the Right (PLN in Costa Rica). In Costa Rica, the ideological vacuum was filled by a new leftist party, Partido Acción Ciudadana, which obtained more than a quarter of the votes in each presidential election since 2002. The Peruvian situation is more complex; the Left remains at the margin, despite the existence of Unión por el Perú, the party headed by Ollanta Humala, which is considered more of a personalistic party than a left-wing one (Tanaka 2008).

The "no change" category is made up of those countries in which leftist parties received a small percentage of the votes during the 1980s, 1990s, and 2000s. Colombia and Honduras are cases with some variation, but leftist parties never gained a significant number of votes. In the period 1982–2002 the highest gain that leftist parties obtained in Colombia was 12.74 percent in 1990 (see fig. 1.4).

As this preliminary diagnosis indicates, different countries present different trends. The increase in voter share that leftist parties received in presidential elections since the 1980s in the Southern Cone and to a lesser degree in Mexico, Guatemala, and El Salvador, as well as the recent increase in Paraguay, Bolivia, Ecuador, and Venezuela, cannot be generalized to the whole of Latin America.

I deological cycles have existed, and still exist, in Latin America in the same way that they exist in American politics. The alternation in power of the Left and the Right since 1945 indicates that there was no hegemonic ideology, and the current dominance of the Left can be understood as the beginning of another cycle.

The Left ideology also prevailed in the region from 1969 to 1976. Those years were characterized by dissatisfaction with the economy, unhappiness with the ISI model, rising inequality in income distribution, high levels of unemployment, and a growing informal sector. These factors are similar to those currently blamed for "reform fatigue" in Latin America. Consequently, one possible argument to test empirically is that these factors favor the vote for the Left. Or, to frame the argument based on more current events: the failure of the neoliberal model has led to the rise of the Left in Latin America.

Although leftist parties are not increasing their electoral support in every Latin American country, the Left is the current dominant ideology in the region, as this chapter shows. On the other hand, there is evidence indicating that the implementation of market-oriented economic reforms during the 1980s and 1990s has failed to achieve sustainable economic growth and employment. In order to answer whether there exists a causal relationship between the failure of neoliberal policies and the increase in the vote for leftist parties, it is necessary to carry out a multivariate analysis. The next chapter does this by analyzing the impact of neoliberal reforms, economic variables that measure the economic results of the reforms, and political variables in the vote for leftist parties in seventeen Latin American countries.

Chapter 2

ECONOMIC AND POLITICAL CONDITIONS
THAT BENEFIT LEFTIST PARTIES
IN LATIN AMERICA

Are leftist parties the beneficiaries of the failure of market-oriented economic reforms in Latin America? As shown in chapter 1, there is academic consensus that the neoliberal economic reforms implemented in Latin America after the debt crisis of the 1980s have largely failed to produce sustainable economic growth and employment. As a result, presidents such as Evo Morales and Hugo Chávez who campaigned against the neoliberal model may have benefited. But the preceding chapter also indicates that not all countries in the region moved to the left after the implementation of economic reforms in the 1990s. In the Dominican Republic, for example, left-of-center parties did not increase their share of votes.

Taking into consideration that most Latin American countries implemented neoliberal reforms during the 1990s, but that only in some of them have left-leaning parties come to power since the late 1990s, a crucial question is which particular features of these reforms, and what economic conditions such as inflation or unemployment, or political conditions, if any, have helped leftist parties' electoral performance.

If the rise of left-wing parties is a backlash against the neoliberal model, these parties might be cautious about implementing security-oriented policies, or at least polices that have not been seen as part of the problem. But if what matters is performance, leftist governments should focus on the outcomes of their policies, regardless of how market- or state-oriented they are. In this case, they would have greater latitude in setting policies, even in terms of moving to the Right, as some Latin American governments have done (Stokes 2001a). My concern here is the depth of liberalization and its consequences, rather than the mere existence of liberalization, because all countries in the region implemented reforms to some extent.

Market Reforms, Economic Conditions, and Political Context

The question of whether the implementation of market-oriented economic reforms in Latin America has produced an increase in votes for the Left is connected with two scholarly research agendas: the literature on the implementation of the "neoliberal model" in Latin America and voter choice studies, in particular, the research on economic voting.

Students of Latin American politics have produced an impressive body of work, representing a variety of perspectives, on the conditions under which the implementation of harmful economic reforms in the region during the 1990s was possible (Corrales 2002; Gibson 1997; Lodola 2005; Murillo 2001; Stokes 2001a, 2001b; Weyland 2002). On the other hand, research on the consequences of these reforms has only started to flourish more recently (Arnson and Perales 2007; Baker and Greene 2011; Lora and Panizza 2003; Lora and Olivera 2005; Portes and Hoffman 2003; Remmer 2003; Wise and Roett 2003). Within this latter group, three studies ask questions similar to the ones posed here. Remmer (2003) analyzes the electoral fortunes of Latin American incumbents from 1982 to 1999 and finds that those governments that controlled inflation were rewarded by the electorate. On the contrary, when the incumbent party's economic performance was poor, the electorate punished it by voting for another party. These findings show that economic voting also works in Latin America. But they do not add anything new regarding the electoral impact of market-oriented economic reforms because Remmer does not include a measure of neoliberal reforms as an independent variable. In other words, she only tested the performance mandate argument.

The same can be said of Baker and Greene's study (2011); it does not actually test if higher levels of market reforms lead to more votes for the Left. The authors analyze whether leftists' gain is the response to a policy mandate against neoliberalism through an index called "mass support for the market," which is based on aggregate values from public opinion surveys, and find a declining enthusiasm for market reforms, concluding that there is a "moderate policy mandate." Their research examines the impact of opinions on the market rather than the influence of economic reforms on electoral outcomes.

Lora and Olivera's study (2005) is the first to test the impact of neoliberal reforms on the electoral fortunes of the incumbent party. Using their structural reform index (SRI), they analyze the effect of market-oriented economic reforms on the incumbent party's electoral results in presidential and legislative elections in seventeen Latin American countries from the mid-1980s to 2002. Their major finding is that Latin Americans "dislike pro-market policies *irrespective* of their results" (33; my emphasis). In other words, the policy mandate seems to prevail. They also find that the electorate rewards incumbents who control inflation. Ideology enters into their analysis as an independent variable, and it is only significant in legislative elections: "while the electorate dislikes privatization measures, it is more tolerant of them when the largest party in the legislature has a pro-market ideology" (40).

Although Lora and Olivera's study advances knowledge about the political impact of the neoliberal model in Latin America, it is still unknown if the implementation of those reforms has caused (or partially caused) the recent increase in the vote for the Left. Their dependent variable is the incumbent's share of the vote, not the vote for leftist parties.

Leftist parties can be the beneficiaries of the neoliberal model's failure because they traditionally oppose market-oriented economic reforms, and they are more supportive of state intervention in the economy. This argument leads to the hypothesis that higher levels of economic reform generate an increase in the share of the vote for left-leaning parties. But the idea that the mere existence of neoliberal reforms is sufficient to increase leftist votes assumes, first, that voters are policy oriented, a controversial argument among students of Latin America political behavior; and second, that voters do not like market-oriented economic reforms regardless of their results, which is, in fact, the main finding of Lora and Olivera (2005). Hence, two predictions are going to be tested. Given that all countries implemented neoliberal reforms but that left-wing parties do not always succeed, the first hypothesis states that *higher levels of economic reforms, by themselves, do not produce an increase in the share of the vote for leftist parties;* the mere existence of market-oriented reforms is not a sufficient condition to support the rise of left-wing parties. The second hypothesis complements the first one: *higher levels of economic reforms, accompanied by elevated levels of failure of these reforms, lead to an increase in the vote for leftist parties.* In other words, neoliberal reforms indirectly benefit left-of-center parties, because it is the failure of these reforms, or their unwanted effects, that improve leftist parties' electoral chances.

The second research agenda to which this question is connected is the comparative literature on voting behavior in Latin America. Most of the studies in that field focus on economic voting theory and electoral turnover, while research on partisanship voting is performed mainly by case studies. Although Latin American countries, along with other low-income democracies, have been subject to less economic voting research than the United States and Western Europe (Lewis-Beck and Stegmaier 2000), the results provided by comparative studies indicate that the economy is an important determinant of Latin Americans' vote (Echegaray 2005; Remmer 1991; Remmer and Gélineau 2003; Krueger 1994; Roberts and Wibbels 1999; Anderson et al. 2000; Molina 2001). There is extensive evidence that economic voting exists in Latin America, that the economy affects electoral outcomes, and that it is a major explanation for the high electoral volatility and turnover rate that exist in the region. But we do not know what economic conditions favor the vote for the Left.

Evidence from developed countries indicates that leftist governments are more concerned with economic goals such as full employment and a more egalitarian income distribution, whereas right-wing parties favor low inflation and tax control (Hibbs 1979). More recent research in industrialized democracies has found that support for right-wing governments is enhanced by low inflation and hurt by high inflation, whereas support for left-leaning governments increases when there is lower than average unemployment (Powell and Whitten 1993). For Latin America, Stokes (2001b) states that in situations of high inflation and growth, the electorate will vote in favor of efficiency-oriented policies, and under high unemployment, they will choose security-oriented policies. Generally, left-of-center parties support security-oriented policies while right-wing parties support efficiency-oriented ones. According to this evidence for the region, it is expected that *high levels of unemployment will increase the vote for leftist parties when the incumbent party is not leftist and that high levels of inflation will hurt leftist parties' electoral chances.*

Remmer (2003) supports the opposite view: left-wing constituencies prefer low inflation because high levels hurt the poor, and this argument is confirmed by Murillo, Oliveros, and Vaishnav's (2011) finding that voters react more negatively to left-wing administrations when there is high inflation than to right-wing administrations in the same situation. These scholars also find that Latin Americans are more sensitive to inflation than to growth, but that they do not examine the impact of a third crucial element of economic voting theories: unemployment.

Economic conditions matter differently depending on political parties' ideology, but they are not the whole story. Economic reforms and economic outcomes occur in a political context. Are economic factors relevant for understanding the movement of some countries to the left only under certain political conditions? And do political conditions, like having a leftist incumbent, affect the electoral possibilities of leftist parties? The impact of the economy on electoral outcomes is a phenomenon that receives academic consensus. James Carville's famous phrase, "It's the economy, stupid," is a good synthesis of the importance usually given to economic factors to explain the fortune of political parties in elections.[1] Nonetheless, scholars have found it extremely difficult to replicate in cross-national studies the economic voting effects found over time within countries. Adding political conditions to the economic conditions in order to explain how elections work solved this puzzle. Powell and Whitten (1993: 409) recommend that to "explain differences in retrospective economic voting across nations and over time we must take into account the political context within which elections take place."

Following this approach, the ideology of the incumbent is added as a political condition: *if a leftist party is the incumbent, and it has a poor economic performance, the share of the vote for the left will decrease in the following election, not as a consequence of the erosion of being in charge of the government, but as a result of bad economic results.* The incumbent's ideology is considered when testing the impact of unemployment: if the government is already leftist and the unemployment rate is high, left-oriented parties will not be able to take advantage of the situation.

To sum up, these hypotheses add to previous research by testing the argument that the increase in the vote for leftist parties is the political response to the implementation of neoliberal reforms, a policy mandate, or, the contrary, a performance mandate. In addition, they explore the economic and political conditions that favored this partisan vote.

To test these hypotheses, data was pooled from seventeen Latin American countries: Argentina, Bolivia, Brazil, Chile, Colombia, Costa Rica, Dominican Republic, Ecuador, El Salvador, Guatemala, Honduras, Mexico, Nicaragua, Paraguay, Peru, Uruguay, and Venezuela. The analysis covers the period from 1985 to 2004.[2] The decision to start the analysis in the 1980s, and not before or after, is based on two factors. First, the 1980s are considered the decade of democratic transitions in Latin America; before that time most Latin American countries were under authoritarian regimes that did not allow free elections. Second, the 1980s are considered the "lost decade" in economic terms and represent a natural baseline before the bulk of neoliberal economic reforms were implemented. The analysis ends in 2004 because going beyond the end of the century would compromise the empirical test; it cannot be argued that the electoral effects of the reforms could last too long after their implementation, which mainly took place during the 1980s and 1990s.

The dependent variable is computed in two ways: as the share of the vote that Left and Center-Left parties obtained in each presidential election and as the change in the share of votes for the Left and Center-Left parties from one presidential election to the previous one. The analysis only includes presidential elections for two reasons. First, Latin American countries have presidential regimes, and in most of them (Bolivia, Costa Rica, Ecuador, Guatemala, Honduras, Nicaragua, Paraguay, Peru, and Uruguay), legislative elections are concurrent with presidential elections, which means the former are highly influenced by presidential campaigns. Second, in the literature on the United States, which is the most widely researched area on this topic, there is scholarly disagreement over the existence of a macro-level relationship between the health of the national economy and the national congressional vote (see the discussion between Erikson 1990 and Jacobson 1990).

Political parties are classified in the Left-Right ideological dimension following Coppedge's criteria (see introd. and chap. 1). The level of economic reforms is measured by the SRI constructed by Lora (1997, 2001). This index gives scores to policies based on their degree of economic liberalization in five areas: trade, tax collection, financial markets, privatization, and labor markets. Countries receive an average annual score between 0 and 100 on each of these five policies. Those with the most state-centric policies score 0, whereas the most market-oriented ones receive 100. To generate the overall SRI, scores for each policy area are averaged. Based on the SRI, two variables are used in the analysis: the SRI mean for the previous period of government and the SRI change from one election to the previous one.

The argument that more reforms lead to more votes for leftist parties rests on two possible ideas. The first one is the policy mandate, which holds that Latin Americans have an aversion to neoliberal reforms. Lora and Olivera (2005) show evidence in favor of this. The second is the performance mandate, which holds that market-oriented economic reforms have failed, and as a consequence, voters punish those who support them and favor those against them. In order to assess the economic success or failure of market-oriented economic results, three economic variables are used: inflation, economic growth, and unemployment rate. These variables are commonly used in the economic voting literature. The inflation rate is measured on the basis of changes in the consumer price index and logged[3] to control for variations produced during hyperinflationary years. Economic growth is the percentage of change in GDP based on constant local currency. The unemployment rate refers to the share of the labor force that is without work but available for and seeking employment. The data come from World Development Indicators 2005 and BADEINSO-ECLAC 2005. All three variables are included in the analysis in three forms: as the mean for the previous government period (inflation mean, growth mean, and unemployment mean), as the election year value (inflation election year, growth election year, and unemployment election year), and as the change in the value between election years (change in inflation, change in growth, and change in unemployment).

To capture the influence of political context on the vote for leftist parties, the ideology of the incumbent is included.[4] As the hypotheses in the previous section stated, having a leftist incumbent may influence the electoral chances of leftist parties. The incumbent's ideology is a dummy variable that takes the value of 1 when the incumbent belongs to a Left or Center-Left party and 0 in the remainder of the cases. Table 2.1 shows the descriptive information for each variable included in the model.

Assessing the Importance of Competing Explanations

The most straightforward way to determine whether the depth of liberalization affects the level of support for left-leaning parties is to look at the evolution of both variables. There is not a unique pattern for all Latin American countries. In some countries both lines correlate in a positive direction; they have high and positive correlation coefficients: Argentina (0.94), Chile (0.86), Guatemala (0.99), Mexico (0.95), Nicaragua (0.99), El Salvador (0.99), and Uruguay (0.98). In the rest of the countries, each variable moves in a different direction: Bolivia (−0.24) and Colombia (−0.46); or in an opposite direction: Costa Rica (−0.74), Dominican Republic (−0.99), and Peru (−0.91); or the share of the vote for leftist parties and the SRI have a positive but low correlation: Brazil (0.32), Ecuador (0.52), Honduras (0.43), Paraguay (0.47), and Venezuela (0.45). What's more, for the whole region, the share of the vote for leftist parties and the SRI are minimally and negatively correlated (−0.02).

Does a different implementation of the neoliberal reforms lead voters to react differently? As shown in table 2.2, there is no clear pattern of behavior depending on the depth or speed of reform implementation. For example, among the countries that show a high and positive correlation between market reforms and leftist vote, a couple are early reformers (Argentina and Chile); one is a slow reformer (Mexico); another, a recent reformer (El Salvador); and one, a gradual reformer (Uruguay). In other words, there is not a unique voters' reaction to the distinct implementation of the Washington Consensus in the region. Or at least, through this raw way to look at it, Latin Americans did not vote more or less for leftist parties depending on how reforms were implemented.

Table 2.1. Summary Statistics

Variable	No. Obs.	Mean	Std. Dev.	Min.	Max.
Dependent Variables					
Percentage vote for left	85	28.92	23.32	0.00	84.50
Change in left vote share	68	1.43	17.57	−45.56	40.24
Economic Reforms					
Structural reform index	59	47.44	9.87	27.20	69.50
Change in structural reform index	46	5.81	14.77	−80.30	26.30
Economic Results					
Inflation mean	62	3.56	1.59	0.22	8.31
Inflation election year	62	3.24	1.95	−0.69	9.37
Growth mean	62	3.15	2.26	−3.50	7.75
Growth election year	62	3.10	3.75	−7.00	11.00
Unemployment mean	59	8.16	3.50	3.17	19.00
Unemployment election year	59	8.37	3.77	2.00	19.00
Political Variables					
Ideology incumbent	76	0.21	0.41	0.00	1.00

Source: Based on Lora and Olivera 2005; Political Database of the Americas (Georgetown University); World Development Indicators 2005; and BADEINSO-ECLAC 2005.

More extensive market reforms per se did not produce more votes for left-leaning parties; there is no linear relationship between the so-called neoliberal model and the Left's share of the vote. With this preliminary evidence, the SRI should not be significant in the models that predict the vote for leftist parties in Latin America. Table 2.3 reports regression results from several models that test the effect of market-oriented economic reforms, economic outcomes, and political variables on the share of the vote that leftist parties obtain in Latin American countries. All the regressions were run using robust standard errors clustered by country. Model 1 uses the mean for the previous government period for the three independent

Table 2.2. Types of Reformers versus Types of Correlations between Reforms and Leftist Vote in Latin America

	Slow Reformers	*Early Reformers*	*Recent Reformers*	*Gradual Reformers*
Positive and high correlation	Mexico	Argentina, Chile	El Salvador	Uruguay
Positive but low correlation	Brazil, Ecuador, Venezuela		Paraguay	
Negative and high correlation	Costa Rica		Dominican Republic, Peru	
Negative and low correlation			Bolivia	Colombia

variables that test the outcome-oriented argument, unemployment, inflation, and growth, because voters might take into account the performance of each indicator during the whole period when making their voting decisions. An alternative is presented in the second model: voters would be more receptive to the level of inflation, unemployment, and growth at the moment of the election, and so those variables are measured at their levels in the election year to take into account the short-term impact.

The most important finding is that, in agreement with the expectations and the preliminary evidence shown in the correlations, each of the models presents evidence that higher levels of economic reforms, by themselves, do not produce an increase in the vote for the Left. The SRI does not reach statistical significance in any of the models. In conclusion, the level of economic reforms implemented in Latin America does not have a direct impact on the increase in the vote for left-leaning parties in the region.

But market-oriented economic policies may have an impact on the vote for the Left in an indirect way. Previous research indicates that the main problem with the reforms is the social consequences that are produced: an increase in poverty, income inequality, unemployment, and the

Table 2.3. The Impact of Market Reforms, Economic Outcomes, and Political Variables on Share of the Vote for Leftist Parties in Latin America

Dependent variable: Percentage of vote for the ideological Left

Independent variables	(1)	(2)	(3)	(4)
Structural reform index (SRI)	0.108	0.063	−0.015	0.2151
	(0.236)	(0.433)	(0.979)	(0.244)
Inflation mean	3.923		3.803	3.799
	(3.892)		(4.287)	(4.236)
Inflation election year		1.976		
		(4.189)		
Growth mean	0.711		0.733	1.689
	(1.811)		(1.910)	(1.709)
Growth election year		0.061		
		(0.869)		
Unemployment mean	1.566**		0.900	1.992**
	(0.749)		(5.596)	(0.774)
Unemployment election year		1.414		
		(0.845)		
Unemployment*SRI			1.378	
			(11.319)	
Unemployment*Ideology incumbent				−4.629*
				(2.592)
Ideology incumbent*SRI				−0.908
				(0.824)
Ideology incumbent	12.483	12.092	12.428	88.094*
	(9.702)	(10.143)	(9.623)	(44.241)
Constant	−10.373	2.902	−4.089	−22.154
	(22.912)	(34.641)	(54.352)	(21.167)
Number of observations	53	53	53	53
R-squared	0.15	0.11	0.15	0.22
F-test	2.92**	1.73	2.41*	3.18**

Notes:
Robust standard errors in parenthesis.
* significant at 10%, ** significant at 5%, *** significant at 1%.
The data time span used for this regression analysis is 1985 to 1999.

percentage of Latin Americans working in the informal sector (Bogliac-cini 2013; Huber and Solt 2004; Portes and Hoffman 2003). Building on this evidence, economic reforms could have had an *indirect* effect on the vote for the Left through these negative social and economic outcomes. The regression results in Model 1 indicate that there is a degree of truth in this argument. Among the economic variables, the one that reaches statistical significance is the closest to being understood as an indicator of a social outcome: unemployment. More unemployment leads to an in-crease in the vote for leftist parties in Latin America, and in particular vot-ers seem to consider the unemployment rate for the whole period of gov-ernment rather than the rate during the election year. This result lends some further credibility to the argument that the failure or negative effects of neoliberal reforms lead to an increase in the vote for the Left.

In line with European partisan literature, high levels of unemploy-ment have been found to truly benefit left-of-center parties, even after controlling for the ideology of the incumbent. Unemployment is signifi-cant when it is measured as the average unemployment for the whole pe-riod of the previous government. On the contrary, inflation and growth are not significant. High levels of inflation do not hurt the Left, as other scholars have found (Remmer 2003; Murillo, Oliveros, and Vaishnav 2011). Neither inflation nor growth has a systematic connection with the vote for the Left. None of these two variables is significant under any specification. Following this evidence, it is possible to state that Latin Americans' partisan responses to economic outcomes are quite similar to those of Europeans.

One way to test the indirect impact of the Washington Consensus policies on the vote for left-wing parties is by looking at their undesired effects, such as unemployment. There is enough evidence provided by other scholars that one of the negative results of market-oriented reforms implementation was an increase in the unemployment levels in the re-gion. For example, Bogliaccini (2013) shows that among the structural re-forms, the one that had the biggest impact on the destruction of formal employment is trade liberalization. It is a mediating effect: the liberaliza-tion of trade produced high levels of unemployment, which in turn fa-vorably affected the vote for the Left.[5] Table 2.3 clearly shows that an increase in unemployment benefits leftist parties' electoral chances. To summarize, neoliberal reforms indirectly benefit Latin American leftist parties' electoral performance; they have a mediating effect.

But there is an alternative way to test this roundabout effect. It is also possible that the effect of the reforms on the vote is conditional on the level of unemployment. Structural reforms implemented during times with no unemployment problems might not affect the vote for leftist parties, while the opposite would happen when unemployment is high. Model 3 adds an interaction term between unemployment and the SRI. However, the combination of the two variables does not reach significance, indicating that the effect of the SRI does not change in a significant way when unemployment increases. To put it differently, political parties on the left side of the ideological spectrum benefit from poor economic outcomes, mainly unemployment, and neoliberal reforms do not seriously affect this relationship.[6]

Political context has a relevant influence on the electoral chances of the Left, as was expected. Model 4 indicates that for left-leaning parties, being in charge of the government is significantly and positively related to its electoral fortune. This finding could explain the reelection of Concertación in Chile (until 2010), Chávez in Venezuela, Morales in Bolivia, the PT in Brazil, the Kirchners in Argentina, and the Frente Amplio in Uruguay. Because most of these reelections of leftist parties occurred after 1999, they are not covered in this analysis; however, the finding indicates that left-of-center parties do not suffer from being in charge of the national government.

In general, high levels of unemployment help leftist parties' electoral chances. But does this opportunity still occur when the government is already in the hands of the Left? Common sense indicates that in this situation unemployment should have a negative impact on leftist parties' fortunes. However, this is only partially the case. The significance of the interaction term between incumbent's ideology and unemployment in Model 4 shows that an increase in unemployment benefits left-of-center parties only when the incumbent is not from the Left. Thus the effect of average unemployment on the vote for leftist parties varies with the presence or absence of a leftist incumbent. But if the incumbent is already a

Figure 2.1. Marginal Effect of Average Unemployment on Vote for Left,
Leftist, and Nonleftist Incumbents

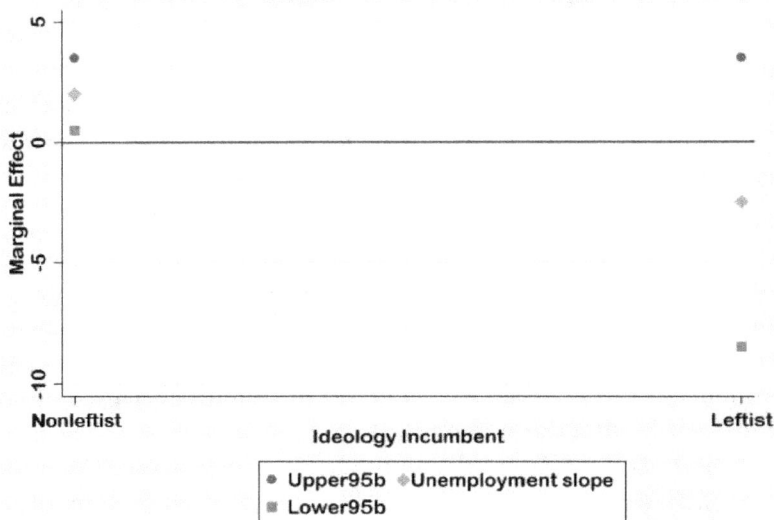

member of a left-wing party, an increase in unemployment does not result
in any significant gain or setback for his or her electoral chances (fig. 2.1).

It is also possible that market-oriented economic reforms have a different impact on leftist parties' electoral performance depending on the
incumbent's ideology. It would not be surprising that the Left gains votes
only when the Washington Consensus was implemented by center or
rightist parties. To test that impact, Model 4 includes the interaction term
between the SRI and the incumbent's ideology, but there is no significant
result. Regardless of who implemented the reforms, incumbent's ideology
does not have a significant impact on leftist parties' electoral fortune.

In order to confirm these results, the regression model was run with
a different measure of the vote for leftist parties. Table 2.4 presents the
results of a model using the change in the vote for the Left between one
election and the previous one. Note that all independent variables, where
possible, are also measured as changes in the value from one election year

Table 2.4. The Impact of Market Reforms, Economic Outcomes, and
Political Variables on Change in the Vote for Leftist Parties in Latin America

Dependent variable: Change in the vote share of the Left

Independent variables	(1)	(2)	(3)
Change in structural reform index	−0.056	−0.043	−0.044
	(0.116)	(0.112)	(0.112)
Change in inflation	0.823	0.810	0.793
	(1.575)	(1.696)	(1.640)
Change in growth	0.036	−0.017	−0.021
	(0.409)	(0.466)	(0.447)
Change in unemployment	1.577	1.535*	1.546
	(0.905)	(0.869)	(0.943)
Ideology incumbent*change	−0.513		−0.179
unemployment	(2.233)		(2.569)
Ideology incumbent*change		−0.488	−0.469
in SRI		(0.704)	(0.876)
Ideology incumbent	−28.888***	−24.036**	−24.333*
	(7.729)	(9.619)	(12.551)
Constant	7.185***	7.148**	7.137***
	(2.350)	(2.489)	(2.426)
Number of observations	42	42	42
R-squared	0.46	0.46	0.46
F-test	5.14***	4.12**	5.67***

Notes:
Robust standard errors in parentheses.
* significant at 10%, ** significant at 5%, *** significant at 1%.
"Ideology incumbent" is still significant when we drop Brazil 1998 and Dominican Republic 2000.

to the previous one. Regression results reinforce some arguments, but they
also reveal some contradictory findings. On the reinforcing side, they
again show that more neoliberal reforms do not generate more votes for
the Left. The evidence is conclusive on this point. Moreover, Model 2
indicates that an increase in unemployment has a significant and positive impact on the fortune of leftist parties. On the other side, under this

model specification, being in charge of the government significantly diminishes the electoral chances of left-leaning parties in the next election. The decrease in votes as a result of governing happens regardless of the implementation of market-oriented policies and the unemployment level, as is shown in the insignificant level of both interaction terms.

In order to test the robustness of these results, two cases that may represent a methodological problem were dropped from the dataset: Brazil, 1998, and the Dominican Republic, 2000. Since the 1998 elections, the Brazilian PSDB has been classified as Center-Right rather than Center-Left as previously. The same occurs with the Partido Revolucionario Dominicano (PRD) in 2000. Both political parties changed their ideology after being in charge of the government. Leaving them in the analysis may increase the negative effect that being an incumbent can have on the future electoral performance of the Left, but even after dropping these cases, the results remain the same.[7]

The strategy of pooling different Latin American countries risks masking the real effects of certain independent variables on the share of the vote for leftist parties. In order to control for any other direct effect of country context on the dependent variable, regressions were run, including country-fixed effects. Some results change. Using country dummies wipes out the significant relationship between unemployment and leftist vote, keeps the positive impact that being in charge of the government has for leftist parties' prospects, and reveals a hidden relationship: when a leftist party was the incumbent and implemented market-oriented economic reforms, the share of the vote for the Left decreased in the next election. In other words, Latin Americans punish leftist parties when they implement neoliberal policies. On the other hand, as shown in figure 2.2, the implementation of neoliberal reforms by rightist or centrist parties does not significantly increase the vote for leftist parties.

This finding contradicts the previous one, which states that when leftist incumbents have a poor economic performance their electoral chances diminish. Neither high levels of inflation nor high levels of unemployment nor low levels of growth hurt left-leaning parties' electoral chances. These differences can be partially explained by the smaller N that the regression models have or by the different specification of the models. Scholars debate the proper way to specify cross-national comparative

Figure 2.2. Marginal Effect of Structural Reform Index on Vote for Left, Leftist, and Nonleftist Incumbents

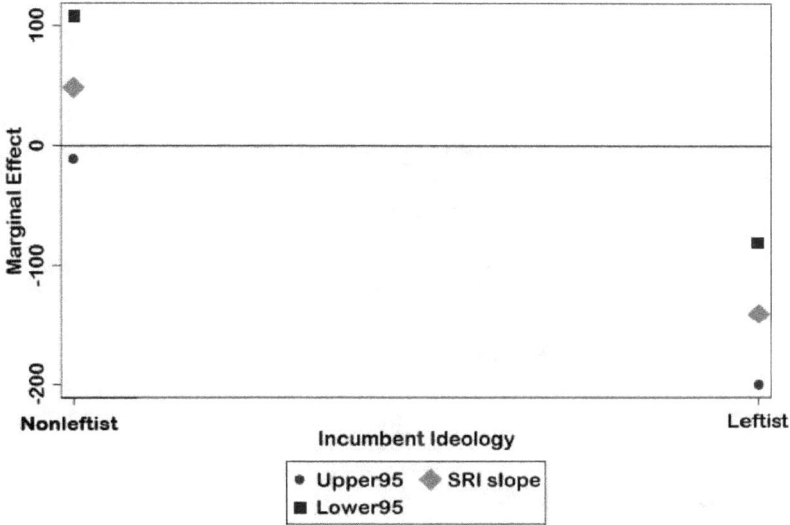

models, and many defend the use of country-fixed effects while working with data sets like this one. Statistically, there is no doubt that introducing country dummies has advantages; for example, it generally increases the explained variance. But theoretically the gains are not so obvious. As Przeworski and Teune (1970) argue, it is better to think less about proper names of countries and more about the relationships among variables such as unemployment, structural reforms, or incumbent ideology.

In conclusion, it is necessary to go beyond the macro-level analysis to fully understand under what economic and political conditions leftist parties increase their share of the vote in Latin America. The differences among results represent another piece of evidence signaling the need to explore the individual level for substantive determinants of left voting.

Going beyond the Macro Level

The main purpose of this chapter is to test the argument that the neoliberal model implemented in the 1990s has a positive impact on the vote for left-of-center parties in Latin America. The findings are conclusive: more market-oriented economic reforms do not produce more votes for political parties on the Left. Despite the fact that Lora and Olivera (2005) found that Latin Americans dislike pro-market policies irrespective of their results, and punish incumbents for implementing those reforms, this macro analysis shows that there is no clear and direct connection between that dislike and voting for leftist parties. But there is one exception: Latin Americans punish left-of-center parties that implemented those reforms.

From the basis of this evidence alone, however, it is not possible to conclude that free-market policies have no effect on the vote for the Left. The structural reform index measures how much a country has liberalized its economy, but it does not say anything about how voters perceive those reforms. Perception of economic reforms, or opinions about them, may not be related to the effective level of reforms. It is possible that in countries where fewer reforms have been implemented, citizens are more tired of them and as a consequence change their voting behavior in favor of those political parties that traditionally oppose efficiency-oriented policies.

Politicians' discourses relating those reforms to the country's well-being might have an impact on voters' perceptions. Hugo Chávez usually ties his country problems, and the troubles of the whole region, to the implementation of the Washington Consensus: "The situation of inequality and social and economic differences that still exists in Latin America as a result of the capitalist and neoliberal policies of the developed countries is the principal obstacle to achieving social cohesion" (Press Conference, Miraflores Presidential Palace, November 13, 2010). Constant repetition of this type of message might have an effect on voters' behaviors. To test whether the perceptions about reforms are more important to understand the vote for the Left than the effective level of reforms, we need a micro-level analysis rather than a macro-level one.

A second purpose of this chapter is to test under what economic and political conditions left-of-center parties increase their share of the vote. The main finding is that unemployment helps leftist parties' electoral chances. Leftist parties gain votes when unemployment rises. The positive effect that unemployment has on the vote for the Left can also be understood as an indicator of the indirect effect of market reforms, leading to the theory that it was not the reforms themselves but one of their impacts, unemployment, that generates the rise of the Left. As shown in the previous chapter, loss of jobs was one of the undesired effects of implementation of the Washington Consensus. Therefore, neoliberal economic reforms, through the rise in unemployment, *indirectly* benefited left-of-center parties. This finding helps us to understand why not all neoliberal reforms produced leftist governments.

Regarding the political conditions that benefit leftist parties, the effect of being in charge of the government is not conclusive, but the analysis sheds some light on what kind of outcomes and policies leftist governments should look for in order to survive. First, on the outcome side, they should avoid high levels of unemployment because their electoral chances are hindered when people lose their jobs. And second, on the policy side, they cannot implement market-oriented reforms since Latin Americans do not view favorably the association between the Left and neoliberal reforms.

In conclusion, the evidence provided by the macro analysis depicts a sophisticated image of Latin Americans. On one side, they are outcome oriented when voting for leftist parties because they respond to unemployment. However, when the Left is already in charge of the government, citizens also act in a policy-oriented way and punish left-wing parties that implement neoliberal reforms. Taking into consideration these diverse findings, it is possible to argue that the electoral rise of leftist parties in the region comes from a diverse set of causal mechanisms.

Macroeconomic and political explanations are relevant to understanding what macro conditions are favorable to the Left, but they do not allow us to answer questions regarding the factors that influence voters to choose a leftist party. The assumption that explanations at the macro level also work at the individual level (the so-called ecological fallacy) is one of the dangers implicit when researchers want to link the individual and the collective. Only a micro-level analysis can shed further light on the reasons leftist parties have recently increased their share of the vote in Latin American countries. In order to ascertain the determinants of Latin Americans' vote for leftist parties, if Latin Americans are voting against reforms, moving ideologically toward the Left, or behaving as policy oriented, or on the contrary, if they are just punishing the incumbent governments for poor economic results and acting outcome oriented, it is necessary to ask these questions at the individual level. The following chapters do this.

Chapter 3

MICRO EXPLANATIONS FOR VOTING LEFT
IN LATIN AMERICA

L atin American voting behavior is usually understood as being highly volatile and unpredictable due to the lack of strong party and ideological identifications. Latin Americans seem mainly to base their votes on short-term factors such as economic conditions (Roberts and Wibbels 1999; Cantón and Jorrat 2002) and candidate image (Echegaray 2005; Weyland 2003). It is in this context that recent victories of leftist parties are puzzling. If ideology and party identification are not relevant voting clues in Latin America (Echegaray 2005), why are voters choosing parties identified with the ideological Left? Is the vote for leftist parties another example of economic voting theory according to which voters punish the incumbent party for poor economic results? Are electorates in Latin America mainly choosing leftist parties because their candidates are, on average, more appealing than those of the Center and Right parties? Or, alternatively, are Latin Americans becoming more ideologically and policy-oriented by voting for the Left because ideology does indeed matter and voters are rejecting the neoliberal paradigm?

It is important to take note that this is not the first time in the history of Latin America that leftist parties have won elections. As chapter 1 showed, the prevalent ideology was leftist during part of the 1960s and 1970s. The main difference is that the meaning of voting Left is not as clear today. For example, when Salvador Allende, leader of the Chilean

Socialist Party, won the presidential election in 1970, his voters identified themselves with a socialist ideology, and they were largely in favor of nationalizing major companies, broadening the public sector, and other "leftist" policies (Baviskar 2004). At present, in Brazil, for example, we do not know whether Brazilians voted for Inácio "Lula" da Silva because they had become more leftist or because they were punishing incumbent Fernando H. Cardoso for not reducing unemployment.

In the view of many political analysts, the current increase in the vote for the Left in Latin America is a consequence of "reform fatigue." Simply stated, this argument holds that because voters are tired of market-oriented economic reforms and their consequences, they are voting in favor of parties that allow more state intervention in the economy. Data from the Latinobarómetro 2002 (*Economist* 2002) support this argument and indicate that the percentage of those who strongly agree or agree that the state should leave economic activity to the private sector diminished from 1998 to 2002 in all Latin American countries except for Mexico. This tendency of a decline in enthusiasm for market reforms was also recently stated by Baker and Greene (2011).

Following the same argument, AmericasBarometer 2010 data showing high levels of support for an active role for the national government in owning enterprises and industries, creating jobs, implementing policies to reduce income inequality, providing retirement pensions and health care services, and even ensuring the general well-being of the people in every Latin American country are quite impressive. Figure 3.1 presents the results of an index that measures government interventionism in the economy through the items listed above; values above 50 indicate that people prefer that the state, rather than the market, manage different aspects of the economy and their own welfare. Paraguay is the country in the region with more pro-state attitudes, followed by Uruguay, Costa Rica, and Chile. The only country included in the survey that has a majority pro-market attitude is not Latin American: it is the United States. As Tussie and Heidrich argue, speaking about the leftist tide, "if we are to point out the single coincidence in this diversity, there is a very significant one: the emergence of a pragmatic belief in a role for state management" (2008: 64).

Figure 3.1. Support for State Management by Country

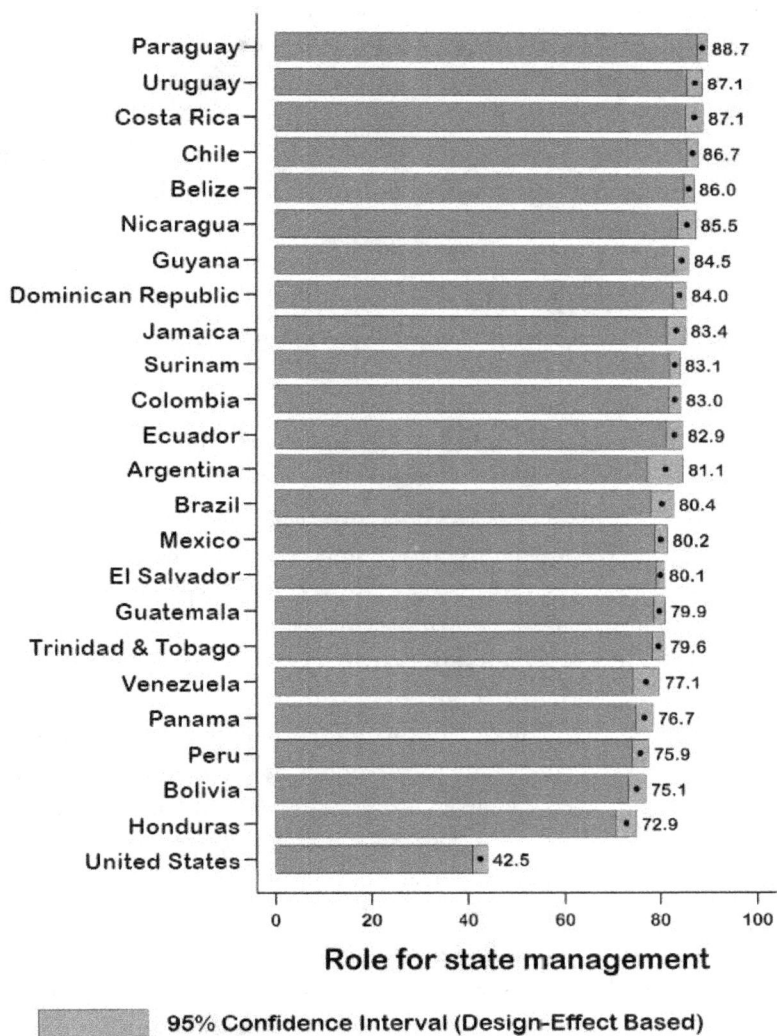

Paraguay	88.7
Uruguay	87.1
Costa Rica	87.1
Chile	86.7
Belize	86.0
Nicaragua	85.5
Guyana	84.5
Dominican Republic	84.0
Jamaica	83.4
Surinam	83.1
Colombia	83.0
Ecuador	82.9
Argentina	81.1
Brazil	80.4
Mexico	80.2
El Salvador	80.1
Guatemala	79.9
Trinidad & Tobago	79.6
Venezuela	77.1
Panama	76.7
Peru	75.9
Bolivia	75.1
Honduras	72.9
United States	42.5

Role for state management

95% Confidence Interval (Design-Effect Based)

Source: AmericasBarometer by LAPOP.

On the other hand, the aggregate analysis displayed in chapter 2 shows that the implementation of neoliberal reforms did not favor leftist parties in Latin America. At least at the macro level, there is no relationship between the level of market-oriented reforms implemented and the share of the vote that leftist parties receive in presidential elections. Only when the incumbent was a member of a leftist party and implemented market-friendly policies did the percentage of vote for leftist parties diminish in the next election. This does not necessarily mean that neoliberal reforms, and in particular their failure to produce sustainable economic growth and employment, have nothing to do with the recent voting behavior of Latin Americans. These findings prove only that even though the relationship does not exist at the aggregate level, it may be possible to find it at the individual level.

In the view of many scholars who study voting behavior and public opinion, perceptions are what really count when trying to understand why citizens act in the way they do. Individuals make their political decisions based on the way they perceive things rather than on any objective reality. Yeric and Todd explain that "the 'real' world is distorted by the individual to fit the already existing elements of the cognitive structure" (1989: 39). This assertion is further reinforced by Duch, Palmer, and Anderson's (2000) finding that public evaluations of the national economy are shaped by an individual's access to or possession of information as well as by a variety of political and socioeconomic factors. As a consequence, economic assessments can by no means be considered objective. Citizens can judge the country's economic performance negatively even though macro indicators show that the economy is doing fine. The same may happen with Latin Americans' perceptions of neoliberal economic reforms. The perception of economic reforms, or the opinion about them, may not be related to the actual level of reforms. It is possible that, contrary to conventional wisdom, in countries where fewer reforms have been implemented inhabitants are more tired of them and, consequently, change their voting behavior in favor of political parties that traditionally oppose efficiency-oriented policies. Independently, whether or not these perceptions are false, it is important to test their impact on the vote for the Left. And this requires micro-level analysis.

Micro-level analysis also allows one to test the impact of other voting determinants such as economic evaluation. At the aggregate level, unemployment is the only significant factor that explains the vote for leftist parties. Evidence presented in chapter 2 indicates that as the unemployment rate increases, so do the electoral chances of leftist parties. The relevance of the economic voting theory can be further appraised by a micro-level analysis because electorates may react to economic promises rather than to past performance and because individualistic pocketbook-oriented reasoning, which is not captured by any sociotropic aggregate measure, may be at play.

Once again, the two main possible explanations of the leftist tide are on the table: backlash against neoliberalism or performance mandate. So it will be tested if Latin Americans are policy oriented (ideology and policy issues are significant determinants of the vote), outcome oriented (economic evaluations are the significant predictors of the vote), or both. But the array of possible voting determinants of Latin Americans is much broader than the one set out thus far. In Fabián Echegaray's (2005) book, which can be considered the most comprehensive attempt to tackle Latin Americans' voting decisions, economic and extraeconomic factors are found to be important voting clues. At the aggregate level, Echegaray finds that candidate appeal is the most important factor shaping support for the incumbent party at the ballot box, while economic variables rank second. At the individual level, the results are different: in addition to economic voting, partisan inclinations are found to be relevant. The variation between the relevant voting clues at the aggregate and individual level can be explained by the different model specifications. While the aggregate model includes variables to measure candidate voting, in the individual-level model those variables are absent. What is more, while the aggregate model has been tested in forty-one competitive presidential elections held in Latin America between 1982 and 1995, the micro-level analysis only examines one election in each of three countries: Argentina, Peru, and Uruguay. Although Echegaray's study is quite complete, it is not devoid of problems. One of the most serious is that his theoretical foundations disregard ideology and partisanship as important voting cues for Latin Americans, but later he finds that partisanship is influential

at the individual level in countries with a high level of political institutionalization like Uruguay. In conclusion, to fully explore the voting
determinants of Latin Americans, partisanship and ideology should be
included in the explanatory models.

Taking into account the research on voting behavior done for Western Europe and the United States and building on the results of previous
studies about Latin American voting, five theories are going to be tested
to explain the rise of the Left in Latin America: *economic voting theory*,
social class cleavages (Lipset and Rokkan 1967); *prospect theory* (Kahneman and Tversky 1979); *partisanship theory* (Campbell 1960); and *cleavages created by political processes* (Przeworski and Sprague 1986; Torcal
and Mainwaring 2003). In particular, the individual-level analysis aims to
understand the role of economic evaluations (economic voting theory),
risk propensity (prospect theory), class structure (social class cleavage
theory), partisanship, and ideology and policy issues (cleavages created
by political processes) in the recent rise of the Left in Latin America.
Each of these theories is described below.

Economic Voting Theory

The literature on voting behavior in Latin America is dominated by the
economic voting explanation, which is the best theory to test the performance mandate argument. Economic voting theory states that if the
economy is doing fine, voters will reelect the incumbent party, whereas
in bad times, citizens will punish the incumbent at the ballot box. The
theory has taken four major forms: pocketbook vote, sociotropic vote
(Kinder and Kiewiet 1981), retrospective vote, and prospective vote (Mac-
Kuen, Erikson, and Stimson 1992). These distinctions lead to four possible combinations in which citizens can appraise the economic situation:
how good or bad the economic situation of the country has been during
the past (retrospective sociotropic); voters' expectations of the country's
economic situation in the future (prospective sociotropic); how good or
bad their family's economic situation has been in the recent past (retrospective pocketbook); or expectations for their family's economic future
(prospective pocketbook).

Economic voting theory has noticeably proved its predictive power in the stable economic and political contexts of the United States and Western Europe (Fiorina 1981; Kinder and Kiewiet 1981; Lewis-Beck and Bellucci 1982; MacKuen, Erikson, and Stimson 1992; Nadeau and Lewis-Beck 2001; Lewis-Beck 1986, 1988). And there is a consensus that Americans and Europeans respond more to changes in their country's economic conditions than to changes in their own economic lives (Kinder 1998).

In Latin America, scholars have tested the relationship between economic downturns and voting for incumbent parties in single-country case studies (Cantón and Jorrat 2002; Domínguez and McCann 1995; Mora y Araujo and Smith 1984; Remmer and Gélineau 2003; Roberts and Arce 1998; Seligson and Gómez 1989; Weyland 1998, 2003) and in comparative studies (Echegaray 2005; Remmer 1991; Roberts and Wibbels 1999), but the evidence is far from conclusive. Economic evaluations matter for Latin Americans depending on the election. For example, Weyland found that Venezuelans were pocketbook voters from 1989 to 1993 (Weyland 1998) but sociotropic voters when they elected Hugo Chávez in 1998 (Weyland 2003). Cantón and Jorrat (2002) and Echegaray (2005) also find that the impact of the economy on Latin Americans' vote choice varies across countries and elections. Despite these distinctions, scholars confirm that voters in Latin America tend to treat elections as plebiscites on the economic performance and capabilities of the government.

If economic factors are important determinants of the fortune of incumbents, are there any specific economic conditions that favor leftist parties in comparison with centrist or rightist parties? The aggregate analysis presented in chapter 2 shows that leftist parties gain votes when unemployment increases. At the individual level, according to the economic voting explanation, the expectation is that voters who evaluate the economic situation negatively will punish the incumbent. In countries where the incumbent is a leftist party, citizens will reward or punish it depending on the economic performance. But in countries where leftist parties were never in charge of the government and represent a "credible" or "untainted" opposition, electorates that are economically dissatisfied with the economy will cast their vote in favor of them. In other words: *the more negatively a voter evaluates the national economic situation, the greater the probability he or she will vote for the opposition. In particular, voters who are discontented will reward leftist parties when they were not in charge of the government.* To put it simply, if a voter has a negative economic evaluation (x1) and leftist parties represent a "credible" or "untainted" opposition (x2), he or she will vote for the Left (y).

There are four variables to test the economic voting theory: retrospective sociotropic vote, retrospective pocketbook vote, prospective sociotropic vote, and retrospective sociotropic vote. *Sociotropic vote* measures the evaluation of the country's economic situation; the higher the value, the worse the evaluation. *Pocketbook vote* measures the evaluation of the family's economic situation; the higher the value of the variable, the worse the family's economic assessment is. *Prospective vote* measures the expectations regarding the economic future; *retrospective vote* measures the evaluation of the country's economic situation in comparison with the past. The measurement of these variables is fully described in relation with each dataset in the next chapter. A "credible" or "untainted" party is one that is at least outside the government, a nonincumbent.

Cleavage Created by the Political Process

Ideology is regarded as one of the most influential voting clues. Electorates use the overarching continuum from Left to Right, or from liberal to conservative, as a shortcut to processing political information and making their electoral decisions. Since Converse (1964) there has been a great deal of debate about how readily voters rely on ideology when voting and to what extent citizens organize their political opinions around the ideological dimension. The same doubts are cast regarding the importance of ideology to predict Latin Americans' voting behavior. Echegaray (2005) considers that ideological clues are an irrelevant source of guidance for Latin American voters, but he does not test this contention empirically. Differing from Echegaray's position, this study tests the impact of ideological clues on the vote for leftist parties.

Several reasons make the inclusion of ideology reasonable, but the most important is its relevance to testing the argument that Latin Americans are voting Left as a reaction against the Washington Consensus. In order to do that, two different scholarly understandings of ideology are used to examine the policy performance argument: the "strong" meaning of ideology, which demands high levels of political sophistication and political knowledge from citizens and for that reason is highly controversial as a determinant of voting behavior; and the "weak" meaning of ideology, which is basically the capability that individuals have to place themselves in the ideological spectrum (Conover and Feldman 1980; Inglehart and Klingemann 1976; Zechmeister 2006).

Starting from the weak meaning, as was pointed out earlier, a majority of Latin Americans are capable of placing themselves in the ideological dimension. Data from the AmericasBarometer 2010 dataset indicate that an average of 80 percent of people define their place in the scale but that the percentage varies depending on the country. Despite the fact that Left and Right ideological labels mean more to Uruguayans than to Argentineans, as a first appraisal, ideological thinking is part of Latin Americans' political behavior.

Also, there is empirical research pointing to ideology as a relevant voting clue for Latin Americans. Torcal and Mainwaring (2003: 83) point out that "class emerges as a major cleavage in party systems to the extent that parties of the left emphasize class issues," and they called this phenomenon the cleavage created by political processes (Torcal and Mainwaring 2003; see also Przeworski and Sprague 1986).[1] This theoretical approach to cleavage formation pays attention to how cleavages are created by political elites and political factors. The Left/Right ideological division can also be considered a cleavage created by political process. In other words, politicians can activate this cleavage as a way to get votes. All this suggests that it is appropriate to test for ideological clues: *ideological self-placement is likely to determine the vote for the Left irrespective of social and structural determinants.*

Luna and Zechmeister (2005b), who have shown that elite groups and citizens are linked by ideological commitments, combine elite and mass survey data to create indicators of representation for nine nations: Argentina, Bolivia, Brazil, Chile, Colombia, Costa Rica, Ecuador, Mexico, and Uruguay. The level of representation is quantified by how much congruency exists between congressmen and voters' policy preferences.

In order to measure the extent to which political parties and their con-
stituents have clear and consistent preferences over a set of relevant policy
dimensions, they use data from two sources: the survey of Latin American legislators carried out by the University of Salamanca in 1997 and
the 1998 Latinobarómetro survey. Using these measures of policy preferences, they build the representation scores and find that country differences are also relevant in that respect. Chile and Uruguay present the
highest levels of ideological elite-mass congruency in the region, while
Ecuador ranks in the lowest position. Mexico and Brazil are also among
the countries with low levels of ideological congruency; Mexico scores
lower than Brazil. Regardless of these differences, and some dubious
matching that the authors performed between indicators at the mass
and elite level, what this research indicates is that ideology is a relevant
category for understanding political representation at least in some Latin
American countries.

The alternative way to test the policy mandate or the ideological
cleavage is based on policy preferences: its "strong" meaning. Voting for
the Left is usually associated with support for government involvement
and regulation of the economy, income redistribution, and an increase in
social spending (Inglehart and Klingemann 1976; Fuchs and Klingemann 1990; Kitschelt and Hellemans 1990). In addition, and due to the
difficulty of obtaining survey data that deals with citizens' perceptions
and opinions about market-oriented economic reforms, the analysis of
policy preferences is the best way to approach this issue. Consequently,
the following hypothesis is tested: *those Latin Americans who support government involvement and regulation of the economy, income redistribution,
and an increase in social spending will be more likely to vote for leftist parties,
while those who are against these policy issues will be more likely to vote for
rightist parties.*

Ideology is measured in its weak meaning by the ideological self-
placement of the respondent in a dimension that ranges from 1 (Left) to
10 (Right). The strong meaning is tested with different policy issues used
as independent variables: support for regional integration, support for
privatization, support for agrarian reform, opinion about government re-
sponsibility, support for social spending, and position with respect to the
inflation/unemployment dichotomy.[2]

Prospect Theory

Prospect theory states that individuals act in a risk averse or risk acceptant way depending on whether they are in the domain of losses or in the domain of gains (Kahneman and Tversky 1979). If an individual considers himself in the domain of losses, the theory expects that he will behave as risk acceptant because there is nothing, or little, to lose. On the contrary, individuals under the domain of gains behave more conservatively, are less willing to gamble with their profits, and become risk averse.

Scholars of Latin America have started to test prospect theory in different political phenomena. Weyland (2002) applied this theory in order to understand why politicians implemented market-oriented economic reforms and why citizens supported these reforms in some Latin American countries and not in others. In the voting behavior subfield, many Mexicanists have used prospect theory to understand why Mexicans keep voting for the "known devil" (i.e., the PRI) instead of voting for the opposition parties (Domínguez and McCann 1996; Magaloni 1999). Morgenstern and Zechmeister (2001) also used prospect theory to understand the 1997 midterm Mexican election result in which opposition parties became the majority in the lower chamber. They found that risk acceptant voters were more likely to support the opposition when they perceive economic decline, whereas risk adverse Mexicans tend to stay with the PRI despite being unhappy with its economic performance.

This explanation can help us to understand why Latin Americans vote for leftist parties. In countries where the Left has been outside the government for many years, electorates that make a negative assessment of the government's economic performance will vote for it if they are risk acceptant. This argument leads to the following hypothesis: *when the incumbent is not a leftist political party and leftist parties belong to the opposition, risk acceptant citizens, more than risk adverse ones, will choose the Left at the voting booth. The propensity to vote for the Left will increase if a voter is in the domain of losses and if he or she is risk acceptant.* To simplify, if leftist parties represent a "credible" or "untainted" opposition (x2), voters who are risk acceptant (x3), and consider themselves in the domain of losses, which is equivalent to having a negative economic evaluation (x1), will tend to vote for leftist parties (y). The model should test the effect of each of these variables separately and also interacting with one another in order to analyze how voters who are risk acceptant increase their propensity to vote Left if they feel they are in the domain of losses ($x3^*x1$).

Prospect theory is tested here by means of different variables that capture voters' risk propensity. One set of variables tackles citizens' opinions about how different political parties would manage the economy, deal with the issue of job creation, negotiate with other countries, organize public security, and control social unrest. Another set of variables measures how risky it is to vote for different candidates. Finally, the question that is commonly used to gauge risk propensity asks respondents to agree with one of the two following aphorisms: "Más vale malo conocido que bueno por conocer" (Better the devil you know than the saint you don't) or "El que no arriesga no gana" (Nothing ventured, nothing gained).[3]

Social Class Cleavage

The theoretical approach linking the existence of social cleavages with voters' behavior has been developed principally for Western European political parties. Lipset and Rokkan (1967) argue that the stability of party systems in Western Europe is a consequence of the historical roots that political parties have in class, religion, and nationality cleavages. The social cleavage literature was extended in various ways. This study examines two of those extensions: the class causal linkage proposition and the cleavage created by political process. The latter is described above.

The "class causal linkage proposition" states that the social position that an individual has in society determines his or her political preferences (Lipset and Rokkan 1967). Belonging to the working class increases the probability of voting for Left parties, whereas being part of the capitalist class reduces this probability. This hypothesis goes against the general understanding of Latin American voting behavior as being highly volatile and unpredictable due to the lack of strong party and ideological identification (Remmer 1993; Ames 2001). It is also contrary to the literature that points out that class cleavages do not matter as social bases of the vote in Latin America except in the Chilean case. Moreover, the Chilean case is open to debate. Scholars agree that in the pre-authoritarian

Chilean party system, class cleavage had an important role; but in the post-authoritarian period, class-based voting appeared less relevant, and there is no consensus about how determinant it is in predicting behavior at the ballot box (Roberts and Wibbels 1999; Torcal and Mainwaring 2003). Another argument that undermines the relevance of social position as a possible voting predictor are the severe transformations during the 1980s and 1990s that affected Latin Americans' well-being and structure of production, which would have weakened social class identities (Echegaray 2005).

Nevertheless, there are two reasons for testing this argument. First, the previous characterization of party systems as unstable cannot be applied to all Latin American countries or political parties since many countries, such as Uruguay and Chile, have highly institutionalized party systems (Mainwaring and Scully 1995). Second, most of the studies that test social cleavage as an explanation of voting behavior and find no evidence rely on aggregate data. In particular, the work by Roberts and Wibbels (1999) uses very crude proxies (union density, informal sector) to measure the structure of sociopolitical cleavages. Moreover, more recent research indicates that social class matters as a vote's predictor (Roberts 2003, for the Venezuelan case under Hugo Chávez; and Cantón and Jorrat 2002, for the Argentinean case using survey data). Therefore, the hypothesis states: *the position that a person occupies in the social structure determines his or her vote. Workers and members of the popular sectors are more likely to vote for leftist parties, while those who belong to the dominant sectors are more likely to vote for rightist parties.*

In reality, there is no doubt that the classical social class cleavage explanation has been brought into question by the structural transformations of national economies and the contraction of the working class. Przeworski and Sprague (1986), for instance, argue that in the mid-1980s the support for leftist parties in Europe weakened due to the shrinking of the working class, but political leaders had the opportunity to appeal to a broader electorate by addressing other issues. Leftist parties always had to attract support beyond the working class in order to win elections; in other words, their electorates include workers but also people from other social classes. Kitschelt (1994) also demonstrates in his study of European social democracy that the electoral prospects of the Left are not necessarily undermined by the social transformations and policy constraints associated with market-oriented reforms. Party leaders can appeal to new electorates and become allies of new social sectors.

Latin America after the implementation of neoliberal economic reforms resembles the description by Przeworski and Sprague and Kitschelt for Europe. In most Latin American countries, the working class remained stagnant or shrank as a result of market liberalization, public sector cutbacks, and privatizations that were implemented during the 1990s. Most of the formal workers who lost their jobs moved into the informal economy, with the result that informal workers became the largest class in every Latin American country (Portes and Hoffman 2003). Evidence of the shrinkage suffered by the formal workers' sector in Latin America is abundant. In Bolivia, formal workers were 31.4 percent of the economically active population (EAP) in 1989 and 24.8 percent in 1997; in Costa Rica, 60.1 percent in 1981 and only 49.9 percent in 1998; and in Mexico, 63.1 percent in 1984 and 47.3 percent in 1998 (Portes and Hoffman 2003, based on ECLAC). As a countereffect, informal employment increased from 44.6 percent of the Latin American urban EAP in 1990 to 47.9 percent in 1998 (Portes and Hoffman 2003).

Taking this into account, the recent increase in the vote for leftist parties may not be explained by the social class cleavage theory because the class that traditionally voted for the Left, the working class, has diminished. An alternative explanation is possible. Building on Portes and Hoffman's (2003) research on the changes in Latin American social structures, this book argues that informal workers are increasingly voting for leftist parties. Preliminary evidence from Venezuela shows that getting the support of the augmented informal sector is becoming an efficient strategy for winning elections in Latin America (Roberts 2003). Hence, *voters who belong to the informal sectors will be more likely to vote for the Left.*

Social class cleavage is tested using a set of five dummy variables; each of these represents one category of social class defined in terms of occupation: dominant class, petty bourgeoisie, formal workers, informal workers, and the nonemployed. This categorization is built on Portes and Hoffman's (2003) definition of Latin American class structure. These scholars argue that it is better to add a separate category for informal workers to understand Latin America social structure. Each category is entered into the model as a dummy variable that takes the value of 1 when the person belongs to it and 0 when he or she does not.[4]

Partisanship

Since publication of *The American Voter* (Campbell 1960), the influence of party identification has become one of the central theoretical concepts in voting research. Partisanship or party identification "acts to filter individual's views of the political world, providing them not only with a means for making voting decisions but also with a means for interpreting short-term issues and candidacies since parties are central actors in most political conflicts" (Dalton and Wattenberg 1993: 197).

In Latin American voting behavior, party identification does not always work as a strong predictor of the vote. Mainwaring and Scully (1995) point out that in Uruguay, Chile, and Colombia, between 60 and 70 percent of citizens mention a party preference, while in Brazil no more than 40 percent declare themselves to have a party identification. More recent data report that only 32 percent of Latin American citizens have a partisan identification (AmericasBarometer Dataset 2010). In addition to cross-national variation, there is cross-party variation in each country. Preliminary evidence from Brazil (Samuels 2004) indicates that the PT receives higher party preference than the rest of Brazil's parties do.

What is the relevance of partisan clues to explaining the vote for leftist parties in Latin America? Extant research indicates that Latin American leftist parties help structure party systems along ideological lines, and they are associated with higher levels of representation (Luna and Zechmeister 2005b). Consequently, partisanship can be more important to predict the vote for leftist parties than for rightist ones. Hence, *partisanship is a more relevant voting clue for those who vote for leftist parties than for voters who choose centrist or rightist parties.*

A strong party identification can influence other voting clues. For example, a Brazilian who feels very close to the PT may evaluate the economic performance of the government through partisanship lenses and be more negative on his or her assessments of Cardoso's economic performance. It is probable that economic evaluations weigh less for those who have party identification than for those with none.[5] Taking into consideration this possibility, I test the argument that *voters with party identification are less likely to take into consideration economic evaluations than those without party preferences.*

These alternative, but not exclusive, explanations have never been tested together for Latin America. In that sense, this study makes two contributions. First, it sheds light on which factors are involved in determining the recent rise of the Left in Latin America. In particular, it compares the possible impact of neoliberal economic reforms as against performance evaluations, and also other more traditional voting clues such as class identifications and partisanship against new ones like propensity risk. Second, and more broadly, it tells us about the most important voting determinants for Latin American electorates because it tests the five theories over the 1980–2004 period for three country cases: Brazil, Mexico, and Uruguay.

Chapter 4

LATIN AMERICANS ARE VOTING LEFT

Evidence from Brazil, Mexico, and Uruguay

Methodologically, an ideal strategy for investigating why Latin Americans are voting for leftist political parties would be to conduct one public opinion poll for every election held in each Latin American country from 1980 to 2004. Moreover, all surveys would include the same variables to test all the theories proposed in the previous chapter. But survey data for Latin America, as well as many other regions of the world, are far from ideal. A vast majority of surveys on voting determinants are carried out by private pollsters who are mainly interested in predicting electoral results and do not provide information necessary to examine voting theories. Taking into account these constraints, I follow a most-different systems research strategy (Przeworski and Teune 1970) to test the hypotheses presented in chapter 3. For each of the three countries studied, it was possible to obtain surveys covering almost the entire 1980–2004 period; furthermore, these surveys have similar questions, which makes it possible to replicate the same explanatory model in each country. In Brazil and Uruguay left-of-center presidents were in charge of the government; in Mexico, a right-of-center candidate won the presidency despite the leftist parties' gain in votes. The question is one of identifying what is sufficiently common among Brazilians, Mexicans, and Uruguayans to produce political events that are fairly similar.

The most-different systems design tests relationships at the individual level across a range of very different countries. Przeworski and Teune (1970) conceived this design to determine how robust any relationship among variables is, independent of other contextual variables. As Peters summarizes it, "The principal task in this design is to find relationships among variables that can survive being transported across a range of very different countries" (1998: 41). If those Brazilians, Mexicans, and Uruguayans who vote for leftist parties have a negative evaluation of the economic situation of their countries, it is possible to infer that behind the leftist electoral trend there is evidence of Latin Americans' performance mandate. On the contrary, if Brazilians, Mexicans, and Uruguayans are voting for left-of-center parties pushed by anti-market demands, the leftist tide would be the result of a policy-oriented citizenry, demanding more state intervention. Finally, if other factors such as party identification, age, or social class are the most relevant predictors of voting behavior, and perceptions about market-oriented economic reforms and economic outcomes are not, the latter can be disregarded as crucial determinants at the individual level to explain the vote for the Left in Latin America.

There are several differences between Brazil, Uruguay, and Mexico that make this case selection relevant and that represent demanding testing scenarios for the two main behavioral arguments. To describe those differences, the focus is on those characteristics that are pertinent for the purpose of this research: party and political systems, level of economic reforms, and economic well-being. These three sets of characteristics correspond to the three groups of independent variables tested in the macro level chapter: political variables, economic reform variables to test the policy mandate, and economic variables for the performance mandate.

The differences between Brazilian, Mexican, and Uruguayan party and political systems are large. Brazil is usually defined as a case of party underdevelopment and weakly established political institutions (Ames 2001; Mainwaring and Scully 1995; Mainwaring 1999). Its multiparty system has been described as "highly fragmented," with comparatively high electoral volatility. "More than one-third of sitting legislators change parties during a term, and individualism, clientelism and personalism rather than programmatic appeals dominate electoral campaigns" (Samuels 2006: 1). Scholars believe that mass partisanship in Brazil is comparatively weak (Mainwaring, Meneguello, and Power 2000), but recent research challenges this view and indicates that Brazilians have higher levels of party identification than many other new democracies, with mass partisanship particularly strong among PT voters (Samuels 2006).

For a long time, Mexico was characterized as a weakly institutionalized political system (Mainwaring 1999) with single-party dominance in the shape of the long-ruling Partido Revolucionario Institucional. The PRI was in charge of the national government from 1929 to 2000, and opposition parties were unable to win a majority in the lower chamber of congress until 1997, when the single, dominant-party system was broken in favor of a multiparty system. It was not until 2000 that the Partido de Acción Nacional (PAN), a right-leaning party, ousted the PRI from the presidency. Uruguay has had a very stable party system (Mainwaring and Scully 1995), with three major political parties, Partido Colorado (PC), Partido Nacional (PN), and Frente Amplio (FA), and one minor party, Partido Independiente (PI). It was with the emergence of the FA in 1971 that the party system experienced a major change, evolving from a two-party system to a multiparty system (Gillespie and González 1989; González 1991). Mass party identification is commonplace; an average of two-thirds of Uruguayans have reported their party identification since the return to democracy in 1985.[1]

To put it simply, Brazil, Mexico, and Uruguay are dissimilar in their levels of party system institutionalization, numbers of political parties, and mass partisanship. Mainwaring and Scully (1995) classify Brazil as an inchoate party system, Mexico as a hegemonic party system, and Uruguay as an institutionalized one. Several things changed by the end of the 1990s—one of them being that Mexico can no longer be considered a hegemonic party system. In terms of the number of parties, Mexico and Uruguay have experienced important transformations by becoming multiparty systems and raising the level of party competition. Recent research shows that the number of parties affects the way in which voters hold governments accountable; multiparty systems strengthen voters' ability to punish several parties at a time, so popular discontent may be lower in countries with more permissive electoral rules that allow small parties to gain congressional representation (Benton 2005). Regarding partisanship, Mexico and Uruguay have higher proportions of their populations with party attachment than Brazil. By having diverse party systems and political systems, these countries made an appropriate case selection to test voting behavior theories.

Market-oriented economic reforms were also implemented very differently in Brazil, Mexico, and Uruguay. Brazil and Mexico are classified as slow reformers: they started reforms later and adopted fewer structural reforms. Uruguay is considered a gradual reformer: reforms were adopted earlier, but they were milder and carried out gradually (Lora 1997, 2001). The differences in the reforms pursued in Brazil, Mexico, and Uruguay also depend on the area being reformed. Brazil presents some of the highest privatization reform and labor reform indexes. On the other hand, Mexico ranks low on tax reform and labor reform indexes but high on the financial reform index. Finally, Uruguay has one of the lowest levels of privatization in the region but one of the highest indexes of trade reform (Lora 1997, 2001).

There are many indicators available to compare the economic well-being of Brazilians, Mexicans, and Uruguayans. To maintain comparability with the macro level section of this study, I compare two indicators: inflation and economic growth. Inflation was an enormous problem in all Latin American countries during the 1980s and mid-1990s, and it was finally brought under control at the end of the 1990s and early 2000s.[2] Among the three countries, Brazil was the one that suffered most from a hyperinflationary crisis: it experienced three-digit inflation from 1980 to 1994. In Mexico and Uruguay hyperinflation was a less common malady, affecting the former in 1983, 1987, and 1988 and the latter in 1990 and 1991. In terms of economic growth, the three countries experienced several ups and downs during the period of study. Brazil and Mexico have been experiencing an increase in their growth rate since the early 2000s. In Uruguay, economic growth was negative from 1999 to 2003. The 2002 economic crisis worsened the situation, with percentage change in GDP based on constant local currency for 2002 at −10.8.[3] This state of affairs was overcome in 2004 with a positive growth rate of 4.5.

Brazil, Mexico, and Uruguay are all cases of *continuous increase* of the Left,[4] but the electoral trajectories followed by left-of-center parties since the 1980s in each country differ. In Brazil, leftist parties gained access to the government in 2002. Before that, in 1994, the Partido Social

Democracia Brasileira, a social democrat party, carried Cardoso to the presidency. However, when the PSDB was elected to Brazil's national government, it had already moved to the Right of the ideological scale. Therefore, the first time that a left-of-center party gained access to Brazil's national government after the return to democracy was in 2002, with the election of da Silva, the longtime leader of the PT. In Mexico, leftist parties, in particular the Partido Revolucionario Democrático, have increased their share of the vote during the 1990s and, by doing so, have helped to increase competitiveness in the Mexican electoral arena. The PRD received almost one-fifth of the votes cast in the 1994 and 2000 presidential elections, and in 2006 it lost the presidency by just 1 percent of the votes in a highly controversial vote count. In Uruguay, leftist parties have progressively increased their electoral participation since the return to democracy in 1984, and in 2004, after twenty years of democracy, a left-leaning coalition called the Encuentro Progresista–Frente Amplio (EP-FA) won the presidency. All these leftist parties, PT, PRD, and EP-FA, are examples of professional parties: they care about party building, they have relatively strong party organizations, and they mobilize political support in addition to social support. In that sense, they are more similar to Concertación in Chile than to Movimiento al Socialismo (MAS) in Bolivia or Hugo Chávez's party, the Movimiento Quinta República, in Venezuela. They are usually categorized as the "institutional" Left in Latin America, as opposed to the "populist" Left represented mainly by the Movimiento Quinta República.[5]

But why has the Left gained the advantage? One possible answer points to the backlash against neoliberal reforms. The other attributes the main cause to poor economic performance. But why should those insufficient economic outcomes have benefited left-of-center parties and not others? Most Latin Americans have faced economic hardship during successive governments under a variety of political parties, and recent research demonstrates that voters have long-term economic memories (Benton 2005) and punish not only the incumbent party for material suffering. They also rebuke parties that governed before the incumbent came to power. Left-of-center parties were able to take advantage of this popular discontent and capitalized on social and economic dissatisfaction because they could claim to be a "credible" or "untainted" opposition, that is, never in charge of the government and therefore not responsible for the country's welfare. In Brazil, the most credible opposition was embodied by the PT. The search for new alternatives could have led Uruguayans to vote for the Frente Amplio, a left-leaning coalition party that represents the only credible or untainted opposition after a long succession of Partido Colorado and Partido Nacional governments. Mexico could represent a different example of the same phenomenon. The electorate's search for something new ended up with its favoring the two credible and untainted opposition parties: PAN, a Center-Right political party, and the PRD, a leftist party. To summarize, leftist parties would be able to capitalize social discontent when (1) they represent a credible or untainted opposition and even more so when (2) they are the only untainted opposition in the political system.

The following sections describe in greater detail each country's electoral path and how "untainted" the Left is in each.

Uruguay: The Left as the Only Untainted Opposition

In the Uruguayan party system, two political parties are considered left-of-center, the Encuentro Progresista–Frente Amplio and the Partido Independiente.[6] The FA was founded in 1971. It emerged as a coalition of leftist political parties that received support principally from young people, urban sectors, intellectuals, and the middle- and upper-middle classes (Gillespie 1986). The coalition was formed mainly by the Socialist Party, Communist Party, Christian Democratic Party, and splinter groups from the Partido Colorado (Movimiento Pregón and Partido por el Gobierno del Pueblo, PGP) and Partido Nacional (Movimiento Popular Nacionalista).

The Partido Independiente is an offshoot of the Nuevo Espacio, which was the right wing of the FA, that is, the alliance between the Christian Democratic Party and the PGP. This alliance campaigned as part of the FA in 1971 and 1984; in 1989, it became independent from the FA and formed the Nuevo Espacio. In 1994 and 1999, the Christian Democratic Party campaigned again with the FA; one faction of the PGP ran with the Partido Colorado, and the other faction as the Nuevo Espacio. In

2004, one faction of the Nuevo Espacio became part of the Frente Amplio again, and the other ran alone under the Partido Independiente.

The other two major political parties, Partido Colorado and Partido Nacional (also called Partido Blanco or the Blancos), are more closely identified with the Center-Right. The PC has more in common with "the Latin American liberal parties, being more liberal, cosmopolitan, urban-centered, and anti-clerical than the Blancos, which became the Uruguayan conservative party" (González 1991: 13). The PN is associated with the Catholic Church and rural areas but is more economically liberal than the other two. The PC and PN have almost parallel histories: both were established in 1830 and are thus almost as old as the country itself, both are multiclass parties, and between them they held office from the country's independence until 2004. For this reason, both are called "traditional parties."

The military coup in 1973 prohibited all political party activity; however, the political parties managed to survive the eleven years of the authoritarian regime by operating below the government's surveillance. The country returned to democracy in the 1984 general election when, much to the military regime's surprise, the party system had evolved into one that relied on a class-based electorate. The PC received votes mainly from older, less well educated housewives and retirees; the FA maintained its support among youth and voters with high school diplomas and college degrees but also received high levels of support among the working class; and the PN was supported by a broader spectrum of the electorate (González 1991).

Until the mid-1960s, Blancos and Colorados together won about 90 percent of the vote; the party system was clearly a two-party system. With the emergence of the Frente Amplio in 1971, the party system started to change from a two-party system to a multiparty system (Gillespie and González 1989; González 1991). Over the past thirty years, the Frente Amplio has increased its electoral successes from election to election. As shown in table 4.1, the two-party system changed first into a "two-and-a-half-party system" in 1971, then into a three-party system in 1984, and to a multiparty system in 1989. In 2004, the FA obtained the majority of votes, and as a result of the low vote share obtained by the PC, the effective number of parties shrank to two and a half.

Table 4.1. Vote Share in Uruguayan Presidential Elections, 1971–2004 (%)

	1971	1984	1989	1994	1999	2004
Partido Colorado	40.9	41.2	30.3	32.3	32.8	10.6
Partido Nacional	40.2	35.0	38.9	31.2	22.3	35.1
Nuevo Espacio/Partido Independiente*			9.0	5.2	4.6	1.9
Frente Amplio	18.3	21.2	21.2	30.6	40.1	51.7
Other minor political parties	0.6	2.5	0.6	0.7	0.2	0.7
Total	100.0	100.0	100.0	100.0	100.0	100.0
Effective Number of Parties**	2.75	2.92	3.33	3.30	3.08	2.49

Source: Corte Electoral del Uruguay.
*In the 1971 and 1984 elections, the Nuevo Espacio was part of the Frente Amplio. From 1989 to 2004, the Nuevo Espacio was an independent party. In 2004 one faction of the party decided to become part of the Frente Amplio using the name Nuevo Espacio, the rest remained independent and ran under the name Partido Independiente.
**Effective number of parties (ENP) is calculated using the Laakso and Taagepera (1979) formula: ENP = $1/\Sigma p_i^2$. The formula is based on the number of votes.

Scholars who study the Uruguayan party system group political parties into two ideological families: "traditional parties" and "challengers" (González 1999; González and Queirolo 2000). The former are made up of the Partido Colorado and Partido Nacional, both right-of-center parties; while the challengers are Frente Amplio and Partido Independiente, both left-of-center parties that until 2004 were never in charge of the national government. Figure 4.1 shows the electoral evolution of these two ideological families.[7]

The progressive increase in the vote for the Left (challengers) is puzzling enough to require an explanation. Several explanations for the incremental electoral success of the Left, as well as for the decrease in voting for traditional parties, have been offered. They include generational effects (Aguiar 2000; Canzani 2000; González and Queirolo 2000) and the ability of the Left (mainly the FA) to retain party traditions (Can-

Figure 4.1. Electoral Evolution of Ideological Families in Uruguayan Presidential Elections, 1971–2004

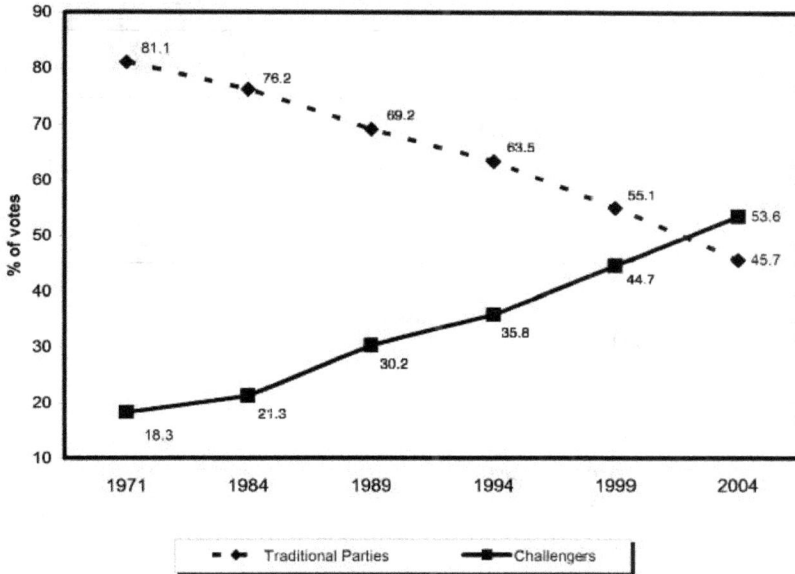

zani 2000; Monestier 2001; Moreira 2000); increasing ideological moderation and pragmatism of the FA (Garcé and Yaffé 2004; Buquet and de Armas 2004); and popular discontent capitalization (González 1999; González and Queirolo 2000; Luna 2004b).

There is sufficient evidence to show that leftist parties benefit from a generational effect. This characteristic of the Frentista electorate is not new; since its foundation, the FA has been a political party that is highly attractive to young people. Moreover, different scholars point out that the electoral growth of the Left is mainly produced by a generational replacement, in which the new voters' preference for the FA supplies an inertial increment of 1 percent per year.[8] Not only did the FA successfully obtain votes from young people, but it demonstrated the ability to retain party traditions (Monestier 2001; Moreira 2000). In other words, those who were young supporters of the FA in 1971 continued to vote for it in 2004. With each successive election, leftist parties have continued to win

Table 4.2. Mean Ideology by Different Electorates in Uruguay, 1984–2004

	1984*	1989		1994		1999		2004	
	Mean	Mean	Std Dv.	Mean	Std Dv.	Mean	Std Dv.	Mean	Std Dv.
Frente Amplio	3.1	3.0	1.4466	3.8	1.4589	3.5	1.6857	3.4	1.8112
Left-of-center parties	3.1	3.6	1.7246	4.0	1.4718	3.6	1.6628	3.6	1.8634
All the electorate	4.8	5.8	2.4624	5.7	2.1192	5.5	2.5294	5.1	2.5732
(N)	(855)	(1310)		(1646)		(1228)		(1470)	

Source: González 1993.
* This mean represents only the electorate in Montevideo. This postelection survey was carried out in March 1985, after the 1984 national election.

young voters who remained in the party as they became older; the age effect coincides with a cohort effect. But this explanation does not tell us *why* the Left is so successful in capturing new voters and keeping the older ones in their ranks.

The explanation that points out the ideological moderation and increasing pragmatism of the Left argues that leftist parties incrementally gained more votes because their leaders chose to moderate their political stances in order to capture voters from the ideological Center. One way to test the validity of this argument is to analyze the ideological identification of FA voters. If FA's electorate or the leftist parties' electorate in general became more centrist over time, we can argue that the Left has grown by capturing votes from the Center. Table 4.2 shows that the FA electorate was more centrist in 2004 than it was in 1989, but those who vote for left-of-center parties are not significantly more centrist in 2004 than they were in 1989. In addition, aggregate evidence shows that during the 1990s the electorate became more leftist in ideology. The mean ideological self-placement of the electorate in 1989 was 5.8,[9] and fifteen years later it was 5.1. Considering this preliminary evidence, we can argue that the increase in the vote for leftist parties cannot be fully explained by the ideological moderation of their leaders because the electorate also moved to the Left ideologically. As a result, it is necessary to look for alternative explanations.

As argued in other studies (González 1999; González and Queirolo 2000; Luna 2004b), the popular discontent capitalization explanation states that leftist parties capitalize on popular discontent with the traditional political parties that have been in charge of the government since the nation's independence. Since the Left was never in charge of the government, it represents an untainted or credible opposition.

Brazil: Voting Left in a Weakly Institutionalized Party System

It can be considered that left-of-center parties in Brazil have reached the presidency twice since the return to democracy in 1985. The first instance was in 1994 with the Partido da Social Democracia Brasileira, the second in 2002 with the Partido dos Trabalhadores. However, there is evidence that when the PSDB became in charge of the national government, it was no longer a party on the Left of the ideological spectrum and was elected as a centrist political party. If this second classification of the PSDB is accepted, leftist parties only won the Brazilian presidency in 2002.

The PSDB was formed in 1988 from a dissident faction of the Partido do Movimiento Democratico Brasileiro (PMDB). This dissident faction was considered the left wing of the PMDB. They supported redistributive policies and, during their first years of existence, voted more times with the Left than with the Right (Power 2001–2002). As a result, the PSDB was considered a Center-Left party in its origins. However, the PSDB moved to the Right even before taking office. In 1994, the PSDB, in coalition with the Partido do Frente Liberal (PFL), won the presidential election and brought Fernando Henrique Cardoso, former finance minister of Itamar Franco, to the presidency. Cardoso immediately took a market-oriented approach and began implementing an ambitious plan of neoliberal reforms that included privatizations and free trade policies. Market-oriented policies were accompanied by the *Plano Real*, a currency reform that was impressively successful in reducing inflation and became the major achievement of Cardoso's government. This movement to the Right was also present among PSDB legislators. Power (2001–2002) shows that in 1990 the mean position of PSDB legislators on the 10-point ideological dimension was 3.52. In 1993 it was 3.81; and in 1997, three years after being in charge of the executive branch, it was 4.77 and for the first time slightly to the right of the congressional mean.[10] To sum up, the PSDB was created as a left-of-center party but was elected in 1994 as centrist and was reelected in 1998 as right-of-center.

Therefore, the first time that a leftist party was elected to preside over the Brazilian national government was in 2002 with the PT. The PT was created in 1980 from the "bottom up" and "united a hodgepodge of Marxists of all shades of red: liberation theology-oriented Catholics, base community activists, moderate intellectuals, and union and social movement leaders" (Samuels 2004: 1002), as well as left-wing congressmen and members of the Movimiento Democratico Brasileiro. Despite the ideological heterogeneity of its members, the PT was clearly identified as "socialist" and an advocate of radical land reform, workers' government, the repudiation of external debt, and the nationalization of the country's banks and mineral wealth (Meneguello 2002; Samuels 2004).

In 2002, Inácio Lula da Silva, the PT's presidential candidate, won the election with 61.3 percent of the vote. Many scholars have pointed out that this success of the PT can be explained by the ideological transformation the party has undergone, in particular, since its 1994 electoral defeat (Hunter 2003, 2007; Meneguello 2002; Samuels 2004). The "deradicalization" of the PT can be traced through its party platform: it changed from supporting "economic socialism" in 1982 to favoring "democratic socialism" or "democratic revolution," with an emphasis on making the state more transparent and accountable, in 2002. In its 2002 presidential campaign the PT even insisted that a PT government would maintain price stability and budget surplus while fighting unemployment and poverty. There were no references to the nationalization of natural resources. Regardless of the ideological moderation, and after four years in charge of the government, the PT can still be considered a left-of-center party.

To sum up, leftist parties have been in charge of the Brazilian national government only once since the end of the authoritarian regime. Figure 4.2 shows the electoral evolution of left, center, and right-wing parties in Brazilian presidential elections. In 1989, the stacked bar does

Figure 4.2. Electoral Evolution of Ideological Blocs in Brazilian Presidential Elections, 1989–2002

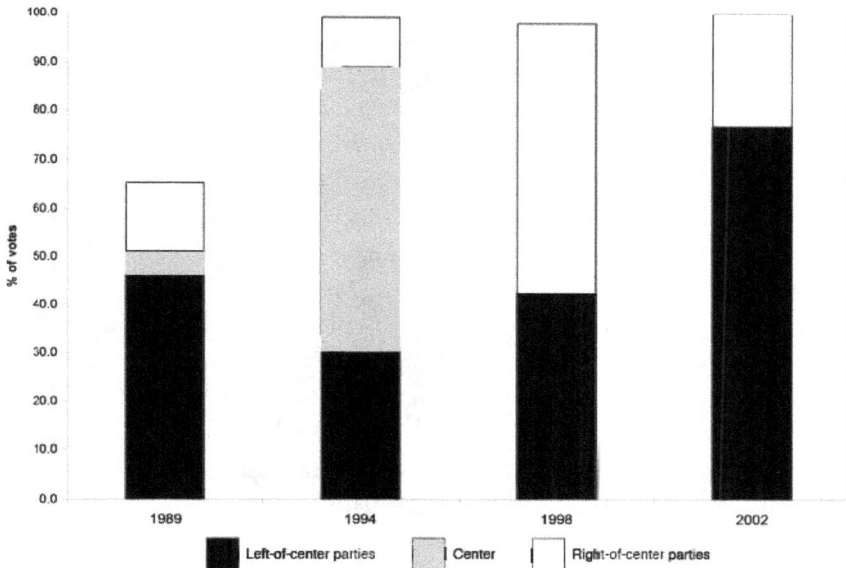

not reach 100 percent because Fernando Collor and his party were classified as Personalist. In the following election, 1994, the centrist PSDB won the election. Four years later it was reelected, but in 1998 the PSDB was considered a right-of-center party. Finally, in 2002, the PT won the presidential elections, and for the first time since the return to democracy a leftist party took over the Brazilian national government.

Are the factors that led Brazilians to vote for leftist parties in 1989, 1994, or 1998 similar to the ones that persuaded them to vote for Lula in 2002? There is a large body of literature explaining why Brazilians vote the way they do, assessing the impact of partisanship (Carreirão and Kinzo 2004; Kinzo 1992; Samuels 2006), ideology (Carreirão 2002b; Singer 2002), economic evaluations (Baker 2002; Camargos 2001), personalism and candidates' personal attributes (Meneguello 1995; Carreirão 2002a), and political discussion within social networks (Baker, Ames, and Renno 2006) on voters' decisions. Most of these studies analyze the vote for political parties. There has been no research on the factors that influence Brazilians to vote for a particular ideological bloc.

One possible explanation for this lack of research on ideological voting is that Brazilian electoral behavior is usually considered highly volatile and weakly determined by ideology or partisan identifications. If this is the case, voting for the Left would be indistinguishable from voting for the Right. However, recent research tends to counter this point. Carreirão and Kinzo (2004) argue that partisanship is a relevant predictor of voting for the ideological bloc to which the party belongs. Samuels (2004) found that party attachment is important for explaining the vote for the PT. Singer (2002) and Carreirão (2002b) claim that despite the fact that not all Brazilian voters are able to place themselves on the ideological scale, ideology is a significant vote predictor for many Brazilians, in particular, those with more education. Furthermore, Singer (2002) finds evidence that in the 1994 national election, Brazilians voted for the candidate who was closer to their party's ideological position.

Including Brazil as a country case makes it possible to explore the determinants of voting Left in a weakly institutionalized and highly fragmented party system. My argument is that the vote for leftist parties in Brazil is an indicator of social and economic discontent, as it is in Uruguay. Voting for the PSDB in 1989 or the PT in 1994 was voting for a credible opposition. Neither party had been in charge of the government. Therefore, it makes no sense for voters to punish them for hyperinflation, unemployment, or poverty.

Mexico: Between Two Credible Oppositions

During the past two decades Mexican politics pivoted on a democratization process different from the one experienced by Brazil and Uruguay. While Brazil and Uruguay in the mid-1980s left behind authoritarian regimes led by the military, the Mexican political system started to move toward democratization by increasing party competition and undermining the dominance of the Partido Revolucionario Institucional, which had ruled since 1929. As a result, many scholars have pointed out that the most relevant political spectrum to understand Mexicans political behavior is the pro-regime/anti-regime cleavage rather than the Left-Right ideological spectrum (Domínguez and McCann 1995, 1996; Greene 2002; Klesner 2004, 2005; Magaloni and Poiré 2004b; Moreno 1998, 1999).

The pro-regime/anti-regime cleavage was summarized by Domínguez and McCann (1995) with the following question: "Am I for or against the party of the state and its leader?" These authors argue that Mexicans' voting decisions can be analyzed through a two-step model. First, Mexicans decide if they are against or in favor of the PRI. Second, and only in the case of those who are against the PRI, they decide between the opposition parties, depending on their policy preferences and social cleavage attachments.

From 1929 to 2000, the "party of the state" was the PRI, whose traditional electoral base is stronger in rural areas, among older Mexicans with low levels of formal education, peasants, public employees, and owners of large businesses (Ames 1970; Lawson 1999; Klesner 2004). The opposition, or those "against the party of the state," until 2000 was represented by the Partido Revolucionario Democrático and the Partido de Acción Nacional. The PRD was founded in 1989 by Cuauhtémoc Cárdenas, a former PRI member who splintered from the party before the 1988 presidential election and who competed for the presidency in that election with a coalition of political parties named Frente Democrático Nacional (FDN). After the 1988 election, Cardenistas merged with the Mexican Socialist Party to create the PRD, a left-of-center political party with strong electoral support in southern states, among Mexicans with low income but a high literacy rate who were skeptical of economic reforms but interested in politics (Bruhn 1999; Domínguez 1999; Klesner 2004; Lawson 1999). The PAN is older than the PRD. It was founded in 1939 and combines a socially conservative strain linked to the Catholic Church with a younger fiscally conservative tendency (*neopanistas*) associated with northwestern business interests in favor of free markets (Klesner 2004, 2005; Lawson 1999; Shirk 2005). The PAN's electoral base is urban, Catholic,[11] educated, and primarily middle class.

Ideologically, the PAN and the PRI can be considered parties on the right half of the ideological spectrum, while the PRD is a left-of-center party. However, there is some discussion regarding the meaning of the ideological dimension in Mexican politics. First, for most of the 1980s and 1990s the ideological dimension was considered a "second-level" dimension, subsumed under the regime cleavage. Second, some scholars argue that during the 1990s the Left-Right spectrum was defined in non-economic terms. Being leftist in Mexico only meant being in favor of opposition and change, while being on the Right corresponded to supporting the status quo. Again, the prevalent dimension was democracy versus authoritarianism rather than economic policy (Moreno 1998, 1999). But Moreno (1999) also recognizes that Mexicans who placed themselves on the Left were stronger supporters of economic equality and state intervention in the economy, while those that placed themselves on the Right were in favor of economic liberalism. Finally, and as a result of the previous arguments, Mexican politics have been structured by two dimensions. According to the ideological dimension based on economic policy, the PRD is placed on the Left and the PRI and PAN on the Right, while the political-regime dimension positions the PRD and the PAN together (Magaloni and Poiré 2004a).

Regardless of these caveats, the PAN and the PRI are parties on the right side of the ideological spectrum, and there is no doubt that the PRD can be taken as a leftist party (Moreno 1999; Zechmeister 2006). What's more, it was expected that as soon as the PRI's dominance ended, the regime dimension would disappear, and the ideological spectrum would regain its importance in Mexican politics (Greene 2002). The PRI's dominance was gradually becoming weaker. Until 1982 the party of the state always occupied no fewer than 80 percent of the seats in the Chamber of Deputies; opposition parties had to wait until 1997 to win a majority in this chamber. Until 1989, no opposition party won a gubernatorial election, but in 1997 Cárdenas was chosen as the first elected mayor in Mexico City. The PRI's dominance finally ended in 2000 when it lost the presidency to PAN.

It is proper to ask why the right-wing PAN and not the left-wing PRD beat the PRI in 2000. Considering that the economic crisis and the failure of the free market economic model to provide for stable economic growth had eroded the PRI's long-term support, these same factors could have buttressed the electoral chances of parties in favor of economic equality and state intervention in the economy. In that sense,

Figure 4.3. Electoral Evolution of Ideological Blocs in Mexican Presidential
Elections, 1982–2006

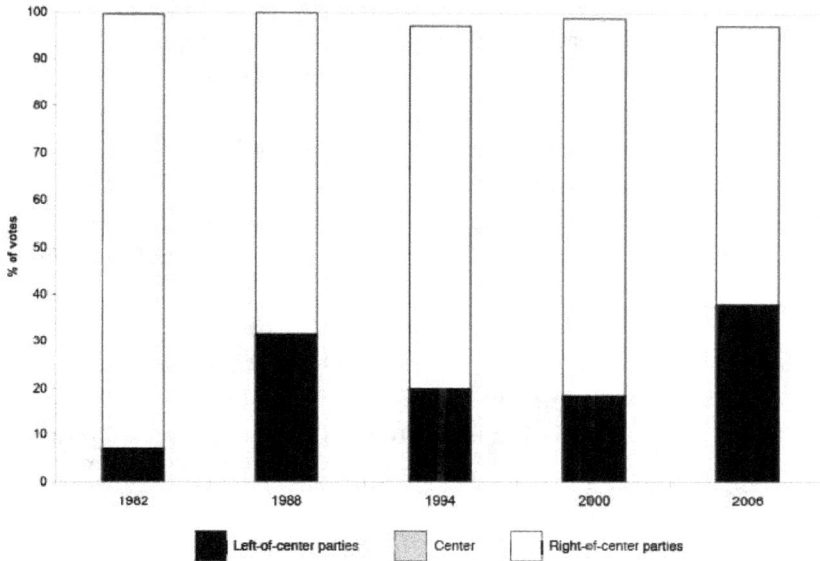

Mexico represents a different case from Brazil and Uruguay: the party that
finally defeated the long-ruling party was on the right-of-center ideological dimension rather than Left-oriented. Figure 4.3 shows the percentage
of vote obtained by each ideological bloc in the presidential elections
from 1982 to 2006.[12] In each of these presidential elections, rightist parties at least doubled the percentage that leftist parties gained. Only in the
2006 election were leftist parties close to winning the presidency with a
plurality of vote, but they finally lost to the right-wing PAN.[13]

Contrary to the Brazilian and Uruguayan cases where only leftist parties represented a credible or untainted opposition, Mexican voters could
choose between two parties representing the untainted opposition. Despite the PAN and PRD having governmental experience at the state and
city levels, neither party had been in charge of the national government
before 2000, and as a result, Mexicans could not blame them for material
scarcity. Why, then, if both parties represented a credible opposition, was
PAN the one that got the credit in 2000?

A few reasons can be mentioned. First, several students of Mexican politics have emphasized the relevance of prospect theory in explaining why voters elected the PRI for so many years. Their argument is that Mexicans believed that voting for the inexperienced opposition was a highly risky enterprise and therefore continued to vote for the "known devil." Between the PAN and the PRD, the former was considered more competent to manage the economy, fight crime, and reduce corruption. In conclusion, it was less risky to vote for the PAN (Cinta 1999; Domínguez 1999; Klesner 2004; Magaloni 1999; Magaloni and Poiré 2004b). Other scholars have pointed out that campaign effects were extremely important in defining the 2000 Mexican presidential election. Vicente Fox's personal characteristics (the PAN's presidential candidate in 2000), as well as high levels of campaign exposure, increased the PAN's electoral chances (Bruhn 2004; Domínguez 2004; Lawson 2004; Lawson and McCann 2004; Moreno 2004). To put it simply, the PAN was preferred over the PRD in 2000 because it was considered the party with higher probabilities of defeating the PRI and more capable of leading the country.

With the PRI's defeat, the regime cleavage was superseded as expected (Bruhn 1999; Greene 2002). As a result, and as long as elections leave aside their transitional character, it is highly probable that other voting clues will become relevant to understand Mexican voting behavior. For example, it is probable that with democratization, the Left-Right spectrum will recover its policy distinction, or that voters will pay more attention to retrospective and prospective economic assessments than before (Poiré 1999).

The argument states that voting Left in Mexico was always a way to vote for the untainted opposition. In other words, the outcome mandate prevails. But not only for the Left. Contrary to Magaloni (1999), who argues that the "uncertain opposition" (those outside the government and inexperienced) had fewer probabilities of being elected, the argument here is that those parties that were always in the opposition have the opportunity to capitalize on social discontent. In Mexico, the PAN and the PRD had this chance before 2000, but after 2000 only the PRD has remained in that position.

Chapter 5

THE REASONS FOR VOTING LEFT

Outcomes, Policies, and Choices

The relevance of understanding what might have caused the so-called leftist tide is twofold. First, the prevalent image of Latin American voters as highly susceptible to clientelism, vote buying, and irrational behaviors does not correspond to a wave of any kind. It is simply not possible to think that the electorates of so many countries in the region had elected left-of-center governments randomly. In other words, unpredictable voters could not have generated an ideological movement such as that which exists in Latin America. There must be something else behind this political phenomenon. That "something" could lead us to outcome-oriented or policy-oriented voters, but it is highly improbable that it would lead to erratic ones. By looking for that "something," it is possible to gain a better understanding of how Latin Americans decide their vote.

But the academic interest in voting behavior is just one of the forces driving the question. As Stokes (2001a: xii) states in the preface to *Mandates and Democracy,* "Latin America in the last decades of the twentieth century faced two major challenges: to strengthen and deepen democracy and to stabilize and reorient economic life." Knowing if Latin Americans' leftist vote is a demand for more government intervention in the economy or better economic results, or both, gives us a clue to how to manage these two challenges, which are, as Stokes clearly states, still pertinent in the first decades of the twenty-first century.

My analysis below is structured in two sections for each country case. The first deals with the main performance mandate versus policy mandate argument; the second explains the role of alternative voting behavior theories in voting Left.

Uruguay

More Outcome Oriented than Policy Oriented?

The Uruguayan data come from five preelection surveys conducted by two well-known public opinion polling firms in that country. The 1984 and 1989 surveys were carried out by Equipos/Mori; the 1994, 1999, and 2004 surveys by CIFRA, González, Raga y Asociados.[1] The 1984 survey includes 400 respondents and covers only the urban population in the Uruguayan capital, Montevideo. The other four are national surveys that include between 1,200 and 1,500 respondents.[2] All the data were collected by personal, door-to-door interviews in the respondents' homes. Missing values were imputed using ICE imputation method from STATA and following the procedures indicated by Royston (2004 and 2005). The same method was used with the Brazilian and Mexican surveys. In all the cases, the imputation was done on the independent variables, never on the dependent variable as this is a highly controversial procedure.

The comparison between the proportions intending to vote for leftist parties in these surveys and the proportions that actually voted for the Left when the elections were held strengthens the validity of the analysis. In the 1989 presidential election, 30 percent of the electorate voted for leftist parties, and the preelection survey registered 35 percent; in 1994, 36 percent voted for the Left, and the survey's proportion was also 36 percent; in 1999, the electoral result was 45 percent and the surveyed result was 52 percent; and finally, in 2004, the election result was 54 percent and the survey predicted 60 percent. Despite the overrepresentation of leftist voters in almost every sample, a well-known problem for Uruguay's pollsters, the survey data used in this chapter represent with sufficient precision the preferences of Uruguayan voters.

only one factor in each election year (1984: Eigenvalue = 1.657; 1989: Eigenvalue = 1.687; 1994: Eigenvalue = 1.597; 1999: Eigenvalue = 2.081; 2004: Eigenvalue = 1.627).[4] The values of this factor were saved as a new variable named *Socioeconomic status (SES)* and were entered into the model as an independent variable.

Other variables are included in the model as control variables: *Age, Education, Family income, Household level,* and *Urban voter (residence).* *Age, Education,* and *Family income* have a straightforward interpretation: low values denote young people, low education, and low income. *Household level* is an ordinal variable that classifies the interviewees in three categories based on an indicator of their household. It takes the value of 1 for low socioeconomic level, 2 for medium socioeconomic level, and 3 for high socioeconomic level. *Urban voter* is a dummy variable representing the region in which the respondent lives; it takes the value of 1 when the person lives in Montevideo and 0 when he or she lives in a rural area or in other smaller cities and towns.

The results of individual-level explanations for voters' behavior in each postauthoritarian election are shown using one Binary Logit for each election year. All the regressions in table 5.1 reach statistical significance.[5] Overall, the models are useful for explaining the factors that lead Uruguayans to vote for left-of-center parties. The coefficients of each variable are reported with their robust standard errors in parentheses.

Which is the prevailing mandate for Uruguayans when voting Left? Ideology is a significant determinant of the vote for the Left in all the elections; a one-unit increase in conservative ideology (one space to the right in the ideological scale that ranges from 1 to 10) *decreases* the probability of voting for leftist parties in comparison to voting for center and right-of-center parties. However, it is not possible to argue that Uruguayans have a policy mandate while voting leftist parties because all that is known is that they care about ideology in its weak meaning. In order to make such an argument, it would be necessary to have questions concerning policy preferences and the "strong" meaning of ideology, but these surveys do not have them. In conclusion, the Uruguayan case provides evidence only to confirm that ideological self-placement determines the vote for the Left irrespective of social and structural determinants. It does not emphasize the existence of an anti-market mandate.

Table 5.1. Vote Determinants for Leftist Parties in Uruguay, 1984–2004 (a)

Independent Variables	1984	1989	1994	1999	2004
Performance Mandate					
Sociotropic Vote	0.369	–	0.534***	0.248	0.465**
	(.303)		(.136)	(.193)	(.148)
Retrospective Sociotropic	–0.095	–	–	–	0.035
	(.254)				(.172)
Prospective Sociotropic	0.262	–	–	–	0.157
	(.199)				(.219)
Pocketbook Vote	–	–0.012	0.088	0.042	0.336**
		(.130)	(.150)	(.202)	(.162)
Retrospective Pocketbook	–	0.174	–	–	–0.079
		(.121)			(.184)
Prospective Pocketbook	–	.329**	–	–	–0.215
		(.130)			(.226)
Policy Mandate					
Ideology	–	–0.812***	–0.654***	–0.792***	–0.710***
		(.079)	(.097)	(.084)	(.086)
Social Class Cleavage (1)					
Dominant Classes	–0.037	–0.161	–0.439	–0.915	0.867
	(.487)	(.275)	(.345)	(.562)	(.627)
Petty Bourgeoisie	–0.578	0.007	–0.569	0.437	0.003
	(.715)	(.466)	(.422)	(.470)	(.395)
Formal Workers	0.205	0.093	–0.049	0.162	0.437
	(.360)	(.206)	(.482)	(.374)	(.275)
Informal Workers	–0.567	0.025	0.015	–0.378	0.139
	(.426)	(.303)	(.262)	(.405)	(.317)
Partisanship (2)					
Partido Colorado	–	–	–2.651***	–3.781***	–2.309***
			(.412)	(.661)	(.469)
Partido Nacional	–	–	–2.634***	–2.364***	–2.613***
			(.393)	(.418)	(.340)
Frente Amplio	–	–	4.525***	3.954***	4.861***
			(.566)	(.662)	(1.042)
Nuevo Espacio/	–	–	2.999***	3.902**	dropped
P. Independiente			(.927)	(1.533)	

Table 5.1. Vote Determinants for Leftist Parties in Uruguay, 1984–2004 (a) *(cont.)*

Independent Variables	1984	1989	1994	1999	2004
Prospect Theory					
Risk Propensity	–	–	–	–	0.436***
					(.099)
Education	0.274**	−0.006	0.204**	0.123	−0.139*
	(.135)	(.078)	(.088)	(.116)	(.075)
Household Level			−0.177	−0.446**	−0.152
			(.157)	(.218)	(.177)
Family Income	−0.042	0.000	–	–	
	(.079)	(.043)			
Age	0.202***	−0.136***	−0.009	0.001	−0.006
	(.059)	(.033)	(.007)	(.008)	(.007)
Urban Voter	–	1.159***	0.899***	0.853**	0.783***
		(.176)	(.232)	(.282)	(.236)
Constant	−2.429	1.971**	0.318	3.248**	2.236
	(1.714)	(.791)	(.976)	(1.137)	(1.442)
Pseudo R squared	0.17	0.48	0.74	0.75	0.52
Wald-chi²	22.8**	132***	252***	217***	188***
Number of Observations	312	1219	1577	1062	1388

Notes:
(1) Includes retired, students, housewives, and unemployed.
(2) Includes those that do not have partisanship or do not want to express it as the reference category.
* p < .10, ** p < .05, *** p < .01.
Dependent variable is Left, a binary measure of whether the respondent intended to vote for
(1) a left-leaning party or (0) nonleftist party.
The null hypothesis of the Wald-chi² test is that all coefficients are jointly equal to zero.

On the other side, the performance mandate finds support in the Uruguayan case. Voters' economic assessments are significant determinants of the vote for leftist parties in all Uruguayan elections following the return to democracy, with the exception of the 1984 and 1999 ones. At least one of the variables included as indicators of performance mandate (*Sociotropic vote, Retrospective sociotropic, Prospective sociotropic, Pocketbook vote, Retrospective pocketbook, and Prospective pocketbook*) reaches significance. Table 5.1 shows that the worse a voter's evaluation of the economic situation, the greater the probability he or she will vote for the opposition. In particular, voters who are discontented will reward leftist parties that were not in charge of the government. As argued in other studies (González 1999; González and Queirolo 2000; Luna 2004b), leftist parties capitalize on popular discontent with the traditional political parties that have been in charge of the government since the nation's independence. Since the FA and the NE or PI were never in charge of the government, they represent an untainted or credible opposition.

Uruguayans are sociotropic oriented rather than egotropic oriented or pocketbook voters. This finding is consistent with most of the literature on economic voting in Western countries, which states that voters take into account their society's economic well-being more willingly than their own welfare. In terms of the temporal distinction on voters' orientations, Uruguayans tend to be closer to "bankers" considering the future expectations of the economy (prospective vote) than "peasants" thinking about what the economy was like over the previous years.[6]

At the aggregate level, the key question is whether the number of people with a negative perception of the country's economic situation has grown over time. The percentage of Uruguayans who negatively evaluated the economy increased from 50.5 percent in 1994 to 69.3 percent in 2004. Negative perceptions of the economy matter at the individual level because they raise the probability of voting for the Left, and also the increase in the aggregate level of discontent is positively correlated with the enlargement of leftist parties' electorate. As these evaluations of the country's economic health worsened, and there is a clear demand for better outcomes, the main beneficiary of this phenomenon continued to be leftist parties, because they represent the untainted or credible opposition in the Uruguayan party system.

Beyond Outcomes or Policies, Partisanship

Party identification is a strong predictor of voting behavior in Uruguay; it reaches statistical significance in every election. This finding is not surprising: scholars have already pointed out the importance of partisanship in Uruguayan politics (Mainwaring and Scully 1995). Uruguay is a case in which the electoral change responds to a realignment rather than a de-alignment (Zuasnábar 2010). What's more, party identification is significant for every political party; there is no cross-party variation, and partisanship is not more important in predicting the vote for leftist parties than for right-of-center or center parties as it was previously hypothesized.

At this point, a caveat is in order. The discussion regarding the possible endogeneity problem between ideology and partisanship, or put differently, that partisan affiliation or ideology have each partly caused the other, either because people leaning one way ideologically choose particular parties or because those loyal to particular parties come to accept certain ideologies, is an old one in the literature on voting behavior. Since Campbell (1960), many scholars have defended the prevalence of partisanship over ideology as a leading voting clue. On the contrary, other scholars, starting from Downs (1957), have pinpointed the importance of ideology because it works as a shortcut or heuristic tool to identify the preferred political party. In any case, the two variables are conceptually different, and they are not always highly correlated. In Uruguay, ideology and party identification are highly correlated only for those with party attachment to the Frente Amplio. In 1994, the correlation was -0.55 and in 1999 and 2004 increased to -0.58. Correlations between ideology and either Colorado identification or Blanco identification are systematically lower.[7] Taking into account these values, the endogeneity problem can be dismissed; ideological preferences and party sympathies in Uruguay are not perfectly aligned.

Urban voter is also significant in all the elections. Since their inception, leftist parties have been identified as urban parties. The Frente Amplio has been extending its electorate to more rural regions of the country, and in the 2004 national election it obtained the majority vote in seven of the nineteen municipalities.[8] Despite this remarkable electoral growth outside Montevideo, the capital city, the urban-rural cleavage continues to influence the party for which Uruguayans vote; leftist parties are mainly preferred by urban Uruguayans.

In addition, some variables are significant in some elections but not in others. One of these is *age*. The changes found from one election to another are unexpected if we take into account the social bases of leftist parties in the past. Age was significant in the first elections after the return to democracy, but it is no longer significant in the 1999 and 2004 elections. Table 5.1 shows that being young increased the probability of someone voting for the FA or NE in the 1984, 1989, and 1994 elections. This characteristic of the leftist electorate in Uruguay is not new; since its founding, the FA has been a political party that is highly attractive to young people. Not only did the FA successfully obtain votes from young people, but it also demonstrated the ability to retain party traditions (Monestier 2001; Moreira 2000). In other words, those who were young supporters of the FA in 1971 continued to vote for it in 1999, and this is the reason age is not more significant in 1999. With each successive election, the FA continued to win young voters who remained in the party as they became older; the age effect coincides with a cohort effect.

The Uruguayan results reinforce the extended idea that social class cleavages are almost irrelevant in understanding voting behavior in Latin America. The social class cleavage theory was tested with two different models. The first, presented in table 5.1, tests the existence of social class cleavages with a set of variables that include a series of dummy variables measuring occupation, a variable measuring education, and another one measuring the household economic level or family income.[9] The results do not support the hypothesis that the position that a person occupies in the social structure determines his or her vote. In Uruguay, workers and members of the popular sectors are not more likely to vote for leftist parties, while those who belong to the dominant sectors do not necessarily vote for rightist parties. Nor are voters who belong to the informal sector more likely to vote for the Left.[10] Education is significant to explain the vote for the Left in 1984, 1994, and 2004. In 1984 and 1994, highly educated citizens had a higher probability of voting for the Frente Amplio; in 2004, this effect was reversed: low education leads to more votes for the Left. Socioeconomic level was only significant in 1999: citizens with a low economic level had a higher probability of voting for the Frente Amplio. The second model to test the social class cleavage is based on a single variable, *Socioeconomic status,* which considers the three indicators simultaneously: occupation, education, and income.[11] Table 5.2 shows that socioeconomic status is not a relevant voting predictor.

These two ways in which the social class cleavage is tested do not rule out the possibility that social class has an indirect impact on leftward voting. It might be possible that social class predicts ideological lean-

Table 5.2. Vote Determinants for Leftist Parties in Uruguay, 1984–2004 (b)

Independent Variables	1984	1989	1994	1999	2004
Performance Mandate					
Sociotropic Vote	0.395	–	0.518***	0.306	0.481***
	(.287)		(.134)	(.194)	(.148)
Retrospective Sociotropic	–0.085	–	–	–	0.004
	(.247)				(.169)
Prospective Sociotropic	0.273	–	–	–	0.128
	(.191)				(.209)
Pocketbook Vote	–	–0.059	0.091	–0.041	0.408**
		(.130)	(.145)	(.207)	(.161)
Retrospective Pocketbook	–	0.183	–	–	–0.092
		(.122)			(.179)
Prospective Pocketbook	–	0.328**	–	–	–0.226
		(.129)			(.218)
Policy Mandate					
Ideology	–	–0.819***	–0.647***	–0.790***	–0.686***
		(.079)	(.100)	(.088)	(.083)
Social Class Cleavage					
SES (socioeconomic status)	0.177	–0.142	0.003	–0.275	–0.050
	(.162)	(.104)	(.103)	(.189)	(.117)
Partisanship (1)					
Partido Colorado	–	–	–2.705***	–3.542***	–2.369***
			(.416)	(.666)	(.482)
Partido Nacional	–	–	–2.588***	–2.274***	–2.651***
	–	–	(.381)	(.434)	(.339)
Frente Amplio			4.465***	3.900***	4.833***
			(.558)	(.641)	(1.039)
Nuevo Espacio/	–	–	3.024***	3.889**	dropped
P. Independiente			(.891)	(1.535)	
Prospect Theory					
Risk Propensity	–	–	–	–	0.419***
					(.097)
Age	–0.257***	–0.141***	–0.014**	–0.005	–0.005
	(.053)	(.029)	(.007)	(.008)	(.006)

Table 5.2. Vote Determinants for Leftist Parties in Uruguay, 1984–2004 (b) (*cont.*)

Independent Variables	1984	1989	1994	1999	2004
Urban Voter	–	0.184***	0.952***	0.915***	−0.667**
		(.175)	(.227)	(.284)	(.229)
Constant	−1.696	2.119**	0.928	2.998**	1.100
	(1.620)	(.686)	(.810)	(.999)	(1.130)
Pseudo R squared	0.10	0.41	0.77	0.76	0.55
Wald-chi²	6.4	59.9***	142.6***	76.2***	103***
Number of Observations	312	1219	1577	1062	1388

Notes:
(1) Includes those that do not have partisanship or do not want to express it as the reference category.
* p < .10, ** p < .05, *** p < .01.
Dependent variable is Left, a binary measure of whether the respondent intended to vote for
(1) a left-leaning party or (0) nonleftist party.
Entries are binary logit coefficients with robust standard errors in parentheses.
The null hypothesis of the Wald-chi² test is that all coefficients are jointly equal to zero.

ings or partisan affiliation, variables that determine the vote for leftist parties in Uruguay. However, the correlation between these independent variables contradicts this possibility. Social class does not have a positive and high correlation with ideology or party choice. In other words, social class is not a key variable, neither in predicting the leftist vote nor in predicting party identification or ideology.

Uruguay is not a case of a class cleavage party system; the traditional social class theory (Lipset and Rokkan 1967) does not explain the vote for the Left in post-dictatorship Uruguay. Since the FA's founding in 1971, its electorate has not only been made up of working-class people; it has received support from students, intellectuals, and the middle and upper-middle classes (Gillespie 1986). The FA became the largest party and won the general election in 2004 because it expanded its electoral base beyond the traditional, left-urban-middle class coalition, without losing the support of these social sectors. The vote for the Left is a multiclass rather than a working-class vote. The vote for leftist parties has increased among different social sectors, not only formal and informal workers. It is possible to understand this change as an indicator of the FA's transformation into a catchall party. In particular, after the 2002 economic crisis, which is con-

Figure 5.1. Ideology and Social Class in Uruguay, 2004

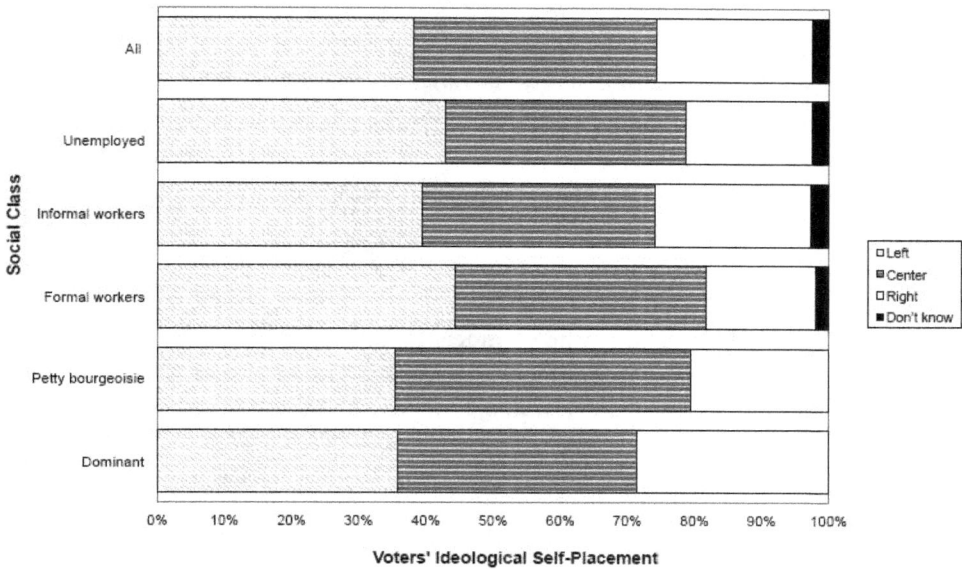

Source: CIFRA 2004.

sidered the severest economic crisis in Uruguayan history and one that affected all socioeconomic sectors, citizens' economic discontent grew. As a result, in the 2004 election citizens voted for left-of-center parties irrespective of their socioeconomic status because they were considered the untainted opposition.

Despite receiving multiclass support, the FA formed a coalition that is ideologically Center-Left. This finding is extremely puzzling because although ideology is an important factor in explaining voting behavior, social class is not. This result goes against the common understanding that ideology and social class are matched: workers are on the Left, and the dominant sectors are on the Right. In Uruguay, this attachment between social class and ideology does not hold, as shown in figure 5.1. Furthermore, as Torcal and Mainwaring (2003) show, this attachment between social class and ideology does not hold in post-dictatorship Chile either.

One possible explanation for this unexpected combination of ideology and catchall parties is that ideology works as a political cleavage used by political parties to mobilize support, as Torcal and Mainwaring suggest. In other words, the ideological cleavage is a political cleavage that becomes active when politicians use it to get votes; it is not a structural cleavage determined by social class. Ideology is a relevant predictor of vote even after controlling for partisanship. Moreover, partisanship is also an extremely important vote determinant in Uruguay for leftist and non-leftist parties. This clear distinction in two ideological families might be reinforced by politicians' agendas.

The impact of economic assessments on voting decisions can be diluted by the effect of party identifications. Voters with party identification might be less likely to take into consideration economic evaluations than those without party preferences. A straightforward way to analyze the combined effect of party identifications and retrospective economic evaluations is by looking at the predicted probabilities shown in table 5.3. In 2004, a voter who identified himself with the Partido Nacional and considers that his own economic situation has improved during the last government has a probability of voting Left of 4.1 percent. This probability increases to 8.4 for those who consider themselves poorer than five years ago. For a Colorado adherent, the impact of getting poorer is similar to that of a Blanco sympathizer: the probability doubles when the voter considers his or her economic situation worse off. The same phenomenon happens among those Uruguayans without party identification. The only situation when personal economic condition has no impact on the decision to vote Left is among those who feel close to the Frente Amplio. Those who consider themselves Frentistas seem to be highly impervious to the economic distress when deciding their vote; or to put it differently, partisanship is what really matters for those individuals, irrespective of their experiences with the economy.

In conclusion, in 2004, those Uruguayans who felt that their economic situation had been impoverished increased their probability of voting for leftist parties, regardless of their party identification. This is another piece of evidence indicating that Uruguayans are outcome oriented. But the probabilities of voting Left are also influenced by party identifications: they are higher for those who lack party identification, moderate for those who despite seeing themselves as "colorados" are disappointed with their party's past performances, and low for the "blancos" who still

Table 5.3. Predicted Probabilities of Voting for Leftist Parties in 2004 Uruguayan Election Depending on Party Identification and Retrospective Egotropic Economic Assessments

Party Identification	Retrospective Egotropic Economic Evaluations		
	Better Off	Same	Worse Off
Partido Colorado	15.4	21.0	27.9
Partido Nacional	4.1	5.9	8.4
Frente Amplio	99.8	99.9	99.9
No party identification	42.6	64.5	81.7

Note: Data are from the 2004 preelectoral national survey of Uruguayan electorate done by CIFRA, González, Raga y Asociados. Cell entries are predicted probabilities of hypothetical individuals voting for left-of-center parties from a logit with the same variables as models presented in tables 5.1 and 5.2. Except for the identified variables, all variables are held constant at their means.

trust their party. However, independently of the base from which each sector starts, the probabilities are doubled when the voter feels economic deterioration. This evidence reinforces the argument that Uruguayan leftist parties grow by capitalizing on the social and economic discontent of those who feel in the domain of losses.

Risk propensity is tested only in 2004, and as a result it is not correct to argue that it was always a strong predictor of the leftist vote, though the evidence from the 2004 election shows that Uruguayans with higher levels of risk acceptance had a higher probability of voting for left-of-center parties than those who were risk averse. In other words, regression results shown in tables 5.1 and 5.2 confirm the argument that *when the incumbent is not a leftist political party, and leftist parties belong to the opposition, risk acceptant citizens will choose the Left at the voting booth.*[12] Economic voting theory and prospect theory work to explain the increase in the vote for the Left in Uruguay. Leftist parties have gained votes from those dissatisfied with the country's economic situation because they have never been in charge of the national government and citizens cannot blame them for economic hardship. By being in the domain of losses, Uruguayans take more risks: they vote against the "known devil" and in favor of the "unknown saint." Figure 5.2 indicates that among those who

Figure 5.2. Risk and Vote Choice in Uruguay, 2004

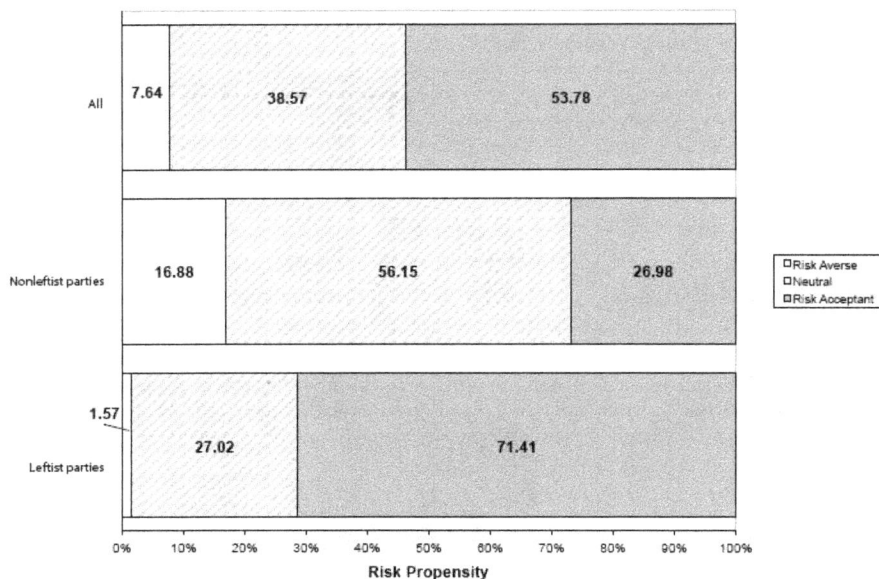

Source: Cifra 2004

intended to vote for leftist parties in 2004, there was a higher level of risk propensity than among those who were going to vote for "traditional" parties. Voting for a party that was never in charge of the government implies higher levels of uncertainty than voting for the parties that had governed the country since its independence.

Moreover, despite the fact that the probability of voting for the Left in 2004 increased with disenchantment with the economic situation, not all voters who were not content with the economy would "gamble" their vote. Table 5.4 shows that a risk averse citizen with a negative evaluation of the country's economy has a probability of voting Left of .42, while a risk-taking voter with the same negative evaluation doubles the probability of choosing the less known opposition (.84). In other words, individuals with a lower risk-taking attitude prefer to stick with the "devil they know" despite their economic discontent.[13]

In conclusion, more than voting against neoliberal reforms, Uruguayans are punishing political parties that produced economic hardship. The main mandate is clearly for better outcomes. Nevertheless, the strength by

Table 5.4. Predicted Probabilities of Voting for Leftist Parties in 2004 Uruguayan Election Depending on Risk Propensity and Sociotropic Economic Assessments

Risk Propensity	Economic Evaluations		
	Positive	*Neutral*	*Negative*
Risk averse	5.7	17.4	42.6
Neutral	13.9	36.3	66.7
Risk acceptant	30.4	60.6	84.4

Note: Data is from the 2004 preelectoral national survey of Uruguayan electorate done by CIFRA, González, Raga y Asociados. Cell entries are predicted probabilities of hypothetical individuals voting for left-of-center parties from a logit with the same variables as models in tables 5.1 and 5.2. Two changes were made in order to produce predicted probabilities: (1) Risk propensity and Sociotropic were merged into three categories to use the prtab STATA command, and (2) Frente Amplio party identification and P. Independiente party identification were dropped from the model. Except for the identified variables, all variables are held constant at their means.

which a performance's command leads a citizen to vote Left depends on his or her propensity to take risks. Risk acceptant individuals double or triple their chances of voting Left in comparison to risk adverse ones. Bearing in mind the value that each theory has to explain the rise of the Left in Latin America, the Uruguayan case shows that outcomes are crucial, but so are others factors such as party identification and risk propensity.

Uruguayan evidence reinforces Benton's (2005) argument that Latin Americans have long memories and punish not only the incumbent party for the material suffering but also parties that governed before the incumbent. Left-of-center parties in Uruguay (or the challengers), and in particular the Frente Amplio, took advantage of this popular discontent and capitalized on social and economic dissatisfaction with the "traditional parties."

Brazil

Outcomes Matter, and Privatization Too

The data analyzed in this section come from different national surveys. In order to analyze the factors that explain the vote for leftist parties in

1989, 1994, and 1998, three preelection national surveys carried out by Datafolha are used. The 1989 survey was conducted in September and includes 2,083 cases; the 1994 survey was done in August and includes 10,459 cases; and the 1998 survey data were collected in July and include 4,380 cases. To test the hypotheses in the 2002 presidential election, Brazil's 2002 National Election Study (BNES), a national postelection voter behavior survey including 2,513 respondents, is used. To complete the analysis, the data from a 2002 four-wave panel study of eligible voters in two midsized Brazilian cities—Caxias do Sul (Rio Grande do Sul) and Juiz de Fora (Minas Gerais)—are also used. Only data from the first wave of the panel, which was conducted in March and April 2002, are used.[14] In all the surveys, data were collected by personal, door-to-door interviews in the respondents' homes.[15] As in the case of Uruguay, Brazilian survey data fit very well the proportion intending to vote Left with the proportion that actually voted Left. The 1989 survey predicted 34 percent of votes for the Left, and the actual figure was 46 percent; in 1994 the survey result was 36 percent, and the actual vote was 30 percent; the 1998 survey anticipated that 43 percent of Brazilian would vote for leftist parties, and the actual percentage was the same; finally, in the 2002 survey, carried out after the election, 68 percent of the respondents said they had voted Left, but the actual figure was 77 percent.[16]

The dependent variable is a dummy variable that measures the intention to vote for a left-of-center party, with 1 meaning that the person intended to vote (or did vote in the case of the postelection survey) for the Left. The following political parties were classified as left of center in each presidential election: in 1989, Partido Democratico Trabalhista (PDT), Partido dos Trabalhadores (PT), Partido da Social Democracia Brasileira (PSDB), and Partido Comunista Brasileiro (PCB); in 1994, PT and PDT; in 1998, PT, Partido Popular Socialista (PPS), and Partido Socialista dos Trabalhadores Unificado (PSTU); and in 2002, PT, Partido Socialista Brasileiro (PSB), and PSTU. The following independent variables, each of which fits within one of the theories discussed in chapter 4, are explored. Several of these variables are composite indexes.[17]

As in the Uruguayan analysis, performance mandate is tested using *Sociotropic vote* and *Pocketbook vote* in the 1994 and 1998 surveys. These variables measure the respondent's evaluation of the *Plano Real* for the country and for voters' own lives. Higher values correspond to negative evaluations. *Prospective inflation, Prospective unemployment,* and *Prospective purchasing power* measure prospective economic assessments; higher values mean that inflation, unemployment, and purchasing power will decrease. In the 2002 panel survey, *Retrospective sociotropic, Prospective sociotropic, Retrospective pocketbook,* and *Prospective pocketbook* measure citizens' evaluations of the country and their own economic situation during the last year, in addition to economic expectations for the next twelve months.

Policy mandate is measured in two ways capturing both the weak and strong meanings of *Ideology.* The first measurement is the respondent's self-placement in the ideological dimension. In the 1989 survey, the ideological scale goes from 1 (Left) to 7 (Right), and in the 2002 survey it goes from 0 (Left) to 10 (Right). Finally, the 2002 panel survey measures ideology with a question with five answer categories: Left, Center-Left, Center, Center-Right, and Right. The second measure of an interviewee's ideology is by means of a series of questions asking citizens' opinions on policy issues: state interventionism, redistribution, socialism, state regulations of private firms, agrarian reform, nationalization, and privatizations. Higher values in each of these policies correspond with liberal positions, which is expected to be negatively correlated with the vote for leftist parties.

Partisanship is tested using a set of five dummy variables, with each dummy representing one category of partisanship: party identification with left-of-center parties, party identification with parties at the center, party identification with right-of-center parties, party identification with parties that cannot be classified in the Left-Right spectrum, and those that lack partisanship. Each category is entered into the model as a dummy variable that takes the value of 1 when the person belongs to it and 0 when the person does not. Those who declare partisanship to unclassified parties are the base category in the regression.

Social class cleavage is tested using a set of five dummy variables. Each dummy represents one category of social class defined in terms of occupation: dominant class, petty bourgeoisie, formal workers, informal workers, and nonemployed. The definition of each category follows the Portes and Hoffman (2003) classification already described. Each category is entered into the model as a dummy variable that takes the value of 1 when the person belongs to it and 0 when he or she does not. Nonemployed people (unemployed, retired, students, and housewives) are taken as the base category. To capture the other dimensions of the socioeconomic status, I include *Education* and *Family income*. Higher values mean higher levels of education and higher family income.

Prospect theory is tested through different variables that capture how risky it is to vote for different candidates. In the 1998 survey, the *Risk Propensity Lula* and *Risk Propensity FHC* (for Fernando Henrique Cardoso) are composite indexes that include the following *hypothetical* questions about the perceived risk implied by a Lula or FHC government: if unemployment increased under Lula/FHC, if the real remained stable under Lula/FHC, and if the country experienced chaos under Lula/FHC. The risk propensity indexes for the 2002 election combines variables that measure which is the most trustworthy candidate, the most honest candidate, the candidate with most experience, the one with the best governmental plan, the best prepared for the task, the candidate who will generate more jobs, and the one who will keep inflation low. Higher values correspond to higher levels of risk.[18] The 2002 panel survey asks respondents to agree with one of the two following aphorisms: "É melhor ter um pássaro na mão do que dois voando" (A bird in the hand is worth two in the bush) or "Quem não arrisca, não petisca" (Nothing ventured, nothing gained), which is a common question used to measure risk propensity.

Finally, *Age* (the higher the value, the older the respondent) and *Urban voter* (a dummy in which 1 is urban and 0 is rural) are added to test for the existence of alternative cleavages. In the 2002 postelection survey, the *Urban voter* variable captures whether the respondent lives in a state capital or not rather than whether the place of residence is urban or rural.

Table 5.5 shows the regression results for each democratic presidential election since the end of the authoritarian regime. The first thing to notice is, as Camargos (2001) pointed out, that Brazilian vote choice is not irrational, random, or merely the result of electoral campaigns as is sometimes described. In each presidential election model, at least five variables attain statistical significance. Overall, the models are useful for explaining the factors that determine voters' behavior in Brazil, in

Table 5.5. Vote Determinants for Leftist Parties in Brazil 1989–2002

Independent Variables	1989	1994	1998	2002
Performance Mandate				
Sociotropic vote	–	0.526***	0.207***	–
		(.048)	(.067)	
Pocketbook vote	–	0.415***	0.506***	–
		(.041)	(.061)	
Prospective inflation	–	–	−0.240***	–
			(.074)	
Prospective unemployment	–	–	−0.203***	–
			(.056)	
Prospective purchasing power	–	–	0.175***	–
			(.062)	
Policy Mandate				
Ideological self-placement	−0.134***	–	–	−0.027
	(.036)			(.018)
Opinion state interventionism	0.036	–	–	0.001
	(.082)			(.011)
Opinion redistribution	0.035	–	–	–
	(.081)			
Opinion socialism	0.088	–	–	–
	(.063)			
Opinion state regulations	–	–	–	−0.006
				(.016)
Opinion agrarian reform	–	–	–	−0.174
				(.126)
Opinion nationalization	–	–	–	−0.002
				(.016)
Opinion privatizations			−0.147***	
			(.051)	
Social Class Cleavage (1)				
Dominant classes	−0.835*	−0.759***	–	0.230
	(.434)	(.243)		(.447)
Petty bourgeoisie	0.214	−0.142	–	−1.622***
	(.178)	(.093)		(.612)
Formal workers	0.103	−0.001	–	−0.027
	(.139)	(.062)		(.149)

Table 5.5. Vote Determinants for Leftist Parties in Brazil, 1989–2002 *(cont.)*

Independent Variables	1989	1994	1998	2002
Informal workers	0.429**	0.021	–	0.271*
	(.207)	(.068)		(.161)
Education	0.104***	−0.122***	−0.043	−0.006
	(.039)	(.041)	(.028)	(.015)
Family income	–	−0.092***	−0.001	−0.000
		(.024)	(.000)	(.000)
Partisanship (2)				
Left	2.658***	1.135***	1.664***	1.115**
	(.281)	(.093)	(.168)	(.532)
Center	0.303	−0.485***	0.151	−1.524
	(.283)	(.105)	(.166)	(1.745)
Right	−0.102	−0.892***	−0.077	−0.844*
	(.304)	(.153)	(.160)	(.504)
No partisanship	0.446*	−0.261***	0.133	−0.449
	(.234)	(.089)	(.136)	(.491)
Prospect Theory				
Risk propensity FHC/Serra	–	–	0.201***	0.090***
			(.019)	(.009)
Risk propensity Lula	–	–	−0.187***	−0.092***
			(.022)	(.012)
Risk propensity Ciro				0.042***
				(.012)
Age	0.159**	−0.008***	0.003	−0.016***
	(.065)	(.002)	(.003)	(.004)
Urban voter	−0.507***	−0.054	–	−0.024
	(.169)	(.052)		(.139)
Constant	−1.422**	−1.064***	−1.695**	0.833
	(.569)	(.174)	(.387)	(.764)
R-squared	0.21	0.14	0.35	0.39
Wald-chi^2	189***	1123***	520***	242***
Number of observations	1771	8617	3644	1878

Notes:
(1) Includes retired, students, housewives, and unemployed.
(2) Includes those with partisanship to political parties that cannot be classified into the Left-Right ideological dimension.
* p < .10, ** p < .05, *** p < .01.
Entries are binary logit coefficients with robust standard errors.

particular, the vote for left-of-center political parties. Brazilian voters take into account short-term factors, such as economic evaluations, as well as long-term ones, such as partisanship and, to a lesser degree, ideological identifications.

Starting from the argument that the left-of-center parties' electoral successes in the region are the result of a backlash against neoliberalism, the Brazilian evidence is twofold. Ideology is a significant predictor of the vote for the Left in one of the two instances in which it was possible to include a direct measure of it: individual self-placement on the ideological scale. In 1989, a one-unit increase in ideology (one space to the right on the ideological scale) decreases the probability of voting for a left-of-center party rather than a centrist or rightist party. However, in 2002, the ideological self-placement does not reach significance. As a result, the evidence is not conclusive to support the argument that Latin Americans who identify themselves with the Left will vote for leftist parties, or to reinforce Singer's (2002) argument, that ideological self-placement is one of the most important factors explaining Brazilians' voting behavior.

Singer (2002) points out that Brazilians have more stable ideological identifications than party identifications and argues that voters use the ideological dimension as a shortcut to distinguish between political parties.[19] He finds that Brazilians who are identified with the Left and those identified with the Right are not very different in terms of their opinions about the role of the state in the economy or even egalitarianism. The majority of both groups favor state interventionism and want a country with more economic and social equality. What really differentiates the two is the best way to achieve equality. Those identified with the Right want the state to be in charge of the process; leftists favor social mobilization. Following Singer's research, the argument was tested that policy issues that usually discriminate Left from Right are irrelevant among Brazilians. Or to put it differently, Brazilians are not policy oriented; they do not care about the "strong" meaning of ideology. To do so, a series of variables that measure citizens' opinions about state interventionism, redistribution, socialism, state regulation of private firms, agrarian reform, nationalization, and privatizations were included. Table 5.5 shows that Singer is not completely right, because one of these variables is a significant determinant of voting for a left-of-center political party: namely, opinion on privatization. Brazilians who oppose privatization have a higher probability of voting for the Left than those who favor that type of economic reform. Taking into account that Brazil is one of the countries in Latin America that carried out the most privatization during the 1980s and 1990s, the electoral effect that opposition to those reforms had generated, at least in the 1998 election, is quite interesting.

In conclusion, the evidence favoring the policy mandate is inconclusive. On one side, the antagonism to privatization reforms that were implemented in Brazil had an effect on the vote for leftist parties, but other policies strongly associated with the Washington Consensus, such as state interventionism or state regulations, did not. On the other side, ideology in its weak meaning is sometimes, but not always, important to explain Brazilians' voting behavior.

As shown in table 5.5, performance matters for Brazilians; economic voting theory explains why they vote for leftist parties. Since the return to democracy, leftist parties seemed to have capitalized on Brazilians' economic discontent. In order to test the influence of economic assessments on vote decisions, two questions were included that asked Brazilians to evaluate how good or bad the *Plano Real* had been for themselves (*Pocketbook vote*) and for the country as a whole (*Sociotropic vote*).

In 1994, Cardoso's short term as President Itamar Franco's finance minister gave him more popular support than opposition. At the time of the presidential election, the great success of the *Plano Real* had just started to become noticeable. Brazilians who negatively evaluated the new monetary policy tended to vote more for left-of-center parties than for center or rightist ones. The same happened in the 1998 election. Citizens who were discontented with the effect the *Plano Real* had on their own lives, or on the country's well-being, voted for left-of-center parties, while those that made a positive evaluation reelected the government. The positive signs on the sociotropic and pocketbook coefficients in table 5.5 indicate that the worse the economic evaluation, the higher the probability of voting for the Left. In 1998 Cardoso was reelected as a result of his successful plan to reduce and control inflation, but Brazilians who were disappointed with the country's economic situation voted against him. Four years later, inflation was no longer a serious problem, and voters were disappointed with the economic consequences of Cardoso's implementation of market-oriented reforms. Therefore, they would continue voting for the Left, now embodied by the PT and other leftist parties but no longer by the PSDB.

Camargos (2001) describes the Brazilian electorate as more sociotropic than pocketbook oriented, and more prospective than retrospective. Table 5.5 indicates that prospective economic assessments have an important influence on voting for leftist parties. In the 1998 presidential election, Brazilians who thought inflation and unemployment were going to increase and purchasing power was going to shrink tended to vote for the Left.

In conclusion, voters' economic assessments, the ones related to the country's welfare as well as the ones related to their own pockets, are significant determinants of the vote for leftist parties in Brazil. As Baker (2002) states, when voting Brazilians take into account the economic dimension. The Brazilian case presents more evidence to support the argument that the worse a voter evaluates the economic situation, the greater the probability he or she will vote for the opposition. In particular, voters who are discontented will reward leftist parties that were not in charge of the government. Guided by these results, there is little doubt that behind the leftist tide there is a huge demand for better outcomes. Even more than for a defense of specific policies.

Partisanship and Risk Propensity Also Influence the Leftist Vote in Brazil

Policies and outcomes do not explain the totality of voting behavior. Party identification is also a strong predictor of choosing leftist parties in Brazil; it reaches statistical significance in every election. Brazilians who identified with a leftist political party tended to vote for a left-of-center party in presidential elections. In contrast, those who identified with a party on the ideological Center or the ideological Right do not necessarily vote within the same bloc. This finding conforms to that of Carreirão and Kinzo (2004), who pointed out that partisanship is a relevant predictor when the outcome to be explained is the vote for an ideological bloc instead of a particular political party. The argument made here goes further by adding that in Brazil party identification is a significant vote predictor *mainly* to explain voting for the Left.

To sum up, party identification is not significant for every ideological bloc but rather is more important for predicting the vote for leftist parties than for right-of-center or center parties. The data used to analyze the 2002 presidential election were collected after the first round of the election; as a result and given the weakness of Brazilian parties, endogeneity might be a problem. For example, PT partisanship could be the result of voting Lula instead of voting Lula being the result of PT partisanship. Ames (2007) overcomes this endogeneity problem for the 2002 election using panel data. By using partisanship values in wave 1 and voting behavior in wave 3, he finds that PT partisanship becomes weaker as a voting determinant while PSDB and PMDB partisanship loses its significance.

One important exception is the 1994 election, when partisanship was significant for every ideological bloc, including for those that lacked any party attachment. In 1994, Brazilians identifying with a left-of-center party tended to vote within the leftist bloc; while those identified with a centrist party or a right-of-center party and those with no partisanship had a significantly higher probability of voting for a center or rightist party. This finding is surprising. Meneguello (1995: 637), for example, has pointed out that in the 1994 presidential election "party identification did not translate into support for the candidates of major parties," and Carreirão (2002a) found that the election was mainly determined by economic evaluations of the *Plano Real.* Contrary to these authors, Singer (2002) has found that in addition to economic voting, the 1994 decisions were influenced by ideology and party identifications. The regressions results presented in table 5.5 confirm Singer's findings: in the 1994 presidential election, economic evaluations were powerful voting determinants, but partisanship was relevant too.

Prospect theory was tested for the 1998 and 2002 presidential elections using voters' judgments about candidates' governing capabilities. The results indicate that in 1998 Brazilians who considered Lula a low-risk candidate tended to vote for leftist parties, while those who believed FHC ranks lower in the risk propensity index tended to reelect him or vote for another nonleftist party. By 2002, the "golden age" of the *Plano Real* was over, and Brazilians had experienced major unemployment problems. The same results are found for the 2002 election: Brazilians who considered Lula the most capable, or less risky, candidate significantly tended to vote for the Left. In contrast, those who believed that José Serra (PSDB-PMDB) or Ciro Gomes (PPS-PDT-PTB) was the most capable tended to vote for a nonleftist party. As pointed out earlier in the Uruguayan case, this way of testing prospect theory is problematic. People can decide to vote Left and later think Lula is a low-risk candidate. However, it is the best proxy available to test the theory for the Brazilian case, and it is frequently used by other scholars (e.g., Cinta 1999).

But prospect theory is also tested using the 2002 panel survey in which citizens are asked to agree with one of these aphorisms: "A bird in the hand is worth two in the bush" or "Nothing ventured, nothing gained." Risk acceptant individuals are the ones who chose "Nothing ventured, nothing gained," and risk averse individuals chose "A bird in the hand is worth two in the bush." Figure 5.3 indicates that among those who intended to vote for leftist parties in 2002 there is a higher level of risk propensity than among those who planned to vote for nonleftist parties. Voting for the Left implied a higher level of risk because leftist parties had never been in charge of the national government.

Voting for a leftist party not only implied higher levels of risk acceptance; it also depended on how strongly voters believed they were in the domain of losses. To put it simply, the probability of an unhappy Brazilian voting for a leftist party in 2002 increased when the voter had a high level of risk acceptance and felt strongly that he or she was in the domain of losses, which is translated as a negative evaluation of the country's economic situation. Table 5.6 shows that a risk-taking citizen with a negative evaluation of the country's economy has a probability of voting Left of .54, while a risk averse voter with the same negative evaluation reduces the probability of choosing the less known opposition to .37. This evidence reinforces what Morgenstern and Zechmeister (2001) pointed out for Mexicans, and was previously shown in the Uruguayan case, that risk averse citizens prefer to stick with the "devil they know" than "gamble" their vote with the inexperienced Left.

The evidence from the Brazilian case reinforces the prevalent idea that social class cleavages are not relevant to predict voting behavior in Latin America. Neither occupation, nor education,[20] nor family income is a stable significant predictor of voting for left-of-center parties. Education was significant only in 1989 and 1994 but in different directions.

Figure 5.3. Risk and Vote Choice in Brazil, 2002

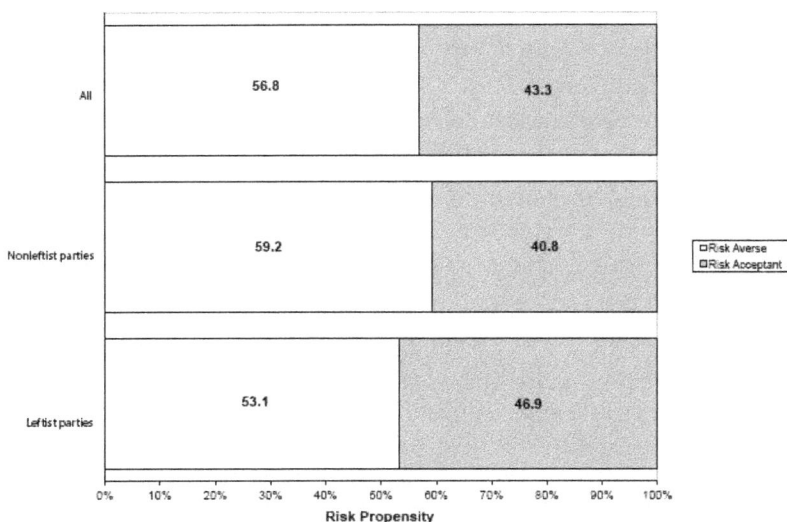

Source: 2002 Panel Survey.

In 1989, voters with high education had higher probabilities of voting Left, while in 1994 those with low levels of formal education and low income tended to vote for leftist parties. Income was only significant in 1994. Workers, formal or informal, are not significantly more inclined to vote for the Left than those who belong to the "dominant" classes, with few exceptions. In 1989 and 1994, those who belong to the dominant classes tended to vote for the Right. The same happened with the petty bourgeoisie in 2002. Informal workers were more inclined to vote for the Left in 1989 and 2002. In other words, Brazilian evidence, in general, supports the notion that the position a person occupies in the social structure does not determine his or her vote.

Leftist parties are usually more appealing to young people and traditionally have more electoral strength within urban electorates. The Uruguayan case supports this traditional view of left-of-center parties' cleavages. However, in Brazil, and despite PT and other leftist parties' electoral support in major cities, it was only in 1989 that the level of urbanization of the place of residence was relevant in explaining the vote for the Left. The age of the respondent is also not a consistent explanatory factor in

Table 5.6. Predicted Probabilities of Voting for Leftist Parties in 2002 Brazilian Election Depending on Risk Propensity and Sociotropic Economic Assessments

Risk Propensity	Retrospective Sociotropic Evaluations		
	Positive	Neutral	Negative
High risk averse	36.9	41.4	46.0
Risk averse	39.2	43.8	48.5
Risk acceptant	41.6	46.3	51.0
High risk acceptant	44.1	48.7	53.5

Note: Data are from the first wave of the 2002 panel survey carried out in Caxias do Sul and Juiz do Fora by Ames, Baker, and Renno. The first wave of the panel was collected during March and April 2002.

Cell entries are predicted probabilities of hypothetical individuals voting for left-of-center parties from a logit with the same variables as the model presented in table 5.5. Except for the identified variables, all variables are held constant at their means.

Brazil. In 1989, the vote for the Left was associated with older people; while in 1994 and 2004, younger voters were more inclined to it.

The analyses of the factors that influence Brazilians to vote for left-of-center political parties have several commonalities with the Uruguayan case. First, the traditional social class theory (Lipset and Rokkan 1967) does not explain the vote for the Left in post-authoritarian Brazil. The vote for the Left in Brazil is a multiclass vote rather than a working-class one.

Second, in a manner similar to Uruguayan leftist parties, leftist parties in Brazil—and mainly the PT—have formed a coalition that is ideologically Center-Left but is catchall in terms of class. This result goes against the common understanding that ideology and social class are matched, with workers on the Left and the dominant sectors on the Right. In Brazil, as in Uruguay, this correspondence between social class and ideology does not hold. It is clear that the meaning of Left and Right categories has changed, but despite this transformation, these categories are still significant in predicting voting behavior even in countries with weakly institutionalized party systems like Brazil. In other words, the Brazilian case provides evidence in favor of Torcal and Mainwaring's (2003) idea that ideology works as a political cleavage used by political parties to mobilize support.

Third, there is a clear performance mandate behind the increase in the vote for the Left in Brazil. Brazilians' dissatisfaction with the economic situation has benefited leftist parties because they were recognized as credible opposition. Immediately after the return to democracy, the Left in Brazil embraced political parties ranging from the social democratic Center-Left PSDB to the socialist PT. All these leftist parties were accepted by the electorate as credible or untainted opposition because, until then, they had not been in charge of the national government. By 1994, the PSDB was no longer considered a left-of-center party: Cardoso had served as finance minister in the Franco government and the PSDB made an electoral alliance with the PFL and had gradually "replaced a traditional social democratic line with a more market-oriented approach" (Power 2001–2002: 625). As a result of its movement to the Right, the PSDB no longer capitalized on social discontent. On the contrary, it captured votes from Brazilians who approved of the results of *Plano Real*, while those Brazilians who were dissatisfied with the economic situation tended to vote for leftist political parties, in particular the PT.[21]

To make a long story short, the analysis of Brazilians' voting behavior has shown that the vote for leftist parties has little to do with voting against neoliberal reforms per se. Only the opinion on privatization, one of the most controversial and unpopular market-oriented reforms, reaches statistical significance. By voting Left, Brazilians are mainly punishing political parties that produced economic hardship and secondarily defending an anti-privatization policy but not any other leftist policy stance. They might have voted for Lula looking for a halt to privatizations, but they did not call for more state intervention in the economy. Basically, they voted for leftist parties because they were the only untainted opposition.

Mexico

Neither Policies nor Outcomes

Three national surveys are used to test the hypotheses for the Mexican case. For the 1988 presidential election, a Gallup/ECO preelection survey is used. This survey was conducted from May 12 to June 1, 1988; it is representative of all the adult Mexican population and includes 2,960 face-to-face cases.[22] The analysis of the 1994 election is performed using a Warren Mitofsky national exit poll that includes 5,635 cases.[23] Finally, the vote for leftist parties in the 2000 presidential election is analyzed using the Post-Electoral Cross-Section survey carried out as part of the Mexico 2000 Panel Study.[24] This survey includes 1,199 cases collected from July 6 to July 9 at respondents' homes.[25] As with Brazil and Uruguay, the proportions intending to vote Left according to the Mexican data correspond very closely with proportions actually voting Left when the elections were held, ensuring the validity of the analysis. In 1988, the survey predicted 23 percent of votes for the Left, and the actual figure was 31 percent. For the 1994 exit poll and the 2000 postelection survey, it is only possible to separate the vote for PRD (not for others leftist parties), and the comparisons between the survey and election proportions are the following: 15 to 20 percent and 15 to 19 percent, respectively.

Each of these surveys has been used by other scholars. The 1988 survey was used in Domínguez and McCann's key 1995 study. The 1994 Mitofsky survey was used by Poiré (1999). And the Mexico 2000 Panel Study is the data source for Domínguez and Lawson's edited volume, *Mexico's Pivotal Democratic Election* (2004), the most comprehensive book analyzing the 2000 election. However, none of these studies ask the question raised here: Why do Mexicans vote for leftist parties?

The dependent variable is a dummy variable that measures the vote or vote intention (in 1988) for a left-of-center party; the value 1 means that the person voted (or intended to vote) for the Left, and 0 captures all other answers. The following political parties were classified as left-of-center in each presidential election: in 1988, Frente Democrático Nacional (FDN), Partido Mexicano Socialista (PMS), and Partido Revolucionario de los Trabajadores (PRT); in 1994 and 2000, only Partido de la Revolución Democrática (PRD) because it was not possible to separate the vote for other leftist parties (these have been put together under the "other" category).

The performance mandate is explored in the same way as in Uruguay and Brazil. *Sociotropic vote* and *Pocketbook vote* in the 1988 survey explore respondents' current economic assessments of the country and their own situation. Higher values correspond to negative evaluations. The 1988 regression model also has a measure of *Prospective inflation* and *Prospective unemployment;* higher values mean that inflation and unemployment are expected to decrease in the following *sexenio* (six-year term). *Prospective sociotropic* in 1988 measures citizens' expectations for the economy at the end of the next government's term in power (next *sexenio*). Higher values correspond to negative expectations. The operationalization of *Retrospective pocketbook* and *Prospective pocketbook* depends on the survey. In the 1988 survey, both variables measure citizens' evaluations of their own economic situation during the last year (*Retrospective pocketbook*) and the economic expectations for the next twelve months (*Prospective pocketbook*). The 1994 and 2000 surveys only ask *Retrospective pocketbook* and *Retrospective sociotropic.* In 1994, the comparison is made with the previous six years (before Salinas's government), while in the 2000 survey it is against the previous twelve months. In all cases, higher values equal negative evaluations.[26]

As in the Brazilian case, the policy mandate is measured in two ways. The first one is the respondent's self-placement on the ideological dimension (the weak meaning of ideology). This indicator is available only in the 2000 survey, and it ranges from 0 (Left) to 10 (Right). The second way to measure an interviewee's ideology is by a series of policy issues. This option tackles the strong meaning and is used to analyze the 1988 presidential election. The 1988 survey asked about foreign investment, imports of foreign products, payment of foreign debt, and privatizations. Higher values in each of these policies correspond to leftist positions.

Social class cleavage is tested using dummy variables; each dummy represents one category of social class defined in terms of occupation following Portes and Hoffman's classification (2003). Because the Mexican surveys did not ask respondents' occupation with the level of specificity that the Brazilian and Uruguayan surveys did, it is not possible to distinguish between formal and informal workers. As a result, only one dummy named *Workers* is entered into the model. The other two dummies in the model are *Dominant class* and *Petty bourgeoisie.* Each category is entered into the model as a dummy variable that takes the value of 1 when the person belongs to it and 0 when he or she does not. Owing to the same problem of lack of specificity, it was also impossible to construct a dummy named *Dominant* for the 1994 election. To capture the other dimensions of socioeconomic status, other variables were included: *Education, Family income* (1994), *Household socioeconomic status* (1988 and 2000) defined by the interviewer's judgment of the house, and 2000 *Household SES* defined by a housewares index that consisted of the ownership of radio, water heater, television, telephone, cellular phone, and oven. Higher values mean higher levels of education, higher family income, and higher socioeconomic status.

Partisanship is tested using dummy variables. Each dummy represents one category of partisanship: party identification with left-of-center parties, party identification with right-of-center parties, and those who lack partisanship. Each category is entered into the model as a dummy variable that takes the value of 1 when the person belongs to it and 0 when he or she does not. The 1994 survey does not have a question about party identification, and the 1988 survey only asks for the "preferred political party," which is slightly different from party identification but is taken as a proxy in the model.

Prospect theory is tested in different ways depending on the presidential election. For 1988, respondents were asked two questions: (1) if Mexican economic conditions would improve, remain the same, or worsen if the opposition were to gain power; and (2) if the country's social peace would be undermined if the opposition were to win the election. In both variables, higher values mean that citizens distrust the capabilities of opposition parties to lead the country along a good path. The 1994 survey captures Mexicans' risk propensity by asking the voter what was the main reason for his vote and giving him as an option the popular saying, "Más vale malo conocido que bueno por conocer" (Better the devil you know than the saint you don't). The question asking the reason for their vote was phrased in the following way: "The presidents who have governed Mexico for the past sixty-five years have come from the PRI. Which of the following reasons motivated you to vote for the party you chose today? a) the PRI is still the best choice, b) in politics it's 'better bad but known than good but unknown,' c) voted opposition to protest, d) want the opposition to win." A dummy variable named *Risk propensity* was coded with 1 when the voter answered this option and 0 for the remaining answer categories. It is important to mention that in this survey, the answer to the voting question was secret (the respondent marked a separate sheet and deposited it in a box), which diminishes the risk of contamination.

In 2000, *Risk propensity* was again measured by respondents' preference for one of two traditional aphorisms: "Better the devil you know than the saint you don't" and "Nothing ventured, nothing gained."[27] This preference was entered into the model as a dummy that takes the value of 1 when respondents mentioned "Better the known devil" and 0 when they chose "Nothing ventured, nothing gained." In addition, to explain the 2000 presidential election, a set of three indexes tackling Labastida's, Fox's, and Cárdenas's capacities to govern were added. Each index combines respondents' opinions on the capacity of each candidate to manage the economy, fight crime and public insecurity, and improve the educational system. Higher values in the index mean worse evaluations of the candidates' abilities to govern. As was pointed out before, this way to test prospect theory through voters' opinions of candidates' capacities is less valid than the one that measure voters' preferences for traditional aphorisms.

Finally, and to keep comparability with the Brazilian and Uruguayan cases, *Age* (the higher the value, the older the respondent) and *Urban voter* (for the 2000 election a dummy in which 1 is urban and 0 is rural, and for the 1988 a variable that ranges from 1 for the most rural areas to 5 for the most urban ones) are added to test for the existence of alternative cleavages.[28] In the 1994 exit poll survey, the *Urban voter* variable does not exist.

Mexicanists have endlessly pointed out that the most important factor to aid understanding of Mexican voting behavior during the past two decades is the regime cleavage, or in other words, voters' position in the pro-PRI/anti-PRI dimension. As a result of this, the relevance of the Left-Right ideological dimension in Mexicans' voting decisions was undermined. If it is really true that the ideological spectrum is not relevant, the factors that lead Mexicans to vote for leftist parties must be different from the ones that influence Brazilians and Uruguayans to vote for the Left. The results presented in table 5.7 are remarkable in showing that Mexicans' vote for the Left differs from other Latin Americans. The following paragraphs discuss these differences and a few similarities.

Table 5.7. Vote Determinants for Leftist Parties in Mexico, 1988–2000

Independent Variables	1988	1994	2000
Performance Mandate			
Sociotropic vote	0.010	–	–
	(.121)		
Sociotropic retrospective	–	0.721***	0.076
		(.056)	(.179)
Sociotropic prospective	0.124	–	–
	(.117)		
Pocketbook vote	0.162	–	–
	(.142)		
Pocketbook retrospective	−0.139	0.331***	0.105
	(.086)	(.061)	(.184)
Pocketbook prospective	dropped (2)	–	–
Prospective inflation	0.015	–	–
	(.121)		
Prospective unemployment	−0.081	–	–
	(.121)		
Policy Mandate			
Ideological self-placement	–	–	−0.018
			(.055)
Opinion external investment	0.094	–	–
	(.089)		
Opinion payment of external debt	0.448***	–	–
	(.172)		
Opinion open economy to imports	0.022	–	–
	(.162)		
Opinion privatizations	0.161	–	0.033
	(.171)		(.075)
Distribution	–	–	−0.012
			(.058)
Social Class Cleavage			
Dominant classes	−0.266	–	−0.231
	(.492)	(.843)	
Petty bourgeoisie	−0.749**	0.167	−1.130*
	(.291)	(.154)	(.738)
Workers	0.093	0.136	−0.815**
	(.170)	(.083)	(.356)
Education	0.165***	0.145***	0.079
	(.045)	(.038)	(.152)
Household SES	−0.298**	–	−0.027
	(.120)		(.199)
Household SES (houseware index)	–	–	0.162
			(.116)
Family income	–	−0.186***	–
		(.046)	

Table 5.7. Vote Determinants for Leftist Parties in Mexico, 1988–2000 (*cont.*)

Independent Variables	1988	1994	2000
Partisanship			
Left	1.545**	–	1.165
	(.703)		(.971)
Right	−2.233***	–	−3.647***
	(.700)		(.895)
No partisanship	−0.989	–	−1.690*
	(.756)		(.921)
Prospect Theory			
Economic risk if opposition wins	−0.772***		
	(.135)		
Social risk if opposition wins	−0.117		
	(.162)		
Risk propensity (1)		−0.560***	−0.229
		(.137)	(.424)
Capacity of Labastida to govern			0.148
			(.095)
Capacity of Fox to govern			0.378***
			(.093)
Capacity of Cárdenas to govern			−0.274**
			(.115)
Age	−0.012	0.032	0.013
	(.008)	(.035)	(.010)
Urban voter	0.030	–	0.093
	(.052)		(.199)
Constant	−0.636	−3.933***	−0.243
	(1.168)	(.189)	(2.230)
R-squared	0.45	0.10	0.68
Wald-chi^2	316***	408	139
Number of observations	1914	5635	950

Notes:

(1) Risk propensity in 1994 is measured by a dummy variable coded 1 for those who said "Better the devil you know" and 0 for the rest. In 2000, it is measured by a question asking respondents to agree with one of the two following aphorisms: (1) "Better the devil you know than the saint that you don't know" or (2) "Nothing ventured, nothing gained."

(2) Dropped due to collinearity.

* p < .10, ** p < .05, *** p < .01.

Entries are binary logit coefficients with robust standard errors in parentheses.

In order for political cleavages to become active, politicians need to emphasize them. Torcal and Mainwaring (2003) point out that political cleavages are created by political elites as a way to get votes. The ideological cleavage only becomes relevant if political leaders and political parties structure political conflict in ideological terms. In other words, voters could behave in a policy-oriented way if politicians frame political debates using ideological categories. As mentioned before, Mexican politics revolved around a regime cleavage at least until 2000. During that time, the ideological dimension remained inactive, or at least was a minor-league dimension (Domínguez and McCann 1995, 1996; Greene 2002; Klesner 2004, 2005; Magaloni and Poiré 2004b; Moreno 1998, 1999). Regression results demonstrate that Mexicans' ideological self-placement does not determine their vote. In 2000, individuals who placed themselves on the Left of the ideological dimension did not significantly differ in their vote from those who placed themselves on the Right.[29] One possible explanation for this finding is the existence of strategic voting in the 2000 presidential election. Because the prevalent cleavage was pro-PRI/anti-PRI and not an ideological one, Mexicans who identified themselves as leftist strategically voted for the PAN because they thought that it had higher probabilities of beating the PRI than did the PRD. The relevance of this explanation can be overstated because the survey was conducted after the election and citizens could have falsely declared their vote as a result of a bandwagon effect. However, the self-reporting error is small.[30]

An alternative way to test the ideological cleavage is to analyze if policy positions are determinants of voting behavior. In the 1988 presidential election, only one of the four policy positions reaches statistical significance: Mexicans who felt that the next government should stop payment of the country's foreign debt were more likely to vote for the Left. Surprisingly, the opinion on privatization of state companies is not a significant voting predictor. Moreover, in the 2000 presidential election, Mexicans' opinion about the privatization of the electric company is not a significant voting predictor for leftist parties. This result indicates that Mexicans who vote Left, at least in 1988 and 2000, did not oppose market-oriented economic reforms.

To sum up, the Mexican case fails to support the argument that the leftist tide was produced by policy-oriented voters angry with the Washington Consensus reforms; ideological considerations were not relevant voting determinants among Mexicans, at least until the 2000 presidential election. This can be explained by the fact that party leaders, who are among the most reliable voting cue providers, have not been interested in priming an ideological debate, focusing instead on the idea of alteration and change (Estrada 2005). It is highly probable that after the 2000 pivotal election, the ideological cleavage became more influential and achieved more explanatory power in the 2006 presidential election.

Mexico might be the country case for which the interplay between economic voting theory and prospect theory has been most fully studied (Cinta 1999; Magaloni 1999; Magaloni and Poiré 2004b; Morgenstern and Zechmeister 2001; Poiré 1999). Scholars have explained that Mexicans kept voting for the PRI despite its poor economic performance because they are risk averse and consequently avoid voting for the inexperienced opposition. Table 5.7 indicates that the economic voting explanation works for some presidential elections but not for all. In the 1988 election, Mexicans did not take into account the prospects for the nation's economy or personal finances when making their voting decisions (Domínguez and McCann 1995). The 1994 election, however, provides strong evidence supporting the argument that the leftist electoral rise could represent a performance mandate: Mexicans who were dissatisfied with the economy cast their vote in favor of leftist parties. Poiré (1999) points out that in the 1994 Mexican elections, retrospective evaluations were crucial factors in determining the vote, and it is not at all surprising after the tremendous economic crisis that the country suffered during that year. Finally, in the 2000 elections, economic assessments neither favored nor undermined leftist parties' electoral chances. As other scholars have pointed out, PRI's defeat in 2000 has nothing to do with the economy; on the contrary, the economic achievements of Zedillo's presidency were acknowledged by most Mexicans (Lawson 2004; Magaloni and Poiré 2004b).

Mexico has undergone a democratization process in which voters decided their vote using a "two-step" model (Domínguez and McCann 1995). First, they asked themselves if they were in favor of or against the PRI. Second, and only among those who decided they were against the PRI, were other voting cues taken into consideration. Could people decide their position on the PRI after deciding for another reason which party or candidate they preferred? Conceptually, it is possible. However, the "usual suspects" that explain voting behavior do not work as well in the Mexican case. Neither pro-state nor anti-market policy opinions are crucial determinants of voting for left-of-center parties. Only the opinion on paying the foreign debt is significant, and just in one election. It seems that there is no anti-neoliberal reform cleavage in Mexico. Not even ideology in its weak meaning, ideological self-identification, is significant. Moreover, the performance mandate does not work better to explain the vote for leftist Mexican parties. Economic assessments were only relevant after the 1994 crisis. Therefore, it is necessary to explore alternative voting determinants to explain the rise of the Left in this country.

More than Anything, Risk Propensity and Expectations of Competence

Social class theory showed no explanatory power for the vote for left-of-center parties in Brazil and Uruguay. The same happens in Mexico. The position that a person occupies in the social structure does not determine his or her vote. Only those who belong to the petty bourgeoisie are significantly less likely to vote for the Left.[31] Even more, workers are not more likely to vote for leftist parties than for rightist ones. In Mexico, the traditional support that left-of-center parties usually receive from workers goes to the PRI. In 2000, workers tended to vote more for rightists than for leftists. But the general idea that in Mexico workers, and in particular, public servants, tended to vote for the PRI (Klesner 2004; Lawson 1999) does not find support in the 1994 election: public servants have a significant and positive influence on voting Left, while being a private employee increases the chances of voting for a nonleftist party.[32] The other way to test for the existence of social class cleavages is through education and indicators of the material well-being of voters. Regression results indicate that Mexicans who vote for leftist parties have high levels of formal education but low income. As Klesner (2004) pointed out, they can be described as the "politically engaged poor."

In contrast to what happens in Uruguay, the vote for the Left in Mexico is not associated with younger voters or with citizens living in urban areas. Age and Urban Voter do not reach significance in any of the three presidential elections analyzed. Other scholars have found that among those characteristics only region is a relevant and consistent voting predictor in Mexico; citizens who live in southern states and Mexico City have a higher probability of voting for the PRD (Magaloni 1999; Poiré 1999; Klesner 2004). To maintain comparability with the Brazilian and Uruguayan models, region was not included in the model shown in table 5.7. In conclusion, sociodemographic cleavages are not significant determinants of the vote for leftist parties in Mexico. The Mexican case provides additional evidence that in Latin America the social class cleavage theory does not work.

Scholars who study Mexican politics are skeptical about the role that partisanship plays in Mexicans' voting decisions. Klesner (2004) states that partisanship used to be stronger among PRI voters than among PAN or PRD voters, but regardless of the party, party identification was not especially strong in Mexico, and besides its importance has tended to decrease with time. In the same way, Magaloni and Poiré (2004a) argue that partisan attachments were weak in the 2000 presidential election. On the other hand, Estrada (2005) and Moreno (2003) provide evidence that party identification is more stable than ideological self-placements and vote choice. The coefficients shown in table 5.7 contribute to the idea that partisanship is an inconsistent explanation for the voting preferences of Mexicans. Partisanship with a leftist or rightist party was a significant predictor of the vote in 1988; individuals who identified with a left-of-center party were more likely to vote for a leftist party, while those attached to a party on the Right significantly tended to vote for a rightist party. But in the 2000 election, having a right-wing partisanship or no party identification reaches significance, while party identification with leftist parties does not, indicating that many Mexicans with attachments to left-wing parties did not vote for the PRD or other left-oriented parties and strategically voted for the PAN.[33] The regression results fail to support the argument that partisanship can be more important for predicting the vote for leftist parties than for rightist ones. The Mexican case indicates that in elections where competition is between a long-ruling party and more than one opposition, party attachments leave their central place to strategic voting decisions that favor the party with higher probabilities of winning.

Prospect theory plays an important role in understanding why Mexicans kept voting for the PRI and the barriers that leftist parties (as well as other opposition parties) had to overcome in order to be seen as a sure alternative. In 1988, voters who considered that voting for the opposition did not represent any economic risk for the country were more likely to vote for the Left. The same happened in 1994, when risk acceptant Mexicans were more likely to choose leftist parties. However, risk propensity does not achieve significance in 2000. One of the reasons might be that Mexicans who were risk takers also voted for the rightist PAN, instead of uniformly voting for the PRD.[34] Nevertheless, figure 5.4 indicates that the pivotal 2000 Mexican election is similar to its counterparts in Brazil and Uruguay: among those who voted for leftist parties, the percentage of risk acceptant voters is higher than among those who voted for nonleftist parties. Voting for the Left, as occurred in the 2002 Brazilian election and the 2004 Uruguayan election, implied a higher level of risk.

On the other side, expectations of the competence that each candidate would have in managing the country were highly significant in the 2000 presidential election. Those who considered that Labastida or Fox was highly capable of managing the economy, fighting crime, and dealing with the educational system voted for rightist parties; those who believed Cárdenas was the candidate with higher capabilities voted PRD. To put it simply, voters evaluated who was the most capable candidate and voted for him.[35]

In conclusion, the 2000 Mexican election partially reinforces prospect theory. On one side, the probabilities of voting for a leftist party increased when the voter is risk acceptant, but on the other side, these probabilities increase when the voter considers himself or herself in the domain of gains, which is translated into a positive evaluation of the country's economic situation. Table 5.8 shows that a risk averse citizen with a highly negative evaluation of the country's economy has a probability of voting Left of .023, while a risk taker voter with the same negative evaluation increases the probability of choosing the PRD to .027.[36] In comparison with the Uruguayan and Brazilian cases, the differences between risk takers

Figure 5.4. Risk and Vote Choice in Mexico, 2000

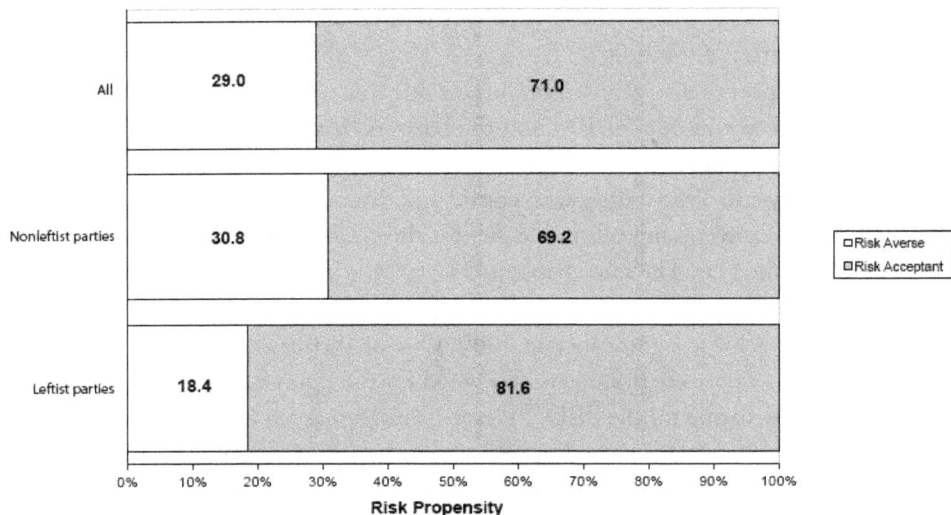

Source: Postelectoral Cross Section, Mexico 2000 Panel Study.

and risk averse citizens are smaller. In addition, a risk acceptant Mexican with a highly positive evaluation of the economy has a probability of voting Left of .059, while a risk averse voter diminishes this probability to .052. In making a decision, the domain of the voter is more important than his or her propensity to take risks. In other words, and in contrast to what happens in Brazil and Uruguay, the probability of voting Left diminishes with bad economic evaluations. This counterfinding can be explained by the fact that there is more than one "credible opposition," one on the Left (PRD) but another on the Right (PAN), and the electorate attributed fewer capabilities to the former than to the latter.

Mexico's regression results indicate that when more than one political party represents a credible and untainted opposition, and despite leftist parties being part of that opposition, risk acceptant citizens will not necessarily choose the Left at the voting booth. In that scenario, voting decisions are not made solely on the basis of the credibility of the opposition. It is also important to judge the capacity to govern that each political party is able to demonstrate. As a result, Mexican leftist parties face a double task. First, they have to convince voters to stop supporting

Table 5.8. Predicted Probabilities of Voting for Leftist Parties in 2000 Mexican Election Depending on Risk Propensity and Sociotropic Economic Assessments

Risk Propensity	Retrospective Sociotropic Evaluations				
	Highly Positive	Positive	Neutral	Negative	Highly Negative
Risk acceptant	5.9	4.9	4.0	3.3	2.7
Risk averse	5.2	4.3	3.5	2.9	2.3

Source: Postelection survey, Mexico 2000.
Note: Cell entries are predicted probabilities of hypothetical individuals voting for left-of-center parties from a logit with the same variables as the model presented in table 5.7. Except for the identified variables, all variables are held constant at their means.

the long-ruling party. Second, they have to persuade anti-PRI Mexicans to cast their vote in favor of the opposition on the Left instead of the opposition on the Right. The Mexican case shows that when the political system has two credible oppositions, the Left is not necessarily the one that is going to receive more support. The ability a party has to capture the votes from a discontented electorate depends on two elements: the skill to articulate an antigovernment message and the capacity to reduce the uncertainty voters usually have toward inexperienced parties. Domínguez (1999: 19) argues that in the 1997 congressional election, "the PAN was defeated because it failed to articulate a clear antigovernment message, for truly convinced opposition voters, the PRD was the only credible option." In the 2000 presidential election, the situation was the reverse: convinced opposition voters chose PAN because it was the more credible opposition as well as the less uncertain option. Again, it remains to be analyzed what happened in the 2006 presidential election when the Left was the only credible opposition.

To put it briefly, the factors that lead Brazilians and Uruguayans to vote for leftist parties do not concur with the ones found in the Mexican case. During the past two decades, Mexicans made their voting decisions based on different reasonings from other Latin Americans. Perceptions of the competence of each candidate and considerations of the risk involved in voting for a certain political party are influential factors in voters' behavior, but this is more the case in Mexico than in other countries of the region. However, economic evaluations, policy stances, and even partisanship are considerations that are still weak among Mexican voters. All of these considerations have faded in comparison to the pro-PRI/anti-PRI cleavage during the 1988, 1994, and 2000 Mexican presidential elections. How this has changed in the first nonregime cleavage election of 2006 remains to be analyzed.

The idea that there is a movement to the Left in the region and that Latin Americans may be punishing governments for the implementation of market-oriented reforms because they are policy oriented, or following a performance mandate generated by the bad economic results of the Washington Consensus model, becomes questionable based on the Mexican evidence provided by the individual-level analysis.

Latin Americans Are Not Random Voters

The most-different system research design made it possible to understand why Latin Americans vote for leftist parties in different political and economic contexts. Table 5.9 summarizes the findings from each of the individual-level analyses. Check marks indicate when a positive or negative significant relationship exists between the predicting theories and voting Left but do not mean that each independent variable that tested that voting theory in every election year reaches significance and in a particular direction. The table just summarizes the general pattern.

The first thing to notice is that Latin Americans are not voting for left-of-center parties because they are against neoliberal reforms. The study of each country suggests that espousing pro-state anti-market options has nothing to do with voting Left but does not necessarily mean that parties' positions on "neoliberal" policies, for or against, have no impact on voters. What it really means is that the impact of certain policy stances or anti-neoliberal discourses is not determinant of Latin Americans' voting decisions. With a few exceptions, most of the time voters are unconcerned with the type of policy politicians propose and even

Table 5.9. Summary of Individual-Level Analysis Findings

Predicting Theories	Uruguay	Brazil	Mexico
Outcome mandate (Economic voting)	√	√	√ (only in 1994)
Policy mandate		√	
Social class cleavage			
Urban-rural cleavage	√		
Partisanship			
with leftist parties	√	√	
with rightist parties	√		√
Prospect theory	√	√	√

enact. The low correlations between policy positions and voters' electoral preferences are just one piece of evidence indicating that Latin Americans are not policy oriented, which is a finding highly congruent with what other scholars have found (e.g., Stokes 2001a). Electorates in the region are voting Left because they are looking for new political alternatives that might provide an improvement in people's economic well-being. The relevance that economic voting theory has to explain leftist vote indicates that Latin Americans might be punishing traditional parties that failed to provide material security to their electorates, and these parties usually are the ones that implemented market-oriented economic reforms, but this opposition is driven less by policy stances than by economic outcomes. Rather than random voters, Latin Americans are proven to be outcome oriented.

Second, the possibilities of leftist parties capitalizing on Latin Americans' social discontent depend on the number of "credible" or "untainted" opposition parties. In countries like Brazil and Uruguay where leftist parties embody the only credible opposition, it is easy to capture votes from those unhappy with the status quo. But in countries where more than one credible opposition exists, as in Mexico, leftist parties have to win over voters who take into account other considerations, mainly the party's capacity to govern. Prospect theory's predicting power to explain voting behavior in the region points to the importance of reducing uncertainty for left-leaning parties' electoral chances. To the extent that leftist parties succeed in reducing the uncertainty that citizens might have voting for an inexperienced party, they will be able to capture the votes of dissatisfied Latin Americans.[37] But it is important to remember that despite being crucial to reducing the uncertainty that the electorate feels about inexperienced parties, the same lack of experience is what makes them more "untainted."

Third, although ideology is an important factor in explaining voting behavior, social class is not. This result goes against the common understanding that ideology and social class are matched: workers are on the Left; the dominant sectors, on the Right. The evidence from Brazil, Mexico, and Uruguay shows that this attachment between social class and ideology does not hold in Latin America. Left-oriented parties in the region have formed a coalition that is ideologically Center-Left but is catchall in terms of class.[38] Despite the fact that ideology and social class are not significantly related, ideology remains an important voting predictor. One possible explanation for this unexpected combination of ideology and catchall parties may be that ideology works as a political cleavage activated by political parties and politicians to mobilize support rather than as a structural cleavage determined by social class.

Finally, the individual-level analysis presented in this chapter provides ample evidence that Latin Americans are not random voters. Regardless of the differences in voting behavior between Brazilians, Mexicans, and Uruguayans, all of them take into account the economic performance of the incumbent, party attachments, and ideological considerations when voting. This is good news for a region demanding a more accountable democracy. Furthermore, the same search for an "untainted opposition," or the vote cast in favor of change regardless of how risky it is, can be seen as a healthy indicator that voters still care about democracy and that they continue to look for institutional ways to fulfill their needs rather than opt for undemocratic ones.

Chapter 6

THE SEARCH FOR UNTAINTED PARTIES

T his book examines the impact of neoliberal economic reforms implemented in Latin America during the 1980s
and 1990s on the shift to the Left. In particular, it seeks to
answer three concrete research questions: (a) is the success of leftist parties in Latin America something new and general in the region? (b) is it
true that market-oriented economic reforms are behind the leftist tide
or, regardless of those policies, that certain economic and political conditions have benefited left-leaning parties' electoral performance? and
(c) what are the determinants of Latin Americans' vote for left-oriented
parties? When citizens in a region well known for its clientelistic prac-
tices vote, are they behaving in a policy-oriented or outcome-oriented
way? All this is relevant to gaining an understanding as to just what the
demand behind the leftist tide is: policies favoring more state intervention or just better economic results?

A combination of methodologies were used to answer these questions. First, a cross-national regression analysis was performed using data
from seventeen countries covering the period from 1985 to 2004. This
dataset, in addition to containing the percentage of votes for each ideological bloc during that period, includes variables that measure the level
of neoliberal reforms implemented in each country, a set of economic
variables that appraise economic well-being, and a series of political
variables that account for the political context. Second, an individual-
level analysis performed in a most-different system design was used to

respond to the question about the factors that lead Latin American voters to choose a leftist party. The three country cases analyzed are Brazil, Mexico, and Uruguay, covering the period from 1980 to 2004. For each of these countries, a multivariate analysis was carried out to test the influence of different factors on the intention to vote for leftist parties.

Examining voting choice both from the macro and micro perspectives has the advantage of overcoming the flaws present in each approach. The aggregate-level examination offers insights into the impact that different levels of market-oriented economic reforms, macroeconomic conditions, and different political contexts have on the electoral fortunes of leftist parties. Put differently, it has the benefit of assessing the impact of objective conditions on political behavior. However, it also has an important shortcoming: individuals do not always behave by taking into account objective conditions. On the contrary, they often act based on their perceptions, which is why it is so important to complement the investigation with an individual-level analysis.

The micro-level perspective takes into account the reasoning processes through which individuals make decisions at the ballot box and makes it possible to examine how macro-level conditions (e.g., reforms, inflation, unemployment) are perceived and valued by citizens (Echegaray 2005). For example, it may be that in a particular Latin American country few neoliberal economic reforms have actually been implemented. Due to an intense campaign against these reforms, however, the electorate perceives them to have been deeply and highly harmful. Perceptions of reality do not necessarily coincide with objective reality; they are highly prone to persuasion from politicians or the media.

But the micro analysis also has some problems. One of the most important is the danger of respondents giving spurious answers (Erikson, MacKuen, and Stimson 2002). By comparing the results of the individual level of analysis with the macro level of analysis, concerns about spuriousness can be overcome or at least reduced.

Several conclusions may be derived from this investigation. First, ideological cycles have existed in Latin America in the same way they have existed in the more developed world. Latin America has experienced four ideological cycles since 1945. The beginning of each cycle correlates with pessimistic popular moods, popular discontent, and dissatisfaction with particular developmental models implemented in the region. Left and Right have switched their predominance since 1945, neither of them being the leading ideology throughout the period. The Left was prevalent from 1969 to 1976, a period in Latin American history that happens to be full of dissatisfaction with the economy, unhappiness with the ISI model, rising inequality in income distribution, high levels of unemployment, and a growing informal sector. In spite of the fact that the region had positive growth rates during some of those years, the sense of failure and unfulfilled expectations was widespread.

The Left became dominant when social discontent was widespread, which also occurred at the beginning of the new wave at the beginning of the twenty-first century. Despite leftist parties not increasing their electoral support in every Latin American country, the Left is the current dominant ideology in the region. Just as before the 1969–1976 leftist predominance there was dissatisfaction with the ISI model, so at the beginning of new millennium the disappointment was with the model promoted by the Washington Consensus. Many things have changed on the Left from the 1960s and 1970s to the 2000s, but perhaps the most relevant one is the attitude toward democracy. Leftist parties in Latin America moved from supporting revolutionary change and underestimating democracy as a tool of the bourgeoisie to defending democratic participation, competing in elections, and demanding a deepening of democracy in the region. The current leading role of the Left in the region suggests a different, and more positive, prospect for democracy.

Second, despite the existing discontent with the neoliberal model, this does not necessarily mean that more market reforms produce more votes for political parties on the Left. The cross-national analysis provides strong evidence against that argument. Even though Lora and Olivera (2005) found that Latin Americans dislike pro-market policies irrespective of their results and punish incumbents for implementing these reforms, this macro-level analysis shows that there is no direct connection between that dislike and the vote for leftist political parties. The key variable in understanding the increase of leftist parties' electoral chances is not the level of neoliberal reforms implemented in each country but rather unemployment. Left-leaning parties in Latin America do increase their electoral chances when unemployment is high. This finding matches the research on the economic conditions that benefit leftist parties in Europe. On the other hand, the implementation of market-friendly reforms by leftist parties hurts their electoral chances in the next election. Leftist parties, when they reach government, lose votes when unemployment increases and also when they implement neoliberal policies. To sum up, from the macro perspective, voters look more outcome oriented than anything else. One exception holds: when leftist parties are already incumbents, they lose votes when there is high unemployment but also when they implement neoliberal economic reforms.

Third, the previous finding is confirmed by the results extracted from the multivariate analysis in Brazil, Mexico, and Uruguay. Latin Americans are not voting for left-of-center parties because they are against neoliberal policies. Policy positions are not among the most influential factors in determining voters' decisions. For example, Brazilians who vote for the Left are not significantly more in favor of state intervention than Brazilians who vote for other ideological blocs. Not even their positions on socialism or egalitarianism determine their vote. Only their posture on privatization reaches significance, which is quite explicable taking into account that Brazil is one of the countries in the region that implemented greater privatization. However, in general, pro-market or pro-state policy stances are not influential factors for Latin Americans when casting their vote.

Electorates in the region are voting Left simply because they want to try new alternatives that might improve their economic well-being. If Latin Americans punish traditional parties that implemented structural reforms, this is less a result of their policy stances against neoliberalism or the market than of bad economic outcomes. In other words, voters are more outcome oriented than policy oriented and punish those parties that they evaluate as having had a negative economic performance. This evidence reinforces the argument that voters, in order to make politicians accountable, do not necessarily need to be policy oriented but rather that it is enough for them to be outcome oriented. The congruency of the findings extracted from the two levels of analysis, the macro and micro, make them more trustworthy. The current shift to the Left in Latin America is more a result of popular discontent with the economic situation than anything else. In particular, espousing pro-state anti-market options has little to do with voting Left.

Finally, and in this context, the electoral possibilities of success that leftist parties have by capitalizing on social discontent depend on the number of "untainted opposition" parties available in the political system. In countries like Brazil and Uruguay where leftist parties embody the only untainted opposition, they needed only to overcome voters' natural resistance to voting for inexperienced parties. On the other hand, Mexico's recent history shows that leftist parties can have a hard time when they have to compete with another untainted opposition party, as was the case between the PRD and the PAN. It is the interplay of macro and micro factors that better explains voting decisions. Voters' economic discontent, a micro-level explanatory factor, can be capitalized on by leftist parties depending on how many parties are seen as untainted opposition, which is a party system characteristic, a macro-level factor.

This argument can be generalized beyond these three country cases. The most-different system design, by testing the relationships between the main variables in highly diverse contexts, makes it easier to translate the findings to other Latin American countries. In Bolivia, the success of Evo Morales indicates that another untainted opposition has become credible enough to merit the chance to govern one of the poorest countries in the region. In Venezuela, Hugo Chávez also embodied a new and distinctive alternative from the traditional COPEI and Acción Democrática (AD). Regardless of the differences between these leftist parties and the more institutionalized Frente Amplio or Partido dos Trabalhadores, they share with them the character of an untainted opposition. Table 6.1 shows other leftist Latin American political parties that have recently reached the presidency and can be classified as untainted. In addition to Movimiento Quinta República (MVR) in Venezuela and Movimiento de Acción Socialista (MAS) in Bolivia, there is Alianza PAIS in Ecuador, Unidad Nacional de la Esperanza (UNE) in Guatemala, Alianza Patriótica por el Cambio in Paraguay, and Frente Farabundo Martí para la Liberación Nacional in El Salvador.

Only Partido Justicialista in Argentina, Frente Sandinista de Liberación Nacional in Nicaragua, and Concertación in Chile cannot be

Table 6.1. "Untainted" Latin American Leftist Parties

Country	Political Party	Period of Government	Government Experience at the National Level	Government Experience at the Local Level	"Untainted"
Venezuela	Movimiento Quinta República	Since 1999	Not before 1999	Not before 1999	Yes
Brazil	Partido dos Trabalhadores	Since 2002	Not before 2002	Yes, since 1985	Yes
Argentina	Partido Justicialista	Since 2003	Yes	Yes	No
Uruguay	Frente Amplio	Since 2004	Not before 2004	Yes	Yes
Chile	Concertación	1990–2010	Yes	Yes	No
Bolivia	Movimiento de Acción Socialista	Since 2005	No	Not before 2005	Yes
Mexico	Partido de la Revolución Democrática	Never	No	Yes, since 1997	Yes
Nicaragua	Frente Sandinista de Liberación Nacional	Since 2006	Yes	Yes	No
Ecuador	Alianza PAIS	Since 2006	Not before 2006	Not before 2006	Yes
Guatemala	Unidad Nacional de la Esperanza	Since 2007	Not before 2007	Not before 2007	Yes
Paraguay	Alianza Patriótica por el Cambio	Since 2008	Not before 2008	Not before 2008	Yes
El Salvador	Frente Farabundo Martí para la Liberación Nacional	Since 2009	Not before 2009	Not before 2009	Yes

considered untainted political parties. The Partido Justicialista or Peronist Party has been in charge of the national government many times during Argentina's independent life. However, as a result of the several factions that the Peronista Party has had, the first time that Kirchnerismo reached the presidency (2003) could be considered "uncontaminated." Mainly so in comparison with Menemismo, the Peronist faction that implemented the bulk of neoliberal reforms in Argentina. Concertación in Chile has had a different trajectory. It has been in charge of the executive branch from the return to democracy to 2010, alternating the presidency between the Partido Demócrata Cristiano and the Partido Socialista. The Socialists had governed the country before the dictatorship, and although at that time they could not be blamed for the implementation of neoliberal reforms (as it was entirely on the hands of the military regime), neither could they be counted as unpolluted or untainted. Finally, the case of Nicaragua with the Frente Sandinista de Liberación Nacional is even more straightforward, because Manuel Ortega, the elected president in 2006, had already been president from 1985 to 1990. A former president can by no means be considered untainted.

This book also contributes to a broadening of our understanding of political behavior, and especially voting behavior, in Latin America. There is a predominant scholarly preconception that depicts Latin Americans as random and unpredictable voters. Voting behavior in the region was traditionally underestimated as a result of unconcealed exchanges of support for particularistic benefits. In addition to the clientelistic motives, candidates' attributes and campaign influence are usually mentioned as relevant voting clues followed by electorates in the region. This project undermines the importance of these factors, despite being well proved for some countries, because the individual-level analysis presented here indicates that other voting clues are also very influential in the way Latin Americans process their voting decisions. Brazilians, Mexicans, and Uruguayans take into account the economic performance of the incumbent, as well as their party attachments and ideological identification, while making their decisions at the ballot box. Put more simply, Latin American electorates are more discriminating than scholars have sometimes considered and, as a consequence, are capable of making politicians accountable.

Perhaps just as important, the findings here can be taken as good news for the future of democracy in the region. Despite the fact that Latin America finished its transition to democracy some years ago, it still needs to consolidate and improve the quality of its democracy (Roberts 1998; Stokes 2001b). In order for democracies to work properly, they need popular support (Easton 1953), and recent research has shown that support for democratic political institutions and democratic systems depends on which side of the winning-losing equation citizens are on (Anderson et al. 2005; Vairo 2012). Citizens who voted for a party that lost the election (losers) tend to have lower levels of support for democracy than winners. As a result, democracies could become unstable if losers are continuously ignored in the political game, excluded from the political process, and always the same people. Furthermore, the gap in support for democracy between winners and losers does not exist at all times for all types of voters. Losers' ideology matters: voters on the extreme Left expressed more negative evaluations of the political system than those on the Right. To make democracy strong and stable, it is better to have alternation in power, and it is preferable to incorporate minorities (Anderson et al. 2005).

Taking all these arguments into account, the findings presented in this book are good news for democracy's prospects for two reasons. First, they show how Latin Americans have changed governments by incorporating left-oriented parties into the political game. The future of democracy could be in danger if certain political actors are always on the losers' side. For many years, several leftist political parties in the region were the losers in the electoral game. Moreover, some of them dismissed democracy as a valid means of achieving power. Therefore, the arrival of left-leaning parties to the governance of several Latin American countries, rather than a cause of concern, should be considered an indicator of a healthy democracy and a mechanism that strengthens democratic support among the citizenry. Second, the results of this project show that when Latin Americans have institutional and democratic means to channel their discontent, they opt for them. At least in Brazil, Mexico, and Uruguay, voters prefer to vote for "untainted parties" rather than look for nondemocratic alternatives to achieve their demands.

Latin Americans are capable of making their political leaders accountable, removing them from office when they do not accomplish what was expected and changing those in charge of the government by voting for untainted parties. The success of untainted parties in Brazil, Mexico, and Uruguay suggests an increase in institutionalization and in political representation and is a sign of political maturity (López 2005). In a region demanding a more accountable and responsive democracy, the examples of Brazil, Mexico, and Uruguay show a particular way this can be done. The recent shift to the Left in Latin America has helped to intensify and strengthen democracy in the region by incorporating losers into the political game.

It is uncertain what might happen after leftist parties have been in charge of national government for a while. Several scholars have anticipated that this "Left Turn" will endure (Castañeda and Navia 2007; Cleary 2006). Cleary points out that "the future of the Left in Latin America will in large part depend on its ability to strike a balance between the pragmatic need for moderation and the moral imperative to pursue strategies of poverty reduction, redistribution, and development" (2006: 48). Castañeda and Navia (2007) agree that moderation is necessary for the Left to stay in power.

Their status as "untainted parties" is lost immediately after gaining access to government. As a result, two possible scenarios may be imagined. In the first, leftist governments succeed in significantly improving the material well-being of Latin Americans and reducing social and economic inequalities and as a result continue to govern for several years. Castañeda and Navia (2007) argue against this scenario. In their view, even if leftist parties do not improve living conditions they will be better positioned than parties on the right because 80 percent of the populace in Latin America live under the median income, so there is a public for redistributive appeals. Although this study does not explore the rationale behind reelection, it is worth mentioning that the majority of the current leftist governments have received a renewed mandate at least once (Venezuela, Brazil, Argentina, Uruguay, Bolivia, and Ecuador). There is some evidence in favor of the continuity argument.

In the second scenario, Schlesinger is right:

> People can never be fulfilled for long either in the public or in the private sphere. We try one, then the other, and frustration compels a change in course. Moreover, however effective a particular course may be in meeting one set of troubles, it generally falters and fails when new troubles arise. And many troubles are inherently insoluble. As political eras, whether dominated by public purpose or by private interest, run their course, they infallibly generate the desire for something different. After a while, it always becomes "time for a change." (Schlesinger 1986: 28)

In this scenario, after several years we would expect another ideological shift in the region, this time to the Right. The recent success of a right-wing party in Chile and the incipient negative slope of the left-wing parties' line in the last ideological cycle indicate that there is also some support for this statement. Time will tell.

APPENDIX 1

Vote Share and Ideological Cycles

The data presented in chapter 2 show the vote share obtained by each ideological bloc (Left, Center, and Right) in congressional elections from 1945 to 2010. A few clarifications about some countries' electoral results are necessary.

Argentina: Includes congressional elections as well as results for national constituent elections.

Brazil: Excludes congressional elections during the military regime because not all parties were allowed to compete.

Bolivia: Elections held before 1956 are not included in the dataset. Before 1956 there was no opposition participation and no universal right to vote (that law was enacted in 1952).

Peru: 1956 election not included because experts said it was fraudulent.

Table A.1.   Political Parties Unclassified in the Left-Right Dimension,
1980–2010

Country	Political Party	Presidential Election Year	Percentage of Vote
Argentina	Partido Justicialista	1983	40.2
	Partido Justicialista	1989	47.3
	Blanco de los Jubilados	1989	1.9
	Partido Justicialista	1995	49.8
	Partido Justicialista	1999	38.1
	Alianza Social Cristiana	1999	0.3
	Frente por la Lealtad (Menem) (PJ)	2003	19.5
	Frente Nacional y Popular (Rodriguez Saa) (PJ)	2003	14.1
	Alianza Unidos o Dominados (Mussa-Suarez)	2003	0.2
	Frente Nacional y Popular (Rodriguez Saa) (PJ)	2007	8.2
Bolivia	Movimiento Indio Tupaj Katari (MITKA)	1980	1.2
	Movimiento Indio Tupaj Katari Uno (MITKA-Uno)	1980	1.3
	Partido de la Unión Boliviana (PUB)	1980	1.2
	Movimiento Revolucionario Tupaj Katari (MRTK)	1985	1.1
	Movimiento Revolucionario Tupaj Katari de Liberación (MRTKL)	1985	2.1
	Conciencia de Patria (CONDEPA)	1989	12.2
	Movimiento Revolucionario Tupaj Katari de Liberación (MRTKL)	1989	1.6
	Frente Único de Liberación Katarista (FULKA)	1989	1.2
	Unión Cívica Solidaridad (UCS)	1993	13.8
	Conciencia de Patria (CONDEPA)	1993	14.3
	Union Cívica Solidaridad (UCS)	1997	16.1
	Conciencia de Patria (CONDEPA)	1997	17.2
	Unión Cívica Solidaridad (UCS)	2002	5.0

Table A.1. Political Parties Unclassified in the Left-Right Dimension,
1980–2010 (*continued*)

Country	Political Party	Presidential Election Year	Percentage of Vote
	LyJ (Libertad y Justicia)	2002	2.7
	Conciencia de Patria (CONDEPA)	2002	0.4
	Frente Patriótico Agropecuario de Bolivia (FREPAB)	2005	0.3
	Unión Social de los Trabajadores de Bolivia (USTB)	2005	0.3
	Alianza Social	2009	2.3
Brazil	Partido da Reconstrução Nacional (PRN)	1989	30.5
	Partido da Reconstrução Nacional (PRN)	1994	0.6
	Partido Verde	2010	19.3
Chile	Partido Unión de Centro Centro Progresista (UCCP)	1989	15.4
	Partido Unión de Centro Centro Progresista (UCCP)	1999	0.4
Colombia	Movimiento Unitario Metapolítico (MUM)	1986	0.6
	Movimiento Unitario Metapolítico (MUM)	1990	0.6
	Movimiento Unitario Metapolítico (MUM)	1994	1.1
	Independiente	1998	27.1
	Partido Verde Oxígeno	2002	0.5
	Movimiento Defensa Ciudadana	2002	0.1
	Movimiento Político. Comunal y Comunidad Colombiano	2002	0.1
	Movimiento Participación Comunal	2002	1.5
	Partido Verde	2010	21.5
Costa Rica	Unión General	2002	0.2
Ecuador	Partido Roldosista Ecuatoriano (PRE)	1992	22.0
	Acción Popular Revolucionaria Ecuatoriana (APRE)	1992	3.1
	Concentración de Fuerzas Populares (CFP)	1992	1.3
	Partido Roldosista Ecuatoriano (PRE)	1996	26.3

Table A.1.   Political Parties Unclassified in the Left-Right Dimension,
1980–2010 (*continued*)

Country	Political Party	Presidential Election Year	Percentage of Vote
	Acción Popular Revolucionaria Ecuatoriana (APRE)	1996	4.9
	Concentración de Fuerzas Populares (CFP)	1996	27.2
	Alianza	1996	3.0
	UCI	1996	1.2
	Revolucionaria Ecuatoriana (PRE-APRE-UPL)	1998	26.6
	Movimiento Ciudadanos Nuevo País (MCNP)	1998	14.8
	Auténtica (MIRA)	1998	5.1
	Partido Roldosista Ecuatoriano (PRE)	2002	11.9
	Movimiento Transformación Social Independiente (TSI)	2002	3.7
	Movimiento Patria Solidaria (MPS)	2002	1.1
	Movimiento Independiente Amauta Jatari (MIAJ)	2002	0.8
	Concentración de Fuerzas Populares (CFP)	2006	0.5
	Partido Roldosista Ecuatoriano	2006	2.1
	Movimiento de Reivindicación Democrática	2006	1.4
	Alianza Alba, Tercera República	2006	0.4
	Movimiento Revolucionario de Participación Popular (MRPP)	2006	0.3
	INA	2006	0.3
Guatemala	Movimiento Emergente de Concordia–Frente de Unidad Nacional (PUA-MEC-FUN)	1985	1.9
	Movimiento de Acción Solidaria (MAS)	1990	24.1
	Partido Democrático de Cooperación Nacional (PDCN)	1990	2.1
	Movimiento Emergente de Concordia (MEC)	1990	1.1
	Partido Liberador Progresista (PLP)	1995	5.2
	Partido Progresista (PP)	1995	1.6

Table A.1.   Political Parties Unclassified in the Left-Right Dimension,
1980–2010 (*continued*)

Country	Political Party	Presidential Election Year	Percentage of Vote
	Partido Reformador Guatemalteco (PREG)	1995	1.1
	Partido Liberador Progresista (PLP)	1999	3.1
	Democracia Social Participativa (DSP)	2003	1.4
	UN	2003	0.4
	Movimiento Social y Político Cambio Nacional (MSPCN)	2003	0.4
Mexico	Partido Social Democrático (PSD)	1982	0.2
	Frente Democrático Nacional (FDN)	1988	31.1
Panamá	Partido Vanguardia Moral de la Patria	2009	2.3
Paraguay	Partido Humanista Paraguayo	2003	0.1
	Partido Humanista Paraguayo	2008	0.4
Peru	CAMBIO 90	1990	29.1
	Frente Popular Agrícola del Perú (FREPAP)	1990	1.1
	CAMBIO 90	1995	64.4
	Frente Popular Agrícola del Perú (FREPAP)	1995	0.8
	Unión por el Perú (UPP)	1995	21.8
	Movimiento Obras Cívicas (MOC)	1995	2.6
	Frente Popular Agrícola del Perú (FREPAP)	2000	0.7
	Unión por el Perú (UPP)	2000	0.3
	Perú 2000	2000	51.0
	Unión por el Perú (UPP)	2006	30.6
	Alianza por el Futuro	2006	7.4
Venezuela	Movimiento Integración Nacional (MIN)	1983	0.3
	Convergencia Nacional	1993	30.4
	Integración, Renovación y Nueva Esperanza (IRENE)	1998	2.8
	Movimiento Integración Nacional (MIN)	2000	1.1

Figure A.1. Ideological Cycles in Latin America, 1945–2010
(excluding Mexico, 1961–1990)

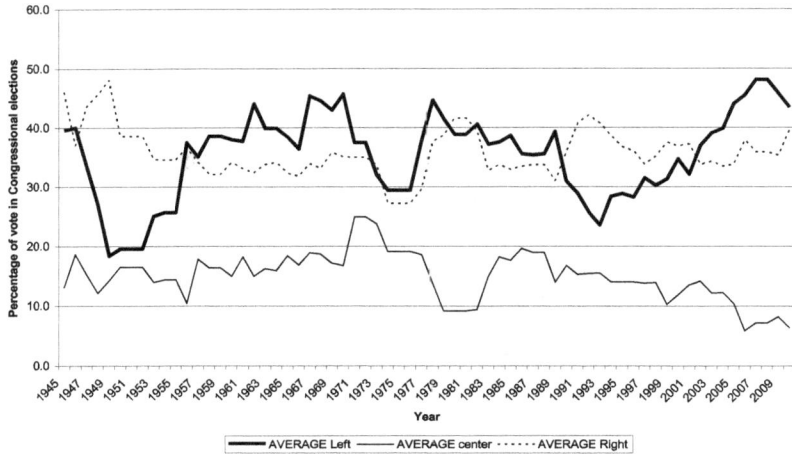

Source: Based on Coppedge 1997; Political Database of the Americas (Georgetown University)

Figure A.2. Ideological Cycles by Country, 1945–2010

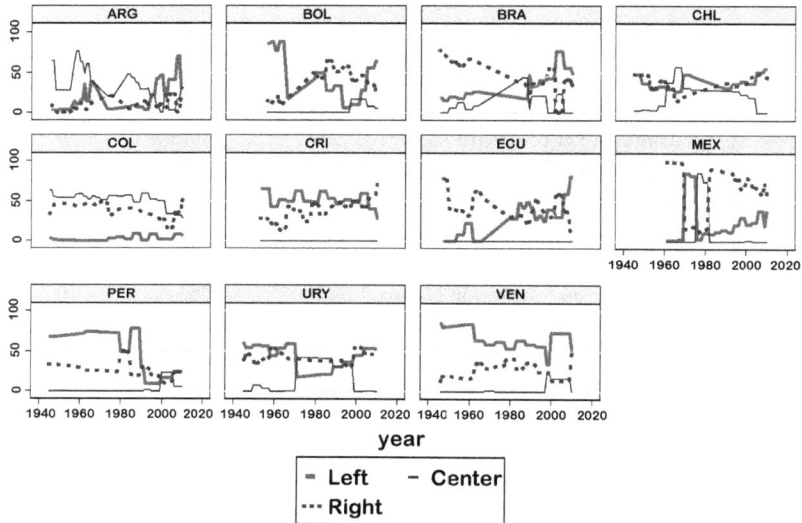

APPENDIX 2

Description of Variables

Description of Variables Used in Chapter 5 for the Uruguayan Case

Dependent variable:
- *Left:* 1 (intention to vote for Frente Amplio or Nuevo Espacio/Partido Independiente) and 0 (intention to vote for the remaining parties).

Independent variables:
- *Sociotropic vote* (measures the evaluation of the country's economic situation at the moment of the interview: the higher the value, the worse the evaluation). Example of question wording: "Ahora cambiamos un poco de tema . . . Pensando la situación económica general del país, ¿Ud. la calificaría como muy buena (1), buena (2), regular (3), mala (4) o muy mala (5)?" (Uruguay 1984).
- *Pocketbook vote* (measures the evaluation of the family's economic situation at the moment of the interview: the higher the value, the worse the evaluation). Example of question wording: "Hablemos ahora de su situación personal. ¿Ud. diría que la situación económica actual de su familia es . . . muy buena, buena, regular, mala o muy mala?" (Uruguay 1989).
- *Retrospective sociotropic* (measures citizens' economic assessments of the country situation in comparison with the past). Example from Uruguay 1984 questionnaire: "¿Y cómo ve la situación económica del país respecto a la de hace un año?" Mucho mejor (1), Mejor (2), Igual (3), Peor (4), Mucho peor (5).

- *Prospective sociotropic* (measures citizens' economic expectations of the country situation for the future). Uruguay 1984: "¿Y cómo cree que será la situación económica del país dentro de un año?" Mucho mejor (1), Mejor (2), Igual (3), Peor (4), Mucho peor (5).
- *Retrospective pocketbook* (measures citizens' economic assessments of their own situation in comparison with the past). Uruguay 1984: "¿Y ud. diría que la situación económica actual de su familia es mejor, igual o peor que la que tenían un año atrás?" Mucho mejor (1), Mejor (2), Igual (3), Peor (4), Mucho peor (5).
- *Prospective pocketbook* (measures citizens' economic expectations of their own situation for the future). Uruguay 1989: "¿Y cómo cree usted que será su situación económica familiar dentro de un año?" Mucho mejor (1), Mejor (2), Igual (3), Peor (4), Mucho peor (5).
- *Ideology:* Ideological self-placement of the respondent in a spectrum that ranges from 1 meaning Left to 10 meaning Right. Example from Uruguay 1989: "Ud. vio que cuando se habla de política se usa decir izquierda y derecha. Aquí tengo esta tarjeta con casilleros que van de izquierda a derecha. De acuerdo a sus opiniones políticas, según se sitúe Ud. más a la izquierda o a la derecha, elija el cuadro que crea corresponde a su posición."
- *Partisanship:* Five dummies: identification with the PC, identification with the PN, identification with the NE/PI, identification with the FA, and no party identification.
- *Risk propensity:* a variable constructed from two questions:
  1. "Hay un refrán que dice 'Más vale malo conocido que bueno por conocer.' ¿Ese refrán le parece más bien verdadero o más bien falso?" 1. Verdadero, 2. Falso.
  2. "Volviendo a los refranes, hay otro dice 'El que no arriesga no gana.' ¿Ese refrán le parece más bien verdadero o más bien falso?" 1. Verdadero, 2. Falso.
- The two questions were combined into a single measurement named "Risk propensity" that ranges from 1 (high risk averse) to 5 (high risk acceptant). Risk averse respondents are those who consider the first statement true and the second false; risk acceptant are those who answered "false" to the first aphorism and "true" to the second. Intermediate values were given to citizens who answered the risk taker option to one question but the risk averse alternative to the other.
- Social class cleavage is tested in two ways:
  1. A set of five dummy variables, each one representing one category of social class defined in terms of occupation: *dominant class, petty bour-*

geoisie, formal workers, informal workers, and *nonemployed.* Each respondent was assigned to one of these categories depending on occupation and following Portes and Hoffman's criteria (2003). For example, the occupational categories used in the 1984 Uruguayan survey were Profesionales y técnicos; Gerentes, administradores y directivos; Empleados de oficina y afines; Vendedores; Agricultores, ganaderos y pescadores; Conductores de vehículos; Obreros y operarios de la industria; Otros obreros y jornaleros; Trabajadores de servicios personales; Miembros de las FFAA; Otros ocupados; Desocupados; Seguro de paro; Busca trabajo por primera vez; Estudiantes; Ama de casa; Jubilados y otros. Later, each category was entered into the model as a dummy variable that takes the value of 1 when the person belongs to this category and 0 when he/she does not.

2. An index of *Socioeconomic status* (SES) that considers three indicators simultaneously: occupation, education, and income. A factor analysis was performed and the values of this factor were saved as a new variable named socioeconomic status (SES) and entered into the model as an independent variable. Higher values represent higher socioeconomic status.

- *Age:* higher values denote older people.
- *Education:* low values represent low levels of education.
- *Family income:* in the 1989 Uruguayan survey, it was measured by asking the "Ingreso total del núcleo familiar (promedio mensual)." Higher values indicate higher income.
- *Household level:* an ordinal variable that classifies the interviewees in three categories based on an indicator of their household. It takes the value of 1 for low socioeconomic level, 2 for medium socioeconomic level, and 3 for high socioeconomic level.
- *Urban voter:* a dummy variable representing the region in which the respondent lives; it takes the value of 1 when the person lives in Montevideo and 0 when he/she lives in a rural area or in other smaller cities and towns.

Description of Variables Used in Chapter 5 for the Brazilian Case

Dependent variable:
- *Left:*
  - 1989: 1 (PDT, PT, PSDB, and PCB) and 0 (intention to vote for the remaining parties).
  - 1994: 1(PT and PDT) and 0 (intention to vote for the remaining parties).

- 1998: 1(PT, PPS, and PSTU) and 0 (intention to vote for the remaining parties).
- 2002: 1 (PT, PSB, and PSTU) and 0 (intention to vote for the remaining parties).

Independent variables:

- *Sociotropic vote:* measures the respondent's evaluation of the *Plano Real* for the country. Higher values correspond to negative evaluations.
- *Pocketbook vote:* measures the respondent's evaluation of the *Plano Real* for his/her life. Higher values correspond to negative evaluations.
- *Prospective inflation:* measures prospective assessment of inflation. The answer categories are 1. Aumentar, 2. Permanecer igual, 3. Disminuir.
- *Prospective unemployment:* measures prospective assessment of unemployment. The answer categories are 1. Aumentar, 2. Permanecer igual, 3. Disminuir.
- *Prospective purchasing power:* measures prospective assessment of purchasing power: 1. Aumentar, 2. Permanecer igual, 3. Disminuir.
- *Retrospective sociotropic* (2002 Panel Survey): measures citizens' evaluations of the country during the last year.
- *Prospective sociotropic* (2002 Panel Survey): measures citizens' economic expectations for the country in the next twelve months.
- *Retrospective pocketbook* (2002 Panel Survey): measures citizens' evaluations of their own situation during the last year.
- *Prospective pocketbook* (2002 Panel Survey): measures citizens' economic expectations for their own situation in the next twelve months.
- *Ideology* (weak meaning): Respondent's self-placement in the ideological dimension.
  1. In the 1989 survey: the ideological scale goes from 1 (Left) to 7 (Right).
  2. In the 2002 survey it goes from 0 (Left) to 10 (Right).
  3. The 2002 panel survey measures ideology with a question with five answer categories: Left, Center-Left, Center, Center-Right, and Right.
- *Ideology* (strong meaning): A series of questions asking citizens' opinions about a series of policy issues: state interventionism, redistribution, socialism, state regulations of private firms, agrarian reform, nationalization, and privatizations. Higher values in each of these policies correspond with liberal positions.
- *Partisanship:* five dummy variables, each dummy representing one category of partisanship: party identification with left-of-center parties, party identification with parties at the center, party identification with right-of-center parties, party identification with parties that cannot be classified in

the Left-Right spectrum, and those who lack partisanship. Each category is entered into the model as a dummy variable that takes the value of 1 when the person belongs to it and 0 when he/she does not.

- *Social class cleavage:* five dummy variables, each dummy representing one category of social class defined in terms of occupation: dominant class, petty bourgeoisie, formal workers, informal workers, and nonemployed, following Portes and Hoffman (2003) criteria.
- *Education:* Higher values mean higher levels of education.
- *Family income:* Higher values mean higher income.
- *Prospect theory:*
    1. In the 1998 survey, *Risk Propensity Lula* and *Risk Propensity FHC* (Fernando Henrique Cardoso) are composite indexes made from these questions: if unemployment increased under Lula/FHC, if the real remained stable under Lula/FHC, and if the country experienced chaos under Lula/FHC. The index varies from 3 to 12. Higher values mean that the candidate is considered a risky one.
    2. The propensity risk indexes for the 2002 election combine variables that measure which is the most trustworthy candidate, the most honest candidate, the candidate with most experience, the one with the best governmental plan, the best prepared for the task, the candidate who will generate more jobs, and the one who would keep inflation low. Higher values correspond to higher levels of risk.
    3. The 2002 panel survey asks respondents to agree with one of the two following aphorisms: "É melhor ter um pássaro na mão do que dois voando" (A bird in the hand is worth two in the bush) or "Quem não arrisca, não petisca" (Nothing ventured, nothing gained), which is a common question used to measure risk propensity.
- *Age:* the higher the value, the older the respondent.
- *Urban voter* (a dummy in which 1 is urban and 0 is rural). In the 2002 postelection survey, the Urban Voter variable captures whether the respondent lives in a state capital or not rather than whether the place of residence is urban or rural.

Description of Variables Used in Chapter 5 for the Mexican Case

Dependent variable:
- *Left:*
    - 1988: 1 (FDN, PMS, and PRT) and 0 (intention to vote for the remaining parties).

- 1994: 1 (PRD) and 0 (intention to vote for the remaining parties).
- 2000: 1 (PRD) and 0 (intention to vote for the remaining parties).

Independent variables:

- *Sociotropic vote* explores respondents' current economic assessments of the country. Higher values correspond to negative evaluations.
- *Pocketbook vote* explores respondents' current economic assessments of their own situation. Higher values correspond to negative evaluations.
- *Prospective inflation.* Higher values mean that inflation is expected to decrease in the following *sexenio* (six-year term).
- *Prospective unemployment.* Higher values mean that unemployment is expected to decrease in the following *sexenio.*
- *Prospective sociotropic* in 1988 measures citizens' expectations for the economy at the end of the next government's term in power (next *sexenio*). Higher values correspond to negative expectations.
- *Retrospective pocketbook* and *Prospective pocketbook:*
  - In the 1988 survey, both variables measure citizens' evaluations of their own economic situation during the last year (*Retrospective pocketbook*) and the economic expectations for the next twelve months (*Prospective pocketbook*).
  - The 1994 and 2000 surveys only ask *Retrospective pocketbook* and *Retrospective sociotropic.* In 1994, the comparison is made with the previous six years (before Salinas's government), while in the 2000 survey it is against the previous twelve months. In all cases, higher values equal negative evaluations. Answer categories for Retrospective Pocketbook are (1) Better, (2) The same, (3) Worse. Answer categories for Retrospective Sociotropic are (1) Improved, (2) The same, (3) Deteriorated.
- *Ideology* (weak meaning): Respondent's self-placement on the ideological dimension. Only available in the 2000 survey, and it ranges from 0 (Left) to 10 (Right).
- *Ideology* (strong meaning): A series of policy issues: foreign investment, imports of foreign products, payment of foreign debt, and privatizations. Higher values in each of these policies correspond to leftist positions.
- *Social class cleavage* is tested using dummy variables; each dummy represents one category of social class defined in terms of occupation following Portes and Hoffman's classification (2003). Each category is entered into the model as a dummy variable that takes the value of 1 when the person belongs to it and 0 when he/she does not.
- *Education.* Higher values mean higher levels of education. Answer categories are None, Primary, Secondary, Prep, University or more.
- *Family income* (1994): ranges from 1 (lower income) to 5 (higher income).

- *Household socioeconomic status* (1988 and 2000) defined by the interviewer's judgment of the house and (2000) defined by a housewares index that consisted of the ownership of radio, water heater, television, telephone, cellular phone, and oven. Higher values represent higher socioeconomic status.
- *Partisanship* is tested using dummy variables, each dummy representing one category of partisanship: party identification with left-of-center parties, party identification with right-of-center parties, and those who lack partisanship. Each category is entered into the model as a dummy variable that takes the value of 1 when the person belongs to it and 0 when he/she does not.
- *Prospect theory:*
    1. In 1988, respondents were asked two questions. First, if Mexican economic conditions would improve, remain the same, or worsen if the opposition were to gain power. Second, if the country's social peace would be undermined if the opposition were to win the election. In both variables, higher values mean that citizens distrust the capabilities of opposition parties to lead the country along a good path.
    2. The 1994 survey captures Mexicans' risk propensity using the following question: "The presidents who have governed Mexico for the past sixty-five years have come from the PRI. Which of the following reasons motivated you to vote for the party you chose today? a) the PRI is still the best choice, b) in politics it's "better bad but known than good but unknown," c) voted opposition to protest, d) want the opposition to win." A dummy variable named Risk propensity was coded with 1 when the voter answered b and 0 for the remaining answer categories.
    3. In 2000, Risk propensity was measured by respondents' preference for one of two traditional aphorisms: "Better the devil you know than the saint you don't" and "Nothing ventured, nothing gained." This preference was entered into the model as a dummy that takes the value of 1 when respondents chose "Better the known devil" and 0 when they chose "Nothing ventured, nothing gained."
    4. Also, three indexes tackling Labastida's, Fox's, and Cárdenas's capacities to govern were used. Each index combines respondents' opinions on the capacity of each candidate to manage the economy, fight crime and public insecurity, and improve the educational system. Higher values in the index mean worse evaluations of the candidates' abilities to govern.
- *Age:* the higher the value, the older the respondent.
- *Urban voter:* in 1988 a variable that ranges from 1 for the most rural areas to 5 for the most urban ones, and in 2000 a dummy in which 1 is urban and 0 is rural.

NOTES

Introduction

1. Their dependent variable is a neat indicator called Vote-Revealed Leftism (VRL), which takes into account the ideological positions and electoral results of all parties or candidates that get votes. There is no doubt that the use of this aggregate measure has several advantages, as Baker and Greene mention; however, it does not allow us to make any inference at the micro level due to the risk of an ecological fallacy.

Chapter 1. Latin American Ideological Cycles in the Postwar Era

1. In the 2009–2010 presidential election, things had changed in Chile with the victory of the right-of-center Coalición por el Cambio.

2. These three types of trends are not exhaustive. It is also possible to find random movements or fluctuations, but these kinds of movements are not usually described as trends. A "random trend" is meaningless. If a trend is random, it does not look like a trend.

3. In those elections in which there are different electoral results for the two chambers (senate and deputies), we use the results for the lower chamber (deputies).

4. Only the results of congressional elections are taken into account. The exception is the results for the Peruvian elections before 1978, which are based on presidential rather than legislative votes.

5. Alexander 1988; Coggins and Lewis 1992; Alcántara and Freidenberg 2001.

6. The extension of this classification was done by Germán Lodola and Rosario Queirolo while studying at the University of Pittsburgh. The following country experts were consulted: Germán Lodola and Belén Amadeo (Argentina), Daniel Moreno Morales and Vivian Schwarz (Bolivia), Lucio Renno and Rachel Meneguello (Brazil), Francisco Díaz and Juan Pablo Luna (Chile), Laura Wills and Miguel García (Colombia), Mitchell Seligson, Juliana Martínez, and Harold Villegas Roman (Costa Rica), Grisel Lerebours (Dominican Republic), Agustín Grijalva and Pablo Andrade (Ecuador), Cynthia McClintock, Ricardo Córdova, and Margarita Correa (El Salvador), Dinorah Azpuru and Margarita Correa (Guatemala), José René Argueta and Margarita Correa (Honduras), Luis Jiménez and Juan Antonio Rodríguez-Zepeda (Mexico), John Booth and Margarita Correa (Nicaragua), Aníbal Pérez-Liñán and José Costa (Paraguay), Cynthia McClintock and Luis E. González (Perú), Juan Pablo Luna, Fernanda Boidi, and Rosario Queirolo (Uruguay), Aníbal Pérez-Liñán and Margarita López-Maya (Venezuela).

7. With the exception of the coding of new parties.

8. A table listing the political parties in each country that do not fit into the Left-Right dimension from 1980 to 2010 appears in Appendix 1. The table also indicates the percentage of the total vote that these unclassified parties obtained in the presidential elections.

9. An election is considered "fraudulent" when there is doubt that the actual electoral results are significantly different from the official ones.

10. Electoral results are taken from different sources. Coppedge's (1997) dataset is used for the 1945–1995 period. Since 1995 the main source of electoral data has been the Political Database of the Americas (PDBA) at Georgetown University. Complementary sources were consulted to fill in blanks or verify the information: www.observatorioelectoral.org, Nohlen 2005, and the Web pages of electoral offices in each country.

11. Mexico fulfills the first three rules set out by Przeworski et al. (2000) to define a democracy, but it does not pass the "alternation rule."

12. Figure A.1 in Appendix 1 shows Latin American ideological cycles excluding these Mexican elections. The main difference between this figure and figure 1.2 is that the predominance of the Left in the second cycle is longer and more pronounced when these controversial Mexican elections are excluded.

13. The graphs for each country are shown in Appendix 1.

14. For the same reason, Mainwaring and Scully (1995) were not able to measure ideological polarization, but taking into account the analysis of the case studies presented in their book, they categorize Costa Rica as a low polarization system; Colombia, Paraguay, and Argentina as systems with moderately

low polarization; Venezuela, Uruguay, Bolivia, Chile, and Ecuador as moderately high polarization; and Mexico, Peru, and Brazil as highly polarized systems. In this classification made in 1993, there are more countries with moderately high to high polarization than countries with low polarization.

15. From 1956 to 1969 and from 1976 to 1979, there are more random movements between Left, Center, and Right than specific trends.

16. Not all Latin American countries opted for ISI, and they embarked on a process of industrialization in different ways. Bulmer-Thomas (2003) considers that Argentina, Brazil, Chile, and Uruguay adopted an inward-looking development model while Colombia, Venezuela, and some of the smaller republics did not.

17. "Reform fatigue" is a concept introduced by Sebastian Edwards (1997) that refers to citizens' difficulty coping with the sacrifices required by economic reforms in their respective countries.

18. Morley et al. (1999) point out that the rise in the trade and financial reform indexes during the 1970s is due mostly to the policies implemented in Chile, Uruguay, Argentina, and Colombia.

19. The main changes introduced by Morley et al. (1999) are made in the privatization and domestic financial reform indexes "to reflect only the presence or absence of government intervention" (10).

20. In the next five years, inflation continued to decrease and reached the regional average of 6.16. However, taking into account the time that had passed since the reforms' implementation, the low inflation during the 2005–2009 period cannot be attributed to them.

21. Only after the second half of the 2000s were these programs, mainly implemented as conditional cash transfers, expanded to other countries in the region such as Brazil, Mexico, Ecuador, Bolivia, Colombia, Chile, and Uruguay (Queirolo 2010). As a result, they did not work as concurrent compensations for the negative effects introduced by market reforms. Most of them have the purpose of alleviating the high levels of poverty prevalent in the region.

22. The percentages presented on figure 1.4 group the vote received by Left and Center-Left parties in presidential elections from the first democratic election in the 1980s to 2010.

23. A different country classification is shown in Queirolo 2008. One of the main differences with the present one is that Paraguay was considered a No Change case.

24. In the 2010 Chilean election, left-of-center parties received more votes than right-wing parties; however, in the second round of the election, the right-wing candidate, Sebastián Piñera, won.

Chapter 2. Economic and Political Conditions That Benefit
            Leftist Parties in Latin America

1. Carville was Bill Clinton's political adviser during the 1992 presidential campaign.

2. The analysis was constrained by the time frame (1985–1999) of one of the main independent variables, structural reform index. Lora and Olivera (2005) extended the SRI to 2002, but data for 2000–2002 are not publicly available.

3. Because it is not possible to obtain the log of a negative number, the following formula to calculate the logs is used: if I>0, LN (1+I); and if I″0, -1*LN(1+|I|). I am grateful to Aníbal Pérez Liñán for suggesting this formula to account for deflationary years.

4. The intention was to also include a measure of ideological polarization, but it was impossible to find a proper one. Ideological polarization is usually measured using voters' self-placement in the ideological dimension (Sani and Sartori 1983), but public opinion data are not available for every election year of every country. An alternative indicator of ideological polarization built by Coppedge (1998) takes into account the share of the vote that each ideological bloc has and measures the dispersion of the vote from the relative center of the party system. Polarization ranges from 0 when all votes are in one ideological extreme to 100 when half of the vote is at each of the ideological extremes, and it is a measure of the system ideological polarization at the time of the election. The formula to calculate the relative center (MLRP) is Right % + .5 Center-Right % - .5 Center-Left % - Left %, and the formula to calculate the ideological polarization is |1-mlrp|*Right % + |.5-mlrp|*Center-Right % + |-.5-mlrp|*Center-Left % + |-1-mlrp|*Left %, where mlrp = MLRP/100. But this measure of ideological polarization is problematic because it is not totally independent of the vote share that each ideological bloc gets. The correlation between polarization and the percentage of vote is 0.51 with the Left, -0.47 with the Center, and 0.02 with the Right. As a result, it was not included to avoid endogeneity.

5. This argument is not statistically proven here because it would imply testing the separate influence of each index dimension on unemployment, something that would overspecify the model taking into account the small N. The correlation between SRI and unemployment is low (0.14 between unemployment and SRI; 0.02 between unemployment change and SRI change), but this might be the result of using the SRI altogether rather than its separate dimensions.

6. The significance of interaction terms was tested using the lincom command in STATA.

7. I have also checked for collinearity problems in the data but found nothing to be concerned about.

Chapter 3. *Micro Explanations for Voting Left in Latin America*

1. Torcal and Mainwaring (2003) test the existence of these political cleavages in the Chilean case with three cultural-ideological divisions that can be used by political leaders to articulate conflict: the authoritarian/democratic cultural division, the perception of social inequality, and religious differences.

2. Further details on variable measurement can be found in chapter 5.

3. A slightly different question is asked in Brazil, but the meaning is the same. See chapter 5 for further description of the variables.

4. A more comprehensive variable description is presented in chapter 5.

5. Partisanship is measured by a question that asked respondents what their party identification was.

Chapter 4. *Latin Americans Are Voting Left*

1. This percentage is especially high for the region. According to data from the Comparative Study of Electoral Systems (CSES), in Peru (2001) only 26 percent of the population have party identification, while in Brazil (2002) 34 percent identify with a particular political party, and in Mexico (2000) the figure is 50 percent.

2. Based on IMF data.

3. Based on IMF data.

4. See chapter 1 for the complete trends classification.

5. Following the same general idea, Castañeda (2006) classifies these cases into Right Left or Wrong Left, but he sees the PRI as a case of Wrong Left.

6. For the sake of simplicity, I use Frente Amplio or FA, instead of Encuentro Progresista–Frente Amplio. Furthermore, after 2004 Encuentro Progresista was no longer used, and Frente Amplio is what most people call it.

7. Luna (2004a) argues that only the "traditional family" exists as an ideological family because Nuevo Espacio's leaders are closer to the traditional parties' leaders than to those of the Frente Amplio. However, he presents evidence that Nuevo Espacio's voters are closer to the FA than to the PC or the PN. Therefore, it is not so clear that they don't belong to the same ideological family.

8. See Aguiar 2000 and Canzani 2000 for the Uruguayan case, and Abramson and Inglehart 1992 for generational replacement.

9. On a 10-point scale: 1 = extreme Left and 10 = extreme Right.

10. Again, 1 = extreme Left and 10 = extreme Right.

11. Against this image of the PAN as the party that receives more votes from religious people, Moreno (2003) provides evidence that the most religious segment of the Mexican population votes for the PRD.

12. The Center does not show up in this graph because there are no parties classified as centrist that received votes during those elections.

13. The 2006 presidential election was extremely competitive: the PAN obtained 14,027,214 votes and the PRD 13,624,506 votes. The PRD's presidential candidate, Manuel López Obrador, argued that the election was fraudulent and mobilized Mexicans to protest the results. The danger of postelection mobilization if the presidential election is too close was predicted well before by Eisenstadt and Poiré (2005).

Chapter 5. The Reasons for Voting Left

1. I would like to thank the directors of CIFRA, Luis E. González and Adriana Raga, and of Equipos/Mori, Agustín Canzani and Ignacio Zuasnábar, for giving me access to these data. González and Raga also generously allowed me to include some specific questions from the 2004 survey.

2. The four national surveys were weighted to correct for an overeducated sample when aggregate statistics are presented but not when binary logit coefficients are shown. Binary coefficients and their significance do not change by weighting the data.

3. A more detailed description of each variable is presented in Appendix 2.

4. For the 1984 and 1989 models, income is measured as family income. For the 1994 and 1999 models, household level is used instead of family income because there is no measure of family income in the 1994 survey and to keep the comparability with the 1999 survey. In the 1999 survey, income and household level are correlated at 0.47 (p < .001).

5. The 1984 survey has a smaller N than the others because it was carried out only in Montevideo.

6. The distinction between "bankers" and "peasants" was introduced by MacKuen, Erikson, and Stimson (1992).

7. In 1994 the correlation between ideology and Colorado identification was 0.34; in 1999, 0.33; and in 2004, 0.29. On the other hand, the correla-

tions between being Blanco and ideology were, for the same years, the following: 0.24, 0.30, and 0.35.

8. The municipalities are Canelones, Florida, Maldonado, Montevideo, Rocha, Salto, and Soriano.

9. Not all surveys have both measures. The household level is an ordinal variable that captures the classification made by the interviewer of the interviewees' households. It takes the value of 1 for low socioeconomic level, 2 for middle socioeconomic level, and 3 for high socioeconomic level. Family income is the self-reported income of the family. In the surveys where both variables are available, I prefer to use family income because it is reported by the interviewee. See Appendix 2 for more details regarding the variables.

10. I also include unemployed people as an independent dummy variable, but it does not reach significance.

11. A factor analysis with these three variables measuring occupation, education, and income was performed, and only one factor was extracted in each election year (1984: Eigenvalue = 1.657; 1989: Eigenvalue = 1.687; 1994: Eigenvalue = 1.597; 1999: Eigenvalue = 2.081; 2004: Eigenvalue = 1.627). Then the values of this factor were saved as a new variable named *Socioeconomic status (SES)* and entered into the model as an independent variable.

12. Prospect theory was also tested in the 1999 election with an alternative indicator: an individual's judgments about the opposition's governing capabilities. This indicator was used by Cinta (1999) to assess uncertainty in the 1997 Mexican congressional election, and he found that Mexicans voted for the party whose governing capabilities they were more certain of. I find the same results for the 1999 Uruguayan elections. Uruguayans who considered Tabaré Vázquez, Frente Amplio's presidential candidate, the candidate most capable of improving the country's situation ("más capaz de sacar al país adelante") significantly tended to vote for the Left. On the contrary, those who believed Jorge Batlle (PC) or Luis A. Lacalle (PN) were the most capable tended to vote for the PC or PN, respectively. Morgenstern and Zechmeister (2001) argue that this variable is highly endogenous to the voters' party preferences. In other words, Uruguayans sympathetic to the opposition are more likely to positively evaluate their party's capacity to govern. I agree with them; it makes sense that those voters who think that a candidate is the better prepared to govern will vote for that candidate. However, because this variable is frequently used in the literature that tests prospect theory, the analysis was run. Results are available on request.

13. This explanation follows the same logic as Morgenstern and Zechmeister (2001), who found that risk propensity directly and indirectly affected voting behavior in the 1997 Mexican congressional election. The indirect effect

is produced by the importance of economic assessments. I included an interaction term between risk and sociotropic to test for the indirect effect of risk, and it is significant.

14. Missing values were imputed using ICE imputation method from STATA.

15. I want to thank Rachel Meneguello and Simone Aranha from the Center for Studies on Public Opinion (CESOP) at the University of Campinas (UNICAMP) in Brazil for giving me access to Datafolha and BNES data. I am also grateful to Barry Ames, Andy Baker, and Lucio Renno for allowing me to use their 2002 Panel Data.

16. This result is counterintuitive because postelection surveys usually overrepresent the winner.

17. A more detailed variable description is available in Appendix 2.

18. As discussed for Uruguay, this method for measuring risk propensity is sensitive to endogeneity problems. Therefore, the results extracted from it should be taken with caution.

19. The correlations between partisanship and ideology are very low in Brazil. For example, in 2002 the correlation between identification with a party on the Left and ideology was -0.12, while the correlation between identification with a right-wing party and ideology was 0.14.

20. Barry Ames pointed out that in the 2002 election education mattered in a different way: neighborhood education dominates individual-level education. To put it differently, poorer neighborhoods voted for Lula, and middle-class people in poor neighborhoods also voted for Lula. This effect cannot be seen in the 2002 data shown in table 5.5 because it does not discriminate between neighborhoods.

21. For the 1994 election, when regressions are run using the vote for PSDB versus the vote for PT as dependent variable, it is the PT that capitalized on the vote of those who were disappointed with their own or Brazil's economic situation. Also, parties identified with the Right get votes from those who are economically unhappy. This shows that the possibility of capitalizing on economic discontent depends on how many alternatives are available in the political system.

22. This survey was obtained through the Roper Center. I am grateful to Jorge Domínguez and James McCann, who helped me reconstruct the codes for several variables on the dataset.

23. Many thanks to Alejandro Poiré for giving me access to these data.

24. Participants in the 2000 Mexico Panel Study included (in alphabetical order): Miguel Basañez, Roderic Camp, Wayne Cornelius, Jorge Domín-

guez, Federico Estévez, Joseph Klesner, Chappell Lawson (Principal Investigator), Beatriz Magaloni, James McCann, Alejandro Moreno, Pablo Parás, and Alejandro Poiré. Funding for the study was provided by the National Science Foundation (SES-9905703) and *Reforma* newspaper.

25. Missing values were imputed using ICE imputation method from STATA.

26. A more detailed description of the variables is available in Appendix 2.

27. In Spanish the exact wording is, "Más vale malo conocido que bueno por conocer" and "El que no arriesga no gana."

28. The exact values are as follows: 1 for populations between 1,000 and 5,000; 2 for populations between 5,001 and 20,000; 3 for populations between 20,001 and 100,000; 4 for populations between 100,001 and 1,000,000; and 5 for populations larger than 1,000,000.

29. This finding holds even when looking at vote determinants by political party (PRD, PAN, and PRI).

30. As mentioned in the 2002 Brazilian election analysis, this is a problem of one-shot surveys taken after the election. People could have decided their position on the PRI after deciding for other reasons which candidate they preferred. Only panel data designed to test this time-sequence counterargument can provide more definite answers.

31. I also try interactions between urban and social class in order to test for the argument that social class has a different impact depending on voters' place of residence. Only the interaction between petty bourgeoisie and urban residence reaches significance for the 1988 election. Although belonging to the petty bourgeoisie diminishes the chances of voting Left, these chances are even lower when the bourgeoisie live in rural areas than when they live in urban ones. In other words, urbanization has a positive but indirect effect on leftist parties' fortune.

32. To keep the comparability among the models in the three country cases, I did not include public servants and private employees as independent variables in table 5.7. The impact of being a public servant or private employee on voting Left is only tested for the 1994 election because the 1988 and 2000 surveys did not ask if respondents work for the government or in the private sector.

33. Results from a multinomial logit provide evidence that party identification with a leftist party increases the probability of voting PRD instead of PRI in 2000 but with a significance level < .10.

34. Regression results show that in 2000, both PRD and PAN voters were more risk takers than were PRI voters.

35. Similar to the Uruguayan and Brazilian cases, these variables are prone to be endogenous.

36. These estimates are much lower partly because there were fewer Mexicans who voted for the PRD in the 2000 election, not only those registered by the survey (15%) but also in the actual vote (19%). In addition, the Risk propensity variable is not significant in the 2000 Mexican model. It is clear that other factors are more relevant to predicting the vote for the Left in that transitional election than is being risk averse or risk acceptant.

37. One way that the leftist parties in the three country cases presented in this chapter have managed to reduce voters' uncertainty is to gain governmental experience at the local, city, municipal, or state level. An alternative is to become more pragmatic and less radical in their party platforms.

38. This relationship is less articulated in Mexico.

BIBLIOGRAPHY

Abramson, Paul R., and Ronald Inglehart. 1992. "Generational Replacement and Value Change in Eight West European Societies." *British Journal of Political Science* 22: 183–228.

Aguiar, César. 2000. "La historia y la Historia: Opinión Pública y opinión pública en el Uruguay." *Prisma* 15: 7–45.

Alcántara, Manuel, and Flavia Freidenberg, eds. 2001. *Partidos políticos de América Latina*. Salamanca: Ediciones Universidad de Salamanca.

Alexander, Robert J., ed. 1988. *Political Parties of the Americas: Canada, Latin America, and the West Indies*. Westport, CT: Greenwood Press.

Altman, David, Juan Pablo Luna, Rafael Piñeiro, and Sergio Toro. 2009. "Partidos y sistemas de partidos en América Latina: Aproximaciones desde la encuesta a expertos 2009." *Revista de Ciencia Política* 29 (3): 775–98.

AmericasBarometer Dataset. 2010. www.lapopsurveys.org.

Ameringer, Charles D., ed. 1992. *Political Parties of the Americas: 1980s to 1990s*. Westport, CT: Greenwood Press.

Ames, Barry. 1970. "Bases of Support for Mexico's Dominant Party." *American Political Science Review* 64 (1): 153–67.

———. 2001. *The Deadlock of Democracy in Brazil*. Ann Arbor: University of Michigan Press.

———. 2007. "Brazil's Presidential Election of 2002: Time and Context." Paper presented at the conference "The Rise of the Left in Latin America," Princeton University, December 6–8.

Anderson, Christopher J., André Blais, Shaun Bowler, Todd Donovan, and Ola Listhaug. 2005. *Losers' Consent: Elections and Democratic Legitimacy*. Oxford: Oxford University Press.

Anderson, Kim, Joe Francois, Tom Hertel, Bernard Hoekman, and Will Martin. 2000. *Benefits from Trade Reform in the New Millennium*. London: Centre for Economic Policy Research.

Arnold, Jason Ross, and David J. Samuels. 2011. "Public Opinion and Latin America's 'Left Turn.'" In *The Resurgence of the Latin American Left*, edited by S. Levitsky and K. Roberts. Baltimore, MD: Johns Hopkins University Press.

Arnson, Cynthia, and José Raúl Perales, eds. 2007. *The "New Left" and Democratic Governance in Latin America*. Washington, DC: Woodrow Wilson International Center for Scholars.

BADEINSO-ECLAC. 2005. www.cepal.org/deype/.

Baker, Andy. 2002. "Reformas liberalizantes e aprovação presidencial: A politização dos debates da politica economica no Brasil." *Dados* 45 (1): 77–98.

Baker, Andy, Barry Ames, and Lucio R. Renno. 2006. "Social Context and Campaign Volatility in New Democracies: Networks and Neighborhoods in Brazil's 2002 Elections." *American Journal of Political Science* 50 (2): 382–99.

Baker, Andy, and Kenneth F. Greene. 2011. "The Latin American Left's Mandate: Free-Market Policies and Issue Voting in New Democracies." *World Politics* 63 (1): 43–77.

Baviskar, Siddharta. 2004. "Political Culture as Leading Indicator of Chile's Democratic Breakdown and Resurrection." PhD dissertation, University of Pittsburgh, Pittsburgh, PA.

BBC News. 2005. "South America's Leftward Sweep." March 2.

Behrman, Jere R., Nancy Birdsall, and Miguel Székely. 2000. *Economic Reforms and Wage Differentials in Latin America*. Washington, DC: Inter-American Development Bank.

Benton, Allyson Lucinda. 2005. "Dissatisfied Democrats or Retrospective Voters? Economic Hardship, Political Institutions, and Voting Behavior in Latin America." *Comparative Political Studies* 38 (4): 417–42.

Bobbio, Norberto. 1995. *Derecha e izquierda: Razones y significados de una distinción política*. Madrid: Taurus.

Bogliaccini, Juan Ariel. 2013. "Trade Liberalization, Deindustrialization and Inequality: Evidence from Latin American Middle-Income Countries." *Latin American Research Review* 48 (2).

Bruhn, Kathleen. 1999. "The Resurrection of the Mexican Left in the 1997 Elections: Implications for the Party System." In *Toward Mexico's Democratization: Parties, Campaigns, Elections, and Public Opinion*, edited by J. I. Domínguez and A. Poiré. New York: Routledge.

———. 2004. "The Making of the Mexican President, 2000: Parties, Candidates, and Campaign Strategy." In *Mexico's Pivotal Democratic Election:*

Candidates, Voters, and the Presidential Campaign of 2000, edited by J. I. Domínguez and C. Lawson. Stanford: Stanford University Press.

———. 2006. "Is Latin America Turning Socialist? The Region's Electoral Trend." *ReVista* (Spring–Summer): 42–43.

Bulmer-Thomas, Victor. 2003. *The Economic History of Latin America since Independence*. Cambridge: Cambridge University Press.

Buquet, Daniel, and Gustavo de Armas. 2004. "La evolución electoral de la izquierda: Crecimiento demográfico y moderación ideológica." In *La izquierda uruguaya entre la posición y el gobierno*, edited by J. Lanzaro. Montevideo: Editorial Fin de Siglo e Instituto de Ciencia Política.

Caballero, Manuel. 1986. *Latin America and the Comintern, 1919–1943*. Cambridge: Cambridge University Press.

Camargos, M. B. 2001. "Economia e voto: Fernando Henrique versus Lula, 1998." *Teoria and Sociedade* 8: 116–45.

Cameron, Maxwell. 1994. *Democracy and Authoritarianism in Peru: Political Coalitions and Social Change*. New York: St. Martin's Press.

Campbell, Angus. 1960. *The American Voter*. New York: Wiley.

Cantón, Darío, and Jorge Raúl Jorrat. 2002. "Economic Evaluations, Partisanship, and Social Bases of Presidential Voting in Argentina, 1995 and 1999." *International Journal of Public Opinion Research* 41 (4): 413–27.

Canzani, Agustín. 2000. "Mensajes en una botella: Analizando las elecciones de 1999/2000." In *Elecciones 1999/2000*, edited by G. Caetano. Montevideo: Ediciones de la Banda Oriental e Instituto de Ciencia Política.

Carreirão, Yan de Souza. 2002a. *A decisão do voto nas eleições presidenciais brasileiras*. Rio de Janeiro: Fundação Getúlio Vargas.

———. 2002b. "Identificação ideológica e voto para presidente." *Opinião Pública* 8 (1): 54–79.

Carreirão, Yan de Souza, and Maria D'Alva G. Kinzo. 2004. "Partidos políticos, preferencia partidária e decision eleitoral no Brasil (1989/2002)." *Dados* 47 (1): 131–68.

Castañeda, Jorge. 1993. *La utopía desarmada: El futuro de la izquierda en América Latina*. Buenos Aires: Ariel.

———. 2006. "Latin America's Left Turn." *Foreign Affairs* (May–June): 28–43.

Castañeda, Jorge, and Marco A. Morales, eds. 2008. *Leftovers: Tales of the Latin American Left*. New York: Routledge.

Castañeda, Jorge, and Patricio Navia. 2007. "The Year of the Ballot." *Current History* (February): 51–57.

CIFRA. 2004. Preelectoral National Survey of Uruguayan Electorate. González, Raga y Asociados. www.cifra.com.uy.

Cinta, Alberto. 1999. "Uncertainty and Electoral Behavior in Mexico in the 1997 Congressional Elections." In *Toward Mexico s Democratization: Parties, Campaigns, Elections, and Public Opinion*, edited by J. I. Domínguez and A. Poiré. New York: Routledge.

Cleary, Matthew R. 2006. "Explaining the Left's Resurgence." *Journal of Democracy* 17 (4): 35–49.

Coggins, John, and D. S. Lewis. 1992. *Political Parties of the Americas and the Caribbean*. Essex: Longman Current Affairs.

Collier, Ruth Berins, and David Collier. 2002. *Shaping the Political Arena: Critical Junctures, the Labor Movement, and Regime Dynamics in Latin America*. 2nd ed. Notre Dame, IN: University of Notre Dame Press.

Colomer, Josep. 2005. "The Left-Right Dimension in Latin America." Economics and Business Working Paper No. 813, Universitat Pompeu Fabra.

Conniff, Michael L., ed. 1982. *Latin American Populism in Comparative Perspective*. Albuquerque: University of New Mexico Press.

Conover, Pamela, and Stanley Feldman. 1980. "The Origins and Meaning of Liberal/Conservative Self-Identifications." *American Journal of Political Science* 25 (4): 617–45.

Converse, Philip E. 1964. "The Nature of Belief Systems in Mass Publics." In *Ideology and Discontent*, edited by D. Apter. Glencoe, IL: Free Press.

Coppedge, Michael. 1997. "A Classification of Latin American Political Parties." Working Paper No. 244, Kellogg Institute, Notre Dame, IN.

———. 1998. "The Dynamic Diversity of Latin America Party Systems." *Party Politics* 4: 547–68.

Corrales, Javier. 2002. *Presidents without Parties: The Politics of Economic Reform in Argentina and Venezuela in the 1990s*. University Park: Pennsylvania State University Press.

Dalton, Russell J., and Martin P. Wattenberg. 1993. "The Not So Simple Act of Voting." In *Political Science: The State of the Discipline II*, edited by A. W. Finifter. Washington, DC: APSA.

Domínguez, Jorge I. 1999. "The Transformation of Mexico's Electoral and Party Systems, 1988–1997: An Introduction." In *Toward Mexico's Democratization: Parties, Campaigns, Elections, and Public Opinion*, edited by J. I. Domínguez and A. Poiré. New York: Routledge.

———. 2004. "Conclusion: Why and How Did Mexico's 2000 Presidential Election Campaign Matter?" In *Mexico's Pivotal Democratic Election: Candidates, Voters, and the Presidential Campaign of 2000*, edited by J. I. Domínguez and C. Lawson. Stanford, CA: Stanford University Press.

Domínguez, Jorge, and Chappell Lawson, eds. 2004. *Mexico's Pivotal Democratic Election: Candidates, Voters, and the Presidential Campaign of 2000.* Stanford, CA: Stanford University Press.

Domínguez, Jorge I., and James A. McCann. 1995. "Shaping Mexico's Electoral Arena: The Construction of Partisan Cleavages in the 1988 and 1991 National Elections." *American Political Science Review* 89 (1): 34–48.

———. 1996. *Democratizing Mexico: Public Opinion and Electoral Choices.* Baltimore, MD: Johns Hopkins University Press.

Downs, Anthony. 1957. *An Economic Theory of Democracy.* New York: Harper & Row.

Duch, Raymond M. 2003. "State of the Latin American Political Economy." Working paper, James A. Baker III Institute for Public Policy, Rice University, Houston.

Duch, Raymond M., Harvey D. Palmer, and Christopher J. Anderson. 2000. "Heterogeneity in Perceptions on National Economic Conditions." *American Journal of Political Science* 44 (4): 635–52.

Easton, David. 1953. *The Political System.* New York: Knopf.

Echegaray, Fabián. 2005. *Economic Crises and Electoral Responses in Latin America.* Baltimore, MD: University Press of America.

Economist. 2002. "A Backlash against the Free Market Reform?" August 17.

———. 2006. "The Battle for Latin America's Soul." May 20.

Edwards, Sebastian. 1995. *Crisis and Reform in Latin America.* New York: Oxford University Press.

———. 1997. "Latin America's Underperformance." *Foreign Affairs* 76 (2): 93–103.

Eisenstadt, Todd, and Alejandro Poiré. 2005. *Campaign Finance and Playing Field "Levelness" Issues in the Run-up to Mexico's July 2006 Presidential Election.* Washington, DC: Center for Strategic and International Studies.

Erikson, Robert S. 1990. "Economic Conditions and the Congressional Vote: A Review of the Macrolevel Evidence." *American Journal of Political Science* 34 (2): 373–99.

Erikson, Robert S., Michael MacKuen, and James A. Stimson. 2002. *The Macro Polity.* Cambridge: Cambridge University Press.

Escaith, H., and S. Morley. 2001. "El efecto de las reformas estructurales en el crecimiento de América Latina y el Caribe: Una estimación empírica." *Trimestre Económico* 272: 469–513.

Estrada, Luis M. 2005. "Party Identification in Mexico." PhD dissertation, University of California, San Diego.

Fiorina, Morris P. 1981. *Retrospective Voting in American National Elections*. New Haven, CT: Yale University Press.

Fuchs, Dieter, and Hans-Dieter Klingemann. 1990. "The Left-Right Schema." In *Continuities in Political Action: A Longitudinal Study of Political Orientations in Three Western Democracies*, edited by M. K. Jennings and J. W. van Deth. Berlin: Walter de Gruyter.

Garcé, Adolfo, and Jaime Yaffé. 2004. *La era progresista*. Montevideo: Editorial Fin de Siglo.

Gibson, Edward L. 1997. "The Populist Road to Market Reform: Policy and Electoral Coalitions in Mexico and Argentina." *World Politics* 49 (3): 339–70.

Gillespie, Charles. 1986. "Activists and the Floating Voter: The Unheeled Lessons of Uruguay's 1982 Primaries." In *Elections and Democratization*, edited by P. W. Drake and E. Silva. San Diego: Center for Iberian and Latin America Studies, University of California, San Diego.

Gillespie, Charles, and L. E. González. 1989. "Uruguay: The Survival of Old and Autonomous Institutions." In *Democracy in Developing Countries,* vol. 4: *Latin America*, edited by L. Diamond, J. Hartlyn, J. J. Linz, and S. M. Lipset. Boulder, CO: Lynne Rienner.

González, Luis E. 1991. *Political Structures and Democracy in Uruguay*. Notre Dame, IN: University of Notre Dame Press.

———. 1999. "Los partidos establecidos y sus desafiantes." In *Los partidos políticos uruguayos en tiempos de cambio*, edited by L. E. González. Montevideo: Fundación de Cultura Universitaria.

González, Luis E., and Rosario Queirolo. 2000. "Las elecciones nacionales del 2004: Posibles escenarios." In *Elecciones 1999/2000*, edited by G. Caetano. Montevideo: Ediciones de la Banda Oriental e Instituto de Ciencia Política.

Greene, Kenneth. 2002. "Opposition Party Strategy and Spatial Competition in Dominant Party Regime: A Theory and the Case of Mexico." *Comparative Political Studies* 35 (7): 755–83.

Halperín Donghi, Tulio. 1993. *The Contemporary History of Latin America*. Durham, NC: Duke University Press.

Hershberg, Eric, and Fred Rosen. 2006. "Turning the Tide." In *Latin America after Neoliberalism: Turning the Tide in the 21st Century?*, edited by E. Hershberg and F. Rosen. New York: New Press.

Hibbs, Douglas A., Jr. 1979. "The Mass Public and Macroeconomic Performance: The Dynamics of Public Opinion toward Unemployment and Inflation." *American Journal of Political Science* 23 (4): 705–31.

Huber, Evelyn, and Fred Solt. 2004. "Successes and Failures of Neoliberalism."

Latin American Research Review 39 (3): 150–64.

Hunter, Wendy. 2003. "Brazil's New Direction." *Journal of Democracy* 14 (2): 151–62.

———. 2007. "The Normalization of an Anomaly: The Workers' Party in Brazil." *World Politics* 59 (3): 440–75.

IDEA. 2004. *Reform Fatigue.* Washington, DC: Inter-American Development Bank.

Inglehart, Ronald, and Hans-Dieter Klingemann. 1976. "Party Identification, Ideological Preference, and the Left-Right Dimensions among the Western Mass Publics." In *Party Identification and Beyond: Representations of Voting and Party Competition,* edited by I. Budge, I. Crewey, and D. Farlie. Chichester: Wiley.

Jacobson, Gary C. 1990. "Does the Economy Matter in Midterm Elections?" *American Journal of Political Science* 34 (2): 400–404.

Kahneman, Daniel, and Amos Tversky. 1979. "Prospect Theory: An Analysis of Decision under Risk." *Econometrica* 47 (2): 263–92.

Kinder, Donald R. 1998. "Opinion and Actions in the Realm of Politics." In *Oxford Handbook of Political Psychology,* edited by D. O. Sears, L. Huddy, and R. Jervis. Oxford: Oxford University Press.

Kinder, Donald R., and D. Roderick Kiewiet. 1981. "Sociotropic Politics: The American Case." *British Journal of Political Science* 11 (2): 129–61.

King, Gary, James Honaker, Anne Joseph, and Kenneth Scheve. 2001. "Analyzing Incomplete Political Science Data: An Alternative Algorithm for Multiple Imputation." *American Political Science Review* 95 (1): 49–69.

Kinzo, M. D'Alva Gil. 1992. "A eleição presidencial de 1989: O comportamento eleitoral em uma cidade brasileira." *Dados* 35 (1): 49–66.

Kitschelt, Herbert. 1994. *The Transformation of European Social Democracy.* New York: Cambridge University Press.

Kitschelt, Herbert, and Staf Hellemans. 1990. "The Left-Right Semantics and the New Politics Cleavage." *Comparative Political Studies* 23 (2): 210–38.

Kitschelt, Herbert, and Stephen Wilkinson, eds. 2007. *Patrons, Clients, and Policies: Patterns of Democratic Accountability and Political Competition.* New York: Cambridge University Press.

Klesner, Joseph L. 2004. "The Structure of the Mexican Electorate: Social, Attitudinal, and Partisan Bases of Vicente Fox's Victory." In *Mexico's Pivotal Democratic Election: Candidates, Voters, and the Presidential Campaign of 2000,* edited by J. I. Domínguez and C. Lawson. Stanford, CA: Stanford University Press.

———. 2005. "Electoral Competition and the New Party System in Mexico."

Latin American Politics and Society 47 (2): 103–42.

Krueger, Anne O. 1994. *The Political Economy of Policy Reform in Developing Countries.* Cambridge, MA: MIT Press.

Kuczynski, Pedro-Pablo, and John Williamson, eds. 2003. *After the Washington Consensus: Restarting Growth and Reform in Latin America.* Washington, DC: Institute for International Economics.

Laakso, Markku, and Rein Taagepera. 1979. "Effective Number of Parties: A Measure with Application to West Europe." *Comparative Political Studies in Comparative International Development* 12: 3–27.

Latinobarómetro, 2004. Annual Report. www.latinobarometro.org/latino/LATContenidos.jsp.

Lawson, Chappell. 1999. "Why Cárdenas Won: The 1997 Elections in Mexico City." In *Toward Mexico's Democratization: Parties, Campaigns, Elections, and Public Opinion,* edited by J. I. Domínguez and A. Poiré. New York: Routledge.

———. 2004. "Mexico's Great Debates: The Televised Candidate Encounters of 2000 and Their Electoral Consequences." In *Mexico's Pivotal Democratic Election: Candidates, Voters, and the Presidential Campaign of 2000,* edited by J. I. Domínguez and C. Lawson. Stanford, CA: Stanford University Press.

Lawson, Chappell, and James McCann. 2004. "Television News, Mexico's 2000 Elections, and Media Effects in Emerging Democracies." *British Journal of Political Science* 35: 1–30.

Levitsky, Steve, and Kenneth Roberts, eds. 2011. *The Resurgence of the Latin American Left.* Baltimore, MD: Johns Hopkins University Press.

Lewis-Beck, Michael. 1986. "Comparative Economic Voting: Britain, France, Germany, Italy." *American Journal of Political Science* 30 (2): 315–46.

———. 1988. *Economics and Elections: The Major Western Democracies.* Ann Arbor: University of Michigan Press.

Lewis-Beck, Michael, and Paolo Bellucci. 1982. "Economic Influences on Legislative Elections in Multiparty Systems: France and Italy." *Political Behavior* 4: 93–107.

Lewis-Beck, Michael S., and Mary Stegmaier. 2000. "Economic Determinants of Electoral Outcomes." *Annual Review of Political Science* 3: 183–219.

Lipset, Seymour Martin, and Stein Rokkan. 1967. "Cleavage Structures, Party Systems, and Voter Alignments: An Introduction." In *Party Systems and Voter Alignments: Cross-National Perspectives,* edited by S. Lipset and S. Rokkan. New York: Free Press.

Lodola, Germán. 2005. "Executives, Legislatures, and the Political Economy of Market Reforms in Latin America, 1985–1999." Paper presented at the

Midwest Political Science Association Conference, Chicago, April 7–10.

López, Santiago. 2005. "Partidos desafiantes en América Latina: Representación política y estrategias de competencia de las nuevas oposiciones." *Revista de Ciencia Política* 25 (2): 37–64.

Lora, Eduardo. 1997. "Structural Reforms in Latin America: What Has Been Reformed and How to Measure It." Working Paper Green Series No. 348, Inter-American Development Bank, Washington, DC.

———. 2001. "Structural Reforms in Latin America: What Has Been Reformed and How to Measure It." Rev. Working Paper Green Series No. 466, Inter-American Development Bank, Washington, DC.

Lora, Eduardo, and M. Olivera. 2005. "The Electoral Consequences of the Washington Consensus." Research Department Working Paper No. 530, Inter-American Development Bank, Washington, DC.

Lora, Eduardo, and Ugo Panizza. 2002. "Structural Reforms in Latin America under Scrutiny." IDB Working Paper No. 34, Inter-American Development Bank, Washington, DC.

———. 2003. "The Future of Structural Reform." *Journal of Democracy* 14 (2): 123–37.

Lora, Eduardo, Ugo Panizza, and Myriam Quispe-Agnoli. 2004. "Reform Fatigue: Symptoms, Reasons and Implications." *Federal Reserve Bank of Atlanta Economic Review* (Second Quarter).

Luna, Juan P. 2004a. "De familias y parentescos políticos: Ideología y competencia electoral en el Uruguay contemporáneo." In *La izquierda uruguaya entre la oposición y el gobierno*, edited by J. Lanzaro. Montevideo: Editorial Fin de Siglo e Instituto de Ciencia Política.

———. 2004b. "¿Entre la espada y la pared? La transformación de las bases sociales del FA y sus implicaciones de cara a un eventual gobierno progresista." In *La izquierda uruguaya entre la oposición y el gobierno*, edited by J. Lanzaro. Montevideo: Editorial Fin de Siglo e Instituto de Ciencia Política.

Luna, Juan P., and Elizabeth J. Zechmeister. 2005a. "Estructuración ideológica e izquierda en los sistemas de partidos Latinoamericanos circa 1996–1998." Unpublished manuscript.

———. 2005b. "Political Representation in Latin America: A Study of Elite-Mass Congruence in Nine Countries." *Comparative Political Studies* 38 (4): 388–416.

MacKenzie, David, and Dilip Mookherjee. 2003. "The Distributional Impact of Privatization in Latin America: Evidence from Four Countries." *Economía: Journal of the Latin America and Caribbean Economic Association* 3:

161–218.

MacKuen, Michael, Robert Erikson, and James Stimson. 1992. "Sociotropic Politics: The American Case." *British Journal of Political Science* 11 (2): 129–61.

Magaloni, Beatriz. 1999. "Is the PRI Fading? Economic Performance, Electoral Accountability, and Voting Behavior in the 1994 and 1997 Elections." In *Toward Mexico's Democratization: Parties, Campaigns, Elections, and Public Opinion*, edited by J. I. Domínguez and A. Poiré. New York: Routledge.

Magaloni, Beatriz, and Alejandro Poiré. 2004a. "Strategic Coordination in the 2000 Mexican Presidential Race." In *Mexico's Pivotal Democratic Election: Candidates, Voters, and the Presidential Campaign of 2000*, edited by J. I. Domínguez and C. Lawson. Stanford, CA: Stanford University Press.

———. 2004b. "The Issues, the Vote, and the Mandate for Change." In *Mexico's Pivotal Democratic Election: Candidates, Voters, and the Presidential Campaign of 2000*, edited by J. I. Domínguez and C. Lawson. Stanford, CA: Stanford University Press.

Mainwaring, Scott. 1999. *Rethinking Party Systems in the Third Wave of Democratization: The Case of Brazil*. Stanford, CA: Stanford University Press.

Mainwaring, Scott, Rachel Meneguello, and Timothy Power. 2000. "Conservative Parties, Democracy, and Economic Reform in Contemporary Brazil." In *Conservative Parties, the Right, and Democracy in Latin America*, edited by K. J. Middlebrook. Baltimore, MD: Johns Hopkins University Press.

Mainwaring, Scott, and Timothy R. Scully, eds. 1995. *Building Democratic Institutions: Party Systems in Latin America*. Stanford, CA: Stanford University Press.

———. 2003. *Christian Democracy in Latin America: Electoral Competition and Regime Conflicts*. Stanford, CA: Stanford University Press.

Meneguello, Rachel. 1995. "Electoral Behavior in Brazil: The 1994 Presidential Elections." *International Social Science Journal* 146: 627–41.

———. 2002. "El impacto de la democratización del Estado en el desarrollo de los partidos brasileños: 1985–1998." In *El asedio a la política: Los partidos Latinoamericanos en la era neoliberal*, edited by M. Cavarozzi and A. Medina. Rosario: Homo Sapiens.

Molina, José E. 2001. "The Electoral Effect of Underdevelopment: Government Turnover and Its Causes in Latin American, Caribbean, and Industrialized Countries." *Electoral Studies* 20 (3): 427–46.

Monestier, Felipe. 2001. "Familia e identidad partidaria: Razones para el éxito de una nueva tradición política en Uruguay." *Prisma* 16: 133–45.

Mora y Araujo, Manuel, and Peter H. Smith. 1984. "Peronism and Economic

Development: The Elections of 1973." In *Juan Perón and the Reshaping of Argentina*, edited by F. C. Turner and J. E. Miguens. Pittsburgh, PA: University of Pittsburgh Press.

Moreira, Constanza. 2000. "Comportamiento electoral y cultura política." In *Elecciones 1999/2000*, edited by G. Caetano. Montevideo: Ediciones de la Banda Oriental e Instituto de Ciencia Política.

Moreno, Alejandro. 1998. "Party Competition and the Issue of Democracy: Ideological Space in Mexican Elections." In *Governing Mexico: Political Parties and Elections*, edited by M. Serrano. London: University of London.

———. 1999. "Ideología y voto: Dimensiones de competencia política en México en los noventa." *Política y Gobierno* 6 (1): 45–81.

———. 2003. *El votante mexicano: Democracia, actitudes políticas y conducta electoral*. Mexico, DF: Fondo de Cultura Económica.

———. 2004. "The Effects of Negative Campaigns on Mexican Voters." In *Mexico's Pivotal Democratic Election: Candidates, Voters, and the Presidential Campaign of 2000*, edited by J. I. Domínguez and C. Lawson. Stanford, CA: Stanford University Press.

Morgenstern, Scott, and Elizabeth Zechmeister. 2001. "Better the Devil You Know than the Saint You Don't? Risk Propensity and Vote Choice in Mexico." *Journal of Politics* 63 (1): 93–119.

Morley, Samuel A., Roberto Machado, and Stefano Pettinato. 1999. *Indexes of Structural Reform in Latin America*. Santiago de Chile Economic Commission for Latin America and the Caribbean.

Murillo, María Victoria. 2001. *Labor Unions, Partisan Coalitions, and Market Reforms in Latin America*. Cambridge: Cambridge University Press.

Murillo, María Victoria, Virginia Oliveros, and Milan Vaishnav. 2011. "Voting for the Left or Governing on the Left?" In *The Resurgence of the Latin American Left*, edited by S. Levitsky and K. Roberts. Baltimore, MD: Johns Hopkins University Press.

Nadeau, Richard, and Michael S. Lewis-Beck. 2001. "National Economic Voting in U. S. Presidential Elections." *Journal of Politics* 63 (1): 158–81.

Narayan, Deepa, and Patti Petesch, eds. 2002. *Voices of the Poor from Many Lands*. Washington, DC, and New York: World Bank and Oxford University Press.

New York Times. 2009. "El Salvador." March 16.

Nohlen, Dieter. 2005. *Elections in the Americas*. Oxford: Oxford University Press.

Okun, A. 1975. "Inflation: Its Mechanics and Welfare Costs." *Brookings Papers on Economic Activity* 2: 301–90.

Panizza, Francisco. 2005. "Unarmed Utopia Revisited: The Resurgence of Left-of-Center Politics in Latin America." *Political Studies* 53: 716–34.

Panizza, Ugo, and Mónica Yañez. 2005. "Why Are Latin Americans So Unhappy about Reforms?" *Journal of Applied Economics* 8 (1): 1–29.

Peters, B. Guy. 1998. *Comparative Politics: Theory and Methods.* New York: New York University Press.

Poiré, Alejandro. 1999. "Retrospective Voting, Partisanship, and Loyalty in Presidential Elections: 1994." In *Toward Mexico's Democratization: Parties, Campaigns, Elections, and Public Opinion,* edited by J. I. Domínguez and. A. Poiré. New York: Routledge.

Political Database of the Americas. http://pdba.georgetown.edu/.

Portes, Alejandro, and Kelly Hoffman. 2003. "Latin American Class Structures: Their Composition and Change during the Neoliberal Era." *Latin American Research Review* 38 (1): 41–82.

Powell, G. Bingham, and Guy D. Whitten. 1993. "A Cross-National Analysis of Economic Voting: Taking Account of the Political Context." *American Journal of Political Science* 38 (2): 391–414.

Power, Timothy. 2001–2002. "Blairism Brazilian Style? Cardoso and the 'Third Way' in Brazil." *Political Science Quarterly* 116 (4): 611–36.

Przeworski, Adam, Michael E. Alvarez, José Antonio Cheibub, and Fernando Limongi. 2000. *Democracy and Development: Political Regimes and Material Well-Being in the World, 1950–1990.* New York: Cambridge University Press.

Przeworski, Adam, and John Sprague. 1986. *Paper Stones.* Chicago: University of Chicago Press.

Przeworski, Adam, and H. Teune. 1970. *The Logic of Comparative Social Inquiry.* New York: Wiley-Interscience.

Queirolo, Rosario. 2008. "The Impact of Neoliberal Economic Reforms on Latin Americans' Voting Behavior." PhD dissertation, University of Pittsburgh, Pittsburgh, PA.

———. 2010. "El rol de los programas de transferencias monetarias en la reelección del Frente Amplio en 2009." In *Del cambio a la continuidad: Ciclo electoral 2009–2010 en Uruguay,* edited by D. Buquet and N. Johnson. Montevideo: Fin de Siglo, CLACSO Coediciones and Instituto de Ciencia Política.

Remmer, Karen. 1991. "The Political Impact of Economic Crisis in Latin America." *American Political Science Review* 85: 777–800.

———. 1993. "The Political Economy of Election in Latin America, 1980–1991." *American Political Science Review* 89 (1): 393–407.

———. 2003. "Elections and Economics in Contemporary Latin America."

In *Post-Stabilibization Politics in Latin America: Competition, Transition, Collapse*, edited by C. Wise and R. Roett. Washington, DC: Brookings Institution Press.

Remmer, Karen L., and François Gélineau. 2003. "Subnational Electoral Choice: Economic and Referendum Voting in Argentina, 1983–1999." *Comparative Political Studies* 36 (7): 801–21.

Roberts, Kenneth M. 1998. *Deepening Democracy? The Modern Left and Social Movements in Chile and Peru.* Stanford, CA: Stanford University Press.

———. 2003. "Social Polarization and the Populist Resurgence in Venezuela." In *Venezuelan Politics in the Chávez Era: Class, Polarization, and Conflict*, edited by S. Ellner and D. C. Hellinger. Boulder, CO: Lynne Rienner.

———. 2008. "The Mobilization of Opposition to Economic Liberalization." *Annual Review of Political Science* 11: 327–49.

Roberts, Kenneth M., and Moisés Arce. 1998. "Neoliberalism and Lower-Class Voting Behavior in Peru." *Comparative Political Studies* 31 (2): 217–46.

Roberts, Kenneth M., and Erik Wibbels. 1999. "Party Systems and Electoral Volatility in Latin America: A Test of Economic, Institutional, and Structural Explanations." *American Political Science Review* 93 (3): 575–90.

Rodríguez Garavito, César A., Patrick S. Barrett, and Daniel Chavez, eds. 2005. *La nueva izquierda en América Latina: Sus orígenes y trayectoria futura.* Bogotá: Grupo Editorial Norma.

Rodrik, Dani, and Francisco Rodríguez. 2001. "Trade Policy and Economic Growth: A Skeptic's Guide to the Cross-National Evidence." In *NBER Macroeconomics Annual 2000*, edited by B. S. Bernanke and K. Rogoff. Cambridge, MA: MIT Press.

Rohter, Larry. 2005. "With New Chief, Uruguay Veers Left, in a Latin Pattern." *New York Times*, March 1.

Royston, P. 2004. "Multiple Imputation of Missing Values." *Stata Journal* 4 (3): 227–41.

———. 2005. "Multiple Imputation of Missing Values: Update of Ice." *Stata Journal* 5 (4): 527–36.

Sabatini, Christopher, and Eric Farnsworth. 2006. "The Urgent Need for Labor Law Reform." *Journal of Democracy* 17 (4): 50–64.

Sachs, Jeffrey D. 2005. "The Development Challenge." *Foreign Affairs* 84 (2): 78–90.

Samuels, David. 2004. "From Socialism to Social Democracy: Party Organization and the Transformation of the Workers' Party in Brazil." *Comparative Political Studies* 37 (9): 999–1024.

———. 2006. "Sources of Mass Partisanship in Brazil." *Latin American Poli-*

tics and Society 48: 1–27.

Sani, Giacomo, and Giovanni Sartori. 1983. "Polarization, Fragmentation, and Competition in Western Democracies." In *Western European Party Systems*, edited by H. Daalder and P. Mair. Thousand Oaks, CA: Sage.

SAPRIN. 2002. www.saprin.org/global_rpt.htm.

Sartori, Giovanni. 1976. *Party and Party Systems: A Framework for Analysis.* New York: Cambridge University Press.

Schlesinger, Arthur M., Jr. 1986. *The Cycles of American History.* Boston: Houghton-Mifflin.

Seligson, Mitchell. 2007. "The Rise of Populism and the Left in Latin America." *Journal of Democracy* 18 (3): 81–95.

Seligson, Mitchell, and Miguel Gómez. 1989. "Ordinary Elections in Extraordinary Times: The Political Economy of Voting in Costa Rica." In *Elections and Democracy in Central America*, edited by J. Booth and M. Seligson. Chapel Hill: University of North Carolina Press.

Shirk, David A. 2005. *Mexico's New Politics: The PAN and Democratic Change.* Boulder, CO: Lynne Rienner.

Singer, André. 2002. *Izquierda y derecha en el electorado brasileño.* Buenos Aires: CLACSO.

Stallings, Barbara, and Wilson Peres. 2000. *Growth, Employment, and Equity: The Impact of Economic Reforms in Latin America and the Caribbean.* Washington, DC: Brookings Institution Press.

Stiglitz, Joseph. 2002. *El malestar en la globalización.* Madrid: Taurus.

Stimson, James A. 1999. *Public Opinion in America: Moods, Cycles, and Swings.* 2nd ed. Boulder, CO: Westview Press.

Stimson, James A., Michael B. MacKuen, and Robert S. Erikson. 1995. "Dynamic Representation." *American Political Science Review* 89: 543–65.

Stokes, Susan C. 2001a. *Mandates and Democracy: Neoliberalism by Surprise in Latin America.* Cambridge: Cambridge University Press.

———, ed. 2001b. *Public Support for the Market Reforms in New Democracies.* Cambridge: Cambridge University Press.

Tanaka, Martín. 2008. "The Left in Peru: Plenty of Wagons and No Locomotion." In *Leftovers: Tales of the Latin American Left,* edited by J. Castañeda and M. Morales. New York: Routledge.

Torcal, Mariano, and Scott Mainwaring. 2003. "The Political Recrafting of Social Bases of Party Competition: Chile, 1973–95." *British Journal of Political Science* 33: 55–84.

Tussie, Diane, and Pablo Heidrich. 2008. "A Tale of Ecumenism and Diver-

INDEX

sity: Economic and Trade Policies of the New Left." In *Leftovers: Tales of the Latin American Left*, edited by J. Castañeda and M. Morales. New York: Routledge.

Vairo, Daniela. 2012. "El 'consenso de los perdedores' y la legitimidad de la democracia en América del Sur." *Política y Gobierno* 19 (1): 41–70.

Weisehomeier, Nina, and Kenneth Benoit. 2009. "Presidents, Parties, and Policy Competition." *Journal of Politics* 71 (4): 1435–47.

Weyland, Kurt. 1998. "Peasants and Bankers in Venezuela? Presidential Popularity and Economic Reform Approval, 1989–1993." *Political Research Quarterly* 51 (2): 341–62.

———. 2002. *The Politics of Market Reform in Fragile Democracies: Argentina, Brazil, Peru, and Venezuela*. Princeton, NJ: Princeton University Press.

———. 2003. "Economic Voting Reconsidered: Crisis and Charisma in the Election of Hugo Chávez." *Comparative Political Studies* 36 (7): 822–48.

Weyland, Kurt, Raúl Madrid, and Wendy Hunter, eds. 2010. *Leftist Governments in Latin America*. New York: Cambridge University Press.

Williamson, J. 1990. "What Does Washington Mean by Policy Reform?" In *Latin American Adjustment: How Much Has Happened*, edited by J. Williamson. Washington, DC: Institution for International Economics.

Wise, Carol, and Riordan Roett, eds. 2003. *Post-Stabilization Politics in Latin America: Competition, Transition, Collapse*. Washington, DC: Brookings Institution Press.

Yeric, Eric, and John Todd. 1989. *Public Opinion: The Visible Politics*. 2nd ed. Itasca, IL: F. E. Peacock.

Zechmeister, Elizabeth. 2006. "Qué es la izquierda y quién está a la derecha en la política mexicana: Un enfoque con el método Q al estudio de las etiquetas ideológicas." *Política y Gobierno* 8 (1): 51–98.

Zuasnábar, Ignacio. 2010. "Las elecciones departamentales de 2010 bajo la lupa de la identificación partidaria." In *El voto en Uruguay 2009–2010*, edited by L. E. González, F. Irazábal, P. Mieres, and I. Zuasnábar. Montevideo: Universidad Católica and Konrad Adenauer Stiftung.

ROSARIO QUEIROLO
is associate professor in the department of social and political science
at Universidad Católica del Uruguay.

www.ingramcontent.com/pod-product-compliance
Lightning Source LLC
Chambersburg PA
CBHW062023270326
41929CB00014B/2296